NARRA
OF REMA
CRIMINAL TRIALS

By

ANSELM RITTER
VON FEUERBACH

Translated from German by

LADY DUFF GORDON

First published in 1846

Read & Co.

Copyright © 2020 Read & Co. History

This edition is published by Read & Co. History,
an imprint of Read & Co.

British Library Cataloguing-in-Publication Data
A catalogue record for this book is available
from the British Library.

Read & Co. is part of Read Books Ltd.
For more information visit
www.readandcobooks.co.uk

CONTENTS

Paul Johann Anselm Ritter von Feuerbach v

PREFACE ix

JOHN PAUL FORSTER;
OR, THE TWO FOLD MURDER 1

THE ANTONINI FAMILY;
OR, THE MURDER ON A JOURNEY 49

FRANCIS RIEMBAUER;
THE TARTUFFE OF REAL LIFE 69

THE UNKNOWN MURDERER;
OR, THE POLICE AT FAULT. 112

ANNA MARIA ZWANZIGER;
THE GERMAN BRINVILLIERS. 142

JAMES THALREUTER;
OR, THE FALSE PRINCE 180

THE KLEINSCHROT FAMILY;
OR, THE PARRICIDES OF THE BLACK MILL. 203

JOHN GEORGE SÖRGEL;
OR, THE IDIOT MURDERER. 233

GEORGE WACHS;
OR, THE SUDDEN TEMPTATION 251

GEORGE RAUSCHMAIER;
OR, THE TELLTALE RING 282

ANDREW BICHEL;
THE WOMAN MURDERER 296

JOHN HOLZINGER;
OR, MANSLAUGHTER, MURDER, AND
SUICIDE, FROM LOVE AND JEALOUSY 313

CASPER FRISCH;
THE MUDERER FROM VANITY.....................335

LUDWIG STEINER;
THE MURDERER FROM REVENGE 346

Paul Johann Anselm
Ritter von Feuerbach

A German jurist and writer on criminal law. He was born at Hainichen near Jena on the 14th of November 1775. He received his early education at Frankfort on Main, whither his family had removed soon after his birth. At the age of sixteen, however, he ran away from home, and, going to Jena, was helped by relations there to study at the university. In spite of poor health and the most desperate poverty, he made rapid progress. He attended the lectures of Karl Leonhard Reinhold and Gottlieb Hufeland, and soon published some literary essays of more than ordinary merit. In 1795 he took the degree of doctor in philosophy, and in the same year, though he only possessed 150 thalers (£22 : 10s.), he married. It was this step which led him to success and fame, by forcing him to turn from his favourite studies of philosophy and history to that of law, which was repugnant to him, but which offered a prospect of more rapid advancement. His success in this new and uncongenial sphere was soon assured.

In 1796 he published *Kritik des natürlichen Rechts als Propädeutik zu einer Wissenschaft der natürlichen Rechte*, which was followed, in 1798, by *Anti-Hobbes, oder über die Grenzen der bürgerlichen Gewalt*, a dissertation on the limits of the civil power and the right of resistance on the part of subjects against their rulers, and by *Philosophische, juristische Untersuchungen über das Verbrechen des Hochverraths.*

In 1799 he obtained the degree of doctor of laws. Feuerbach, as the founder of a new theory of penal law, the so-called "psychological-coercive or intimidation theory," occupied a prominent place in the history of criminal science. His views, which he first made known in his *Revision der Grundsätze und Grundbegriffe des positiven peinlichen Rechts* (1799), were further elucidated and expounded in the *Bibliothek für die peinliche Rechtswissenschaft* (1800–1801), an encyclopaedic work produced in conjunction with Karl L. W. G. Grolmann and Ludwig Harscher von Almendingen, and in his famous *Lehrbuch des gemeinen in Deutschland geltenden peinlichen Rechts* (1801). These works were a powerful protest against vindictive punishment, and did much towards the reformation of the German criminal law. The *Carolina* (the penal code of the emperor Charles V.) had long since ceased to be respected. What in 1532 was an inestimable blessing, as a check upon the arbitrariness and violence of the effete German procedure, had in the course of time outlived its usefulness and become a source of evils similar to those it was enacted to combat. It availed nothing that, at the commencement of the 18th century, a freer and more scientific spirit had been breathed into Roman law; it failed to reach the criminal law. The administration of justice was, before Feuerbach's time, especially distinguished by two characteristics: the superiority of the judge to all law, and the blending of the judicial and executive offices, with the result that the individual was practically at the mercy of his prosecutors. This state of things Feuerbach set himself to reform, and using as his chief weapon the *Revision der Grundbegriffe* above referred to, was successful in his task. His achievement in the struggle may be summed up as: *nullum crimen, nulla poena sine lege* (no wrong and no punishment without a remedy).

In 1801 Feuerbach was appointed extraordinary professor of law without salary, at the university of Jena, and in the following year accepted a chair at Kiel, where he remained two years. In 1804 he removed to the university of Landshut; but on being commanded by King Maximilian Joseph to draft a penal code for Bavaria (*Strafgesetzbuch für das Königreich Bayern*), he removed in 1805 to Munich, where he was given a high appointment in the ministry of justice and was ennobled in 1808. Meanwhile the practical reform of penal legislation in Bavaria was begun under his influence in 1806 by the abolition of torture.

In 1808 appeared the first volume of his *Merkwürdige Criminalfälle*, completed in 1811—a work of deep interest for its application of psychological considerations to cases of crime, and intended to illustrate the inevitable imperfection of human laws in their application to individuals. In his *Betrachtungen über das Geschworenengericht* (1811) Feuerbach declared against trial by jury, maintaining that the verdict of a jury was not adequate legal proof of a crime. Much controversy was aroused on the subject, and the author's view was subsequently to some extent modified. The result of his labours was promulgated in 1813 as the Bavarian penal code. The influence of this code, the embodiment of Feuerbach's enlightened views, was immense. It was at once made the basis for new codes in Württemberg and Saxe-Weimar; it was adopted in its entirety in the grand-duchy of Oldenburg; and it was translated into Swedish by order of the king. Several of the Swiss cantons reformed their codes in conformity with it. Feuerbach had also undertaken to prepare a civil code for Bavaria, to be founded on the Code Napoléon. This was afterwards set aside, and the Codex Maximilianus adopted as a basis. But the project did not become law.

During the war of liberation (1813–1814) Feuerbach showed himself an ardent patriot, and published several political brochures which, from the writer's position, had almost the weight of state manifestoes. One of these is entitled *Über deutsche Freiheit und Vertretung deutsche Volker durch Landstände* (1514).

In 1814 Feuerbach was appointed second president of the court of appeal at Bamberg, and three years later he became first president of the court of appeal at Anspach. In 1821 he was deputed by the government to visit France, Belgium, and the Rhine provinces for the purpose of investigating their juridical institutions. As the fruit of this visit, he published his treatises *Betrachtungen über Öffentlichkeit und Mündigkeit der Gerechtigkeitspflege* (1821) and *Über die Gerichtsverfassung und das gerichtliche Verfahren Frankreichs* (1825). In these he pleaded unconditionally for publicity in all legal proceedings. In his later years he took a deep interest in the fate of the strange foundling Kaspar Hauser, which had excited so much attention in Europe; and he was the first to publish a critical summary of the ascertained facts, under the title of *Kaspar Hauser, ein Beispiel eines Verbrechens am Seelenleben* (1832). Shortly before his death appeared a collection of his *Kleine Schriften* (1833).

Feuerbach, still in the full enjoyment of his intellectual powers, died suddenly at Frankfort, while on his way to the baths of Schwalbach, on the 29th of May 1833. In 1853 was published the *Leben und Wirken Ans. von Feuerbachs*, 2 vols., consisting of a selection of his letters and journals, with occasional notes by his fourth son Ludwig, the distinguished philosopher.

A BIOGRAPHY FROM
1911 *Encyclopædia Britannica, Volume* 10

PREFACE

THE following trials are selected and abridged from a work consisting of 1300 closely-printed pages, by Anselm Ritter von Feuerbach, a man celebrated as a judge, a legislator, and a writer. He was for many years President of the highest criminal court of Bavaria, and the penal code of that country was chiefly framed by him ; his exposition of the criminal law is a text-book for the whole of Germany, where the present work, which was the last he wrote, excited great attention.

For ten years Feuerbach was President of the Central Criminal Court of a province of Bavaria, containing several towns, and inhabited by half a million of souls differing in faith. In the exercise of his judicial functions many remarkable cases were brought before him, and ample opportunity was afforded him, by the form of criminal procedure in Bavaria, for the exercise of his extraordinary power of penetrating the recesses of the human heart, and of divining the secret motives of human action. In Bavaria, on the discovery of any crime, the *Untersuchungs Richter* (examining judge)—and Feuerbach himself once filled that office, which, in fact, combines the duties of public prosecutor with that of judge—instantly sets about collecting evidence. Those against whom he finds any reasonable grounds of suspicion are at once apprehended, and kept in prison until their guilt or innocence be proved. The judge meanwhile endeavours to trace back the prisoner's life to his very cradle, to make himself thoroughly acquainted with his character and disposition, in order thence to infer whether he be or be not a man likely to have committed the crime imputed to him. To this end witnesses are examined.

Children under eight years of age, persons directly interested in the result of the trial, or who have been convicted or even strongly suspected of perjury, falsehood, or suppression of evidence, are incompetent witnesses. Suspicious witnesses are persons under the age of eighteen, accomplices, the injured party, informers, except such as are officially bound to inform, persons of doubtful character, and persons in any way connected with or hostile to the party affected by their testimony.

The evidence of two sufficient witnesses (those against whom none of the above-mentioned objections can be raised), as to facts which they have seen with their own eyes, is taken as proof; that of one sufficient witness as half proof.

The testimony of two suspicious witnesses, if agreeing, is equal to that of one sufficient witness.

Circumstantial evidence amounts to proof when all the circumstances are fully proved by witnesses, and cannot be reasonably accounted for except on the supposition of the prisoner's guilt; but while any other explanation is possible the evidence is deemed imperfect; and even when circumstantial evidence is complete, the conviction of the prisoner, in cases of capital offence, is not followed by sentence of death, unless he confess his crime.

By far the most important evidence is that given by the prisoner himself; he is questioned by the examining judge, in the presence only of a notary employed to take down his replies. The judge begins by exhorting him to tell the truth, hinting that a full confession may soften his punishment. He then asks him whether he knows why he has been arrested; and if the prisoner affects ignorance or gives a false reason, he is again admonished. Should he persist in his assertions the judge closes the examination for that day. At the next examination he reminds the prisoner of the duty of truth and of the danger of persisting in falsehood, and then begins a series of questions calculated to entrap him into admissions inconsistent with innocence. If on the other hand the prisoner states the true cause of his arrest, he is called upon to tell all he knows of the matter. His statement is written down, and the judge afterwards questions him upon every circumstance of his story, important or trifling, taking care that he shall not, if it can be avoided, perceive which questions are important, and that no time be allowed him to consider his replies. During the inquiry the prisoner is kept in ignorance of the charge against him, and any endeavour on his part to gain information on the subject is an offence in law. He is not allowed to see a copy of his own evidence or of that of the witnesses. But when the judge has failed to obtain a confession the prisoner is unexpectedly confronted with one or more of the witnesses against him, or with an accomplice, if there be one, in the hopes of surprising him into a confession. Should the prisoner refuse to answer, he is put on a diet of bread and water. In cases of murder, the accused is led to the spot where the crime was committed, and the bleeding corpse, or, it may be, the mouldering remains are suddenly shown to him. Feuerbach remarks that in cases of infanticide this expedient has never been known to fail; but it is manifest that such terrors can have little or no effect on hardened and resolute criminals. A confession must be formally made before the examining judge, and that not during the first examination; a confession made then cannot be followed by conviction; and a confession made before two sufficient witnesses in the absence of the judge is only half proof, and requires to be confirmed by other evidence.

But even when a confession has been extorted it affords no proof of the *That bestand*, the *corpus delicti*, or fact that the crime has been committed: it is evidence that the prisoner committed the actions which he describes, but it does not prove what were the results of those actions. The *That bestand* must be proved beyond all reasonable doubt, and in cases of murder it must be shown that the injuries inflicted were undoubtedly mortal.

It is the duty of the examining judge to collect evidence for the prisoner as carefully as against him; but when he has got together all that he can find, the prisoner is furnished with a legal defender, who is allowed to confer with him in private, having first sworn to undertake no unrighteous defence. This advocate makes a minute of his objections to the course of procedure, and composes a written defence, which is sent by the examining judge, together with a full report of all the proceedings, to the central criminal court of the district. This court decides by majority upon the guilt of the accused, the nature of his crime, and the punishment to be inflicted; when the punishment is death, or imprisonment exceeding twenty years, the sentence is sent for revision to the high court of appeal, and in other cases the prisoner may appeal, if he desires it. When the appellate court has given its decision, the prisoner, if the sentence be reversed, is instantly set free; if confirmed, it is executed within twenty-four hours.

If, in cases of capital crime, proof fails from mere technical insufficiency, the prisoner escapes the punishment of death; but imprisonment of greater or less duration and severity is inflicted.

The Bavarian system of inquiry and of appeals occasionally prolongs a trial over a space of several years. In one case described in this work, that of Riembauer, the reports filled forty-two folio volumes, and the trial lasted five years, whereas in England it would have been concluded in as many days. The reader, who may be inclined altogether to condemn this German prolixity and deliberation, should remember that in the year 1827 no fewer than six persons, who had been convicted of capital crimes at the Old Bailey, and left for execution, were proved to be innocent, and saved by the zeal and activity of the sheriff.* In the last century the Bavarian criminal procedure was anything but slow. Torture was not abolished until 1806, a reform chiefly owing to the humane exertions of Feuerbach, and extremely distasteful to the judges of the old school, who could not forgive him for having put an end to so simple, expeditious, and easy a mode of obtaining evidence. " What," said they, " could be the use of making so many difficulties about hanging a pack of criminals?" The time lost by the abolition of torture was at first regained by a total disregard of the very slight means of defence afforded to the accused by the Codex Juris Bavarici Criminalis de anno 1751. The doctrine that the sooner criminal cases were disposed of, the better, was acted upon until the 16th of May, 1813, when the criminal code, composed by Feuerbach for the kingdom of Bavaria, received the royal assent. This code was adopted by the

* ' Criminal Law Report,' vol. viii.

duchy of Oldenburg, and forms the basis of new criminal codes for Weimar, Würtemburg, and other German states.

The defects of the mode of procedure used in the following trials are of a kind which cannot fail to strike every English reader—its advantages are far more likely to escape his notice. The minute and searching investigation into the secret motives and inmost feelings, as well as the external actions of the criminal, must give to a Bavarian trial an interest which would be sought in vain in our own courts of law.

Perhaps nothing in the following trials will appear more surprising to English readers than that the criminals should almost always confess their crimes in the most circumstantial manner. Feuerbach was himself so much struck by this circumstance, that he has devoted a chapter of the book from which the following trials have been selected, to an examination of the subject. A few, he says, very few, confess from remorse, some from inability to evade the searching interrogatories of the judge, some from indifference to their fate, others from a desire to put an end to a state of anxiety and suspense; but by far the greater number from dislike to the strict discipline and compulsory silence of a Bavarian prison. One criminal, after three days' imprisonment, confessed, saying, "That he could no longer hold his tongue; that he had been accustomed to social pleasures, and would rather tell all than be condemned to perpetual silence."

Those among my readers who are interested in the comparison of the criminal procedure of Bavaria with that of England, will find the information which I want both space and ability to offer, in the ' Law Magazine,' vol. ix., p. 277 ; the ' Foreign Quarterly Review,' vol. viii. p. 267 ; and the ' Edinburgh Review,' vol. lxxxii., p. 318.

I have selected those trials which appear to me to possess the greatest general interest, and, in obedience to the suggestions contained in a most interesting article in the last-named journal, I have abridged them to little more than half their original length. I hope that I have nevertheless succeeded in preserving the main outline of every trial, filled up with just so much of detail as will serve to give a tolerably faithful picture of crimes common to all nations, treated in a manner very widely differing from our own.

L. D. G.

December, 1845.

REMARKABLE

GERMAN CRIMINAL TRIALS.

―――○―――

JOHN PAUL FORSTER,

THE TWOFOLD MURDER.

CHRISTOPHER BÄUMLER, a worthy citizen of Nürnberg, lived in the Königsstrasse, a wide and much-frequented street, where he carried on the trade of a corn-chandler, which there includes the right of selling brandy. He had lately lost his wife, and lived quite alone with only one maid-servant, Anna Catherina Schütz. He had the reputation of being rich.

Bäumler was in the habit of opening his shop at five o'clock in the morning at latest. But on the 21st of September, 1820, to the surprise of his neighbours it remained closed till past six. Curiosity and alarm drew together a number of people before the house. They rang repeatedly, but no one came to the door. At last some neighbours, with the sanction of the police, entered the first-floor windows by a ladder. Here they found drawers, chests, and closets burst open, and presenting every appearance of a robbery having been committed. They hastened down stairs into the shop, where they discovered in a corner close to the street-door the bloody corpse of the maid; and in the parlour they found Bäumler lying dead beside the stove.

The house stands on the left hand in going along the Königsstrasse from the Frauen Thor, not far from the church of Saint Laurence. Several houses, chiefly inns and shops, flank it on either side; on the right an inn called the Golden Lion stands out several feet beyond it.

Close to this projecting wall is the door of Bäumler's house, which is entered by one low step; the hall serves as a shop, and the walls are lined with shelves, chests, &c. The length of this hall from the street-door to the opposite end, where a door opens into a court, is about sixteen feet; on the left a staircase leads to the floor above. The breadth is unequal, for on the right hand near the door there is a corner about four feet wide and three feet deep, which forms part of the shop. On one side is the wall of Bäumler's parlour; on the other, the main wall of the house towards the street, where a large bow-window, always closed with heavy shutters at night, admits the light into the shop, and thence into the parlour through a window opening into this corner. About seven feet from the entrance to the shop is the door of the small parlour, which is cut off from the street on all sides, and furnished with tables and benches for the convenience of the customers for brandy.

The house-door, as is usually the case in shops of this kind in Nürnberg, is formed of two wings joined together, one of which folds back upon the other, and is fastened by a simple contrivance to the wall. During

the day a glass door is fixed in the half of the doorway thus left open, which in the daytime serves to
light the shop, and in the evening to show passers
by that the host is ready to receive customers. The
door of Bäumler's shop, behind the wing of which
a man could perfectly conceal himself from any one
entering, opens towards the left, exactly opposite to
the corner we have already described, so that any one
coming in would turn his face towards the corner;
and in the event of being attacked by a person hidden
behind the door, would naturally run towards it. A
bell hangs over the entrance, which rings whenever
either the glass or the wooden door* is opened.

As soon as the police were informed of the murder,
a commission was appointed to visit Bäumler's house.
Immediately on entering the shop, to the right of the
door in the corner, between two bins of meal and
salt, the maid-servant Schütz lay on her back, with
her head shattered, and her feet, from which both
her shoes had fallen, turned towards the door. Her
face and clothes, and the floor, were covered with
blood; and the two bins, between which her head lay,
as well as the wall, were sprinkled with it. As no
other part of the shop showed any marks of blood,
it was evident that she had been murdered in this
corner. Not far from the body they picked up a
small comb, and at a little distance from that a larger
one, with several fragments of a second small one.
In the very farthest corner of the parlour, between the
stove and a small table, upon which stood a jug,

* Without this dry description it would be almost impossible to
understand the manner in which this complicated murder was
perpetrated.

they found the body of Bäumler stretched on his back, with his head, which was resting on a small overturned stool, covered with wounds and blood. A pipe and several small coins lay under the body, where they had probably fallen when the murderer ransacked the pocket, which was turned inside out and stained with blood, for money or for keys. The floor, the stove, and the wall were covered with blood, the stool was saturated, and even the vaulted ceiling, which was nine or ten feet high, was sprinkled with it. These circumstances, especially the stool on which Bäumler's head still rested, and the pipe which lay under his body, showed that the murderer must have suddenly attacked him unawares and felled him to the earth, as he sat drinking his beer and smoking his pipe on that very spot.

One drawer of the commode in the upper chamber was pulled out, the doors of two cupboards in the adjoining room were open, and every thing lay scattered about the floor. Several other presses, however, had not been opened, and many things of value, such as clothes, silver ornaments, a gold repeater, &c., were left in them, and even in those which had been opened. The rooms on the second story were found in their usual state.

On the table, in the parlour, stood a wine-glass with some red brandy at the bottom, and a closed clasp-knife stained with blood on the back and sides. Two newly-baked rolls were found near the entrance-door.

The baker Stierhof stated that Bäumler's maid had fetched these rolls from his shop the evening before, at about a quarter to ten. His wife, who was examined the next day on this point, recognised the

rolls as those bought by the unfortunate maid-servant
on the evening of the 20th of September, adding,
" The evening before last, at nearly a quarter to ten,
the maid came to my house and asked for two half-
penny rolls, which I gave her. I did not recognise
her till she was going away, when I said, 'It is you,
is it?' She answered sulkily, 'Yes.' I asked if they
still had guests with them; and she said 'Yes, there
are a few fellows there still.' I then looked out of
the window for a while: there was a death-like silence
in the street, so much so that I remarked it to my
people. At a quarter to ten exactly I closed the shop."

This evidence afforded a strong presumption that
some person or persons who were still in Bäumler's
shop at a quarter to ten had committed this murder.
Furthermore it was certain that the murder of the
maid-servant could not have taken place earlier
than a quarter to ten; the two rolls which she had
fetched about that time from the baker Stierhof, and
which were found on the floor near the entrance,
showed that the murderer had attacked her as she
entered the shop on her return from the baker's,
that she dropped the rolls in her fright, was driven
into the corner of the shop, and there murdered.
There could be no doubt that Bäumler was murdered
before the maid-servant, for he was found beside the
stool on which he usually sat smoking his pipe by the
stove. Had he been alive when the murderer attacked his maid, he would have been alarmed by the
noise, and have gone out into the shop; at any rate
he would not have remained quietly seated for the
murderer to despatch him at his leisure. It was
also evident that Bäumler must have been murdered

during the maid's absence. Now the distance from
Bäumler's house to the baker's shop is at most a
hundred steps; thus, even supposing that Schütz,
angry at being sent out so late, went very slowly, the
walk there and back, including the short conversation
with the baker's wife, could not have occupied above
five minutes, and during this interval the murder of
Bäumler must have been completed, and that of
Schütz prepared. This was proved by the following
circumstance :—as long as the glass door was there
the murderer could neither attack Schütz on her
entrance nor murder her within the threshold, as he
could not possibly hide himself behind the glass door,
which would moreover have exposed him to the risk
of observation from every passer by, and even to the
chance of some stray guest of Bäumler's entering the
shop and surprising him in the act. It was therefore
necessary to take the glass door off its hinges, and to
shut the street-door, before attacking Schütz on her
return to the house,—and this he accordingly did.
Bäumler's house was not usually closed till eleven,
but on the night of the murder a chandler of the
name of Rössel, who lived opposite, happened to
look out at about a quarter to ten, and saw, to his
surprise, that Bäumler's house was then closed—no
doubt by the murderer. It was a quarter to ten
when Schütz was at the baker's shop; at the same
hour Rössel saw Bäumler's house shut: we may
therefore infer that the murderer killed Bäumler soon
after his maid's departure, quickly unhinged the
glass door, lay in wait for the maid behind the street-
door, opened it for her, and attacked her as she came
in : the concurring evidence of two witnesses thus

distinctly proves that the murder of Bäumler and his maid must have taken place during the few minutes before and after a quarter to ten.

We must further remark that the bell over the entrance-door did not ring when the police entered, and was found to be stuffed with paper. Neither Bäumler nor his maid could have had any motive for doing this; but the murderer had every reason: the ringing of the bell might have drawn the attention of a neighbour or a passer by to Bäumler's house at the very moment when the horrible crime was being committed just within the door.

It further appeared that the murderer stayed till at least half-past ten, occupied in ransacking the house, and probably in washing himself and changing his clothes; for a shoemaker of the name of Pühler, who passed by Bäumler's house at that hour, saw a light in the first floor, while the window over the shop-door was quite dark.

Although the two houses adjoining Bäumler's were both inhabited, and two watchmen were guarding some loaded waggons in the street close by,—and although the murders were committed at a time when very few people are in bed and asleep,—and, as the baker's wife stated, when death-like silence prevailed in the street,—not a single person could be found who had heard any outcry or other noise in Bäumler's house.

On examining the body of the maid-servant, a handsome well-shaped girl of twenty-three, the head was found completely shattered; there were also several wounds upon the neck, breast, and hands, and the breast-bone and three of the ribs were fractured. Bäumler's skull was broken into eleven pieces; and although there were no external injuries upon the chest, the sternum and ribs were fractured, as in the maid-servant. There could not be the slightest doubt that the wounds were mortal. The surgeons gave it as their opinion that the wounds on the heads of both victims had been inflicted with a heavy instrument having a flat surface with sharp edges, probably the back of a hatchet. The ribs did not appear to have been broken with the hatchet, but rather by stamping on the bodies.

The evidence of the baker's wife had led to the conclusion that some man who had stayed until late in the evening at Bäumler's house must have been the murderer. Accordingly, all those who had been at Bäumler's house on that evening were examined, and concurred in saying that a stranger had entered the shop very early, had sat at the farther end of the table, alternately smoking and drinking red brandy out of a wine-glass; and that he had remained there alone at nine o'clock, when the others went away. All agreed in their description of his person; that he was about thirty, of dark complexion, and black hair and beard; that he wore a dark-coloured coat (most of the witnesses said a blue one, which afterwards proved to be a mistake), and that he had on a high beaver hat. With the exception of one witness who had conversed with the stranger about the hop trade and other like matters, and had found him a well-informed, agreeable man, they all stated that he had kept his hat pressed over his face, and his eyes constantly fixed on the ground, and that he had said little or nothing. He stated himself to be a hop-merchant, and said that he was waiting at Bäumler's for his companion, another hop-merchant, who had gone to the play. The witnesses recognised the glass produced in court, as exactly similar to that out of which the stranger had been drinking red clove-brandy.

Meanwhile suspicion had fallen upon a certain Paul Forster, who had lately been discharged from the bridewell at Schwabach, and who had been observed for several days before the murder walking about in a suspicious manner before Bäumler's house. His father, a miserably poor day-labourer, lived with two daughters of infamous characters in a cottage belonging to a gardener named Thaler, in the suburb of St. John. Forster did not live with his father; but on the morning after the murder he had left the suburb of St. John quite early, and had gone to Diesbeck, where he lived with a woman called Margaret Preiss, who had been his mistress for many years. At her house he was arrested by the police on the 23rd of September, the third day after the murder. In her room were found, among other things, two bags of money, the one containing 209 florins 21 kreuzers, the other 152 florins 17 kreuzers. Besides these Preiss's illegitimate daughter, a girl of about fourteen, gave up a small purse containing some medals and a ducat which Forster had given to her when he returned to Diesbeck.

On the following day, when the gens d'armes were escorting Forster and his mistress through Fürth, the waiter of the inn recognised the prisoner as the man who had come to the inn at about eight or nine in the morning of the 21st of September, dressed in a dark grey cloth greatcoat, went away again in about an hour, and then returned dressed in a dark blue coat, and gave him a brown one which he carried under his arm to take care of, requesting him to keep it safe, and to be sure not to show it to any one; adding that in a week he would return and claim it. The waiter now informed the magistrate at Fürth of this circumstance, and produced the greatcoat, which was much stained and in some places soaked with blood.

The description given of the suspicious-looking stranger, who had sat out all the others on the evening of the 20th of September, exactly resembled Forster.

As soon as the prisoners reached Nürnberg, at about 4 P.M. of the 24th, they were conducted, according to legal practice, to view the bodies lying in Bäumler's house. The corpses were laid in their coffins, with the faces exposed and the bodies covered with their own bloody garments; Bäumler on the right, and the maid-servant on the left hand, thus leaving a passage open between the coffins.

Paul Forster was brought in first : he stepped into the room, and between the two corpses, without the slightest change of countenance. When desired to look at them, he gazed steadfastly and coldly upon them, and replied to the question whether he knew the body on the right, " No, I know it not; it is quite disfigured : I know it not." And to the second question, " Do you know this one to the left?" he answered in the same manner, " No, she has lain in the grave; I know her not." When asked how he knew that the body had lain in the grave, he replied, pointing to the face, " Because she is so disfigured; the face is quite decayed here!" On being desired by the judge to point out the exact spot which he thought so decayed, with a constrained air, but with the coarsest indifference, he grasped the head of the murdered woman, pressed the brow, the broken nose, and the cheeks with his fingers, and said quite coolly, "Here: you may see it clearly!" He attempted to evade every question addressed to him by the judge, by affecting that the idea of murder was so utterly foreign to him, that in all innocence and simplicity he mistook the deadly wounds for the result of decay.

All the endeavours of the judge to wring some sign of embarrassment or feeling from this man, as he stood between his two victims, were vain: his iron soul was unmoved. Only once, when asked, "Where, then, is the corn-chandler to whom the house belongs?" he appeared staggered, but only for a moment. The judge went so far in his zeal, as to desire him to hold the hands of both corpses, and then to say what he felt. Without a moment's hesitation, Forster grasped the cold hand of Bäumler in his right, and that of Schütz in his left hand; and answered, "He feels cold — ah, she is cold too;" an answer which clearly contained a sort of contemptuous sneer at the judge's question. During the whole scene, the tone of his voice was as soft and sanctimonious, and his manner as calm, as his feelings were cold and unmoved.

His mistress's behaviour was very different: she was much shaken on entering the room. When desired to look at the dead bodies, she did so, but instantly turned away shuddering, and asked for water. She declared that she knew nothing of these persons, or of the manner of their death. She said that she had learned that she was supposed to be implicated in the horrible deed from the populace, who crowded in thousands round the carriage which brought them from Fürth to Nürnberg, calling her a murderess, striking her with their fists and sticks, and ill-using her in every way. But that God would manifest her innocence, and that she could bring witnesses to prove that she had not left her home at Diesbeck for some weeks. Her evident compassion for the victims, and horror of the crime, spoke more in favour of her innocence than her tears and protestations. An alibi was subsequently most clearly proved.

On Forster's examination, he professed himself totally ignorant of the cause of his arrest, adding that he conjectured from the shouts of the mob that he was suspected of a murder. He said that he had been at Diesbeck from the 21st to the 23rd September; and that if the murder was committed before that day, he should he as little able to prove his innocence as others would be to prove his guilt. He had never known the murdered persons. He had passed the 18th, 19th, and 20th September in Nürnberg in search of employment, and had gone on the last-named day through the Frauen Thor to the suburb of St. John. He had not been able to sleep in his father's house on account of the fleas, and had lain in the hay in Thaler's open shed, which he left at one o'clock in the morning when the people got up to begin threshing, and went to Diesbeck, which he reached at about 4 P.M. on the 21st; he gave his mistress two bags of money to keep for him. This money came into his possession in the following manner :—While he was in the bride-

well at Schwabach he had formed a most intimate
friendship with a certain Xavier Beck, a jeweller,
who was confined there for bigamy, and who subsequently died in prison. This man confided to him
that in a particular spot between Fürth and Farnbach
he had buried a large sum of money, half of which
he promised to give to him. After his release, he,
Forster, searched for and discovered the treasure,
which, however, instead of amounting to eight or nine
thousand florins, as Beck had represented, was at most
two hundred and fifty. This money he had concealed
in a stack of wood close by the Frauen Thor at Nürnberg, but on the evening of the 20th September he
had taken it out again, and had carried it on the
following day to his mistress. - The court was forced
to rest satisfied with this tale for the present; but in
the mean time one suspicious circumstance after another rose up in black array against Paul Forster.

Two of the men who had been drinking at Bäumler's house on the 20th September, identified Forster
as the suspicious-looking stranger already described;
the rest would not affirm this on oath, which was
perhaps owing to his having since that day shaved
off his thick beard, and had his hair cut close. Yet
even these declared that "they thought he was the
unknown guest;" or "that he appeared to be one
and the same person;" or that "he was exceedingly
like him."

Margaret Preiss declared that on Thursday the
21st Forster returned home at about 4 P.M.; that
instead of his usual brown coat, in which he had left
her a few days before, he had on a new blue one;
that he wore a pair of large nankeen trowsers which

she had never seen before, over his own old ones, and
new-fashioned Suwarrow boots.   He brought some
money in his handkerchief, and gave it to her to keep
for him, observing that it was not his, but only intrusted to his care; he then took from the pocket of
his trowsers a Nürnberg thaler and a ducat, which he
gave to her daughter.   He was very tired and his
feet were blistered, and, contrary.to his usual habit,
seemed thoughtful and out of spirits; when she asked
him the reason, he answered her drily, that nobody
could always be cheerful.   On the next day he ate
nothing, and continued silent and gloomy.   On the
following Saturday, when they heard a noise and
several men came into the room to apprehend him,
he turned red as scarlet; and when she said "You
have been about some mischief," he merely answered,
" Nay, I have done nothing."

Dörr, a poor lead-pencil maker, who lived in the
same cottage with old Forster and his daughters, gave
evidence as follows: "On Thursday the 21st September, at two o'clock in the morning, Paul Forster
came to the window and called for his father to
come out to him.   Old Forster was in the barn
threshing; but Forster's sister Walburga, on hearing
his voice, exclaimed 'That is my brother John,'
jumped out of bed and fetched her father.   They then
all three stood at the back of the house for about half
an hour, talking together in a low voice.   Next
morning Walburga told his (Dörr's) wife that her
brother was gone hop-picking, and had given her his
old boots, as he had bought some new ones.   Old
Forster also told witness that his son had paid him an
old debt of two or three florins."   It further appeared

that Paul Forster could not have slept in the shed till
one in the morning, as he stated, as Thaler and his
son swore that it was invariably locked at night. His
mysterious nocturnal visit at his father's house tallied
with the time when the murder had been committed;
and his long conversation with his father and sister
appears the more suspicious as the reason which Walburga assigned for calling her father out of the barn
was totally untrue.

In a very short time the instrument was discovered
with which there was every reason to suppose the
crime had been committed, and which furnished a
fresh link in the chain of evidence against Forster.
On the 20th September a certain Margaret Wölflin
saw Catherine, Forster's youngest sister, go into the
churchyard in the suburb of St. John's, come out
again and fetch her elder sister Walburga, who then
went into the churchyard, where Paul Forster was
standing. After talking with him for a short time in
an under-tone, she went home, and soon returned
carrying an axe under her arm as if to hide it.
Margaret Wölflin asked her what she had under her
arm, and she then carried the axe more openly, and
gave it to her brother with the words " Be so good as
to take this axe into town to be ground for me."
Forster took it and went towards Nürnberg, after ex-
changing a few words and casting an angry glance at
Margaret.

On the following morning Walburga met Margaret
Wölflin and told her that the chandler Bäumler had
been stabbed the night before. She had her brother's
boots in her basket, but they had been so washed and
rubbed that she could not find a purchaser for them at

any price. On the same day Walburga met a certain
Roth and told him that her brother had given her the
boots, which she was forced to wear herself, adding,
" If things go well, it will not be long before I have a
new petticoat too."

As soon as the police had received information of
these facts, they searched Forster's house, and found
behind the stack of wood an axe, which one of the
police identified as one which he had seen the night
before (26th September) lying behind the stove
wrapped in a wet rag : there was some red moisture
on the hatchet just where the handle joined the blade.
Margaret Wölflin recognised this as the same which
Walburga had given to her brother by a flaw in the
steel, and the physician declared the reddish stains on
the handle just below the blade to be half-effaced
marks of blood.

Forster's two sisters, Walburga and Catherine, were
apprehended and examined. On her first examination Walburga confessed that her brother had borrowed the axe exactly as Wölflin had stated, under
pretence of wanting it for a burglary ; that between
two and three in the morning he brought it back
to her partly cleaned, and at the same time made
her a present of his boots, which had been washed
up to the ankle, telling her that he had not been
lucky in his burglary, but that whenever he got
any money he would send her some. At Forster's
desire she then fetched their father, to whom he paid
1 fl. 38 kr. which he had borrowed of him a fortnight
before. On her second examination, however, when
pressingly admonished by the judge, she confessed
that her brother had said to her on that night, " I

have committed a crime—I have done a great thing—
I have murdered a man! Fetch my father quickly,
I am going hop-picking. Do you wash the axe and
the boots, and take care of them for me, so that no
one may know anything of the matter." On the
boots she had observed large spots, which disappeared on washing, and which she supposed must
have been blood. She added in a subsequent examination, that the silk tassels of both boots were quite
glued together with blood.

The circumstantial evidence against Forster now
appeared conclusive. The dark brown coat worn
by the accused on the day of the murder, and
left with the waiter at the inn of Fürth, was found
to be much stained with blood. It was further
proved that over it he wore a good grey greatcoat,
which he exchanged at Fürth with a Jewess for the
blue one in which he was apprehended. This grey
coat had belonged to Bäumler, and the white lining
was much stained with blood : the nankeen trowsers and the Suwarrow boots were also identified
as Bäumler's property by the tradesmen who had
made them for him. All these things, and the money-
bags, which could have belonged to no one but
Bäumler, were stronger evidence of his guilt than
the testimony of the most unsuspected witnesses.

Such was the state of the case when Forster sent
to request an audience of the judge. The solitude of
the prison had afforded him leisure to reflect that a
number of damning circumstances were clearly proved
against him. His natural acuteness and long experience of such matters taught him that by persevering
in the affectation of ignorance as well as innocence of

the crime laid to his charge, he would expose himself
to the danger of being compelled step by step to deny
manifest truths, in the teeth of the most conclusive
evidence. This, he saw, would be a difficult and
dangerous game, in which he must be driven from
one retreat to another, and end by being entangled
in snares woven of his own answers and admissions.
He therefore resolved to disarm the judge by making
a confession, which, while it should throw the guilt
on others, might nevertheless accord with the evidence
already in the possession of the judge, or likely to be
still produced. He opened the audience on the 3rd
November by asking " pardon of the judge for all the
untruths of which he had been guilty on the first
examination, and by declaring that he would now relate
circumstances which must lead to the discovery of the
murderer." His statement was shortly this : —

" On Monday the 18th September he had gone
from Diesbeck to Langenzenn, determined in consequence of his misfortunes to leave his native country
and to enlist as a soldier in Bohemia. While sitting
in a melancholy mood by the road side near Langenzenn, two men, followed by a couple of dogs,
came up to him, asked what was the matter, and,
on hearing his distress, expressed great interest in
his fate. They told him that they were hop-merchants, of the name of Schlemmer, from Hersbruck ;
that they were brothers, and had rich relations in
Bohemia, whither they were going with a cargo of
hops, and offered to take him with them to Bohemia,
where he would be sure to find employment. They
added that on the morrow or the next day (Wednesday, the day of the murder) they should be going

with a hop-cart into Nürnberg, where they had a
cousin, a corn-chandler, of the name of Bäumler,
who lived near the church of St. Laurence. On the
following day, the 19th September, he went to Nürnberg, walked up and down the street near the church
of St. Laurence, inquired of a barber for Bäumler,
and asked ' who the woman in the house might be.'
He was told it was the maid. He waited in vain till
six in the evening for the Schlemmers; and then returned to the suburb of St. John's and slept in the
shed. On the following morning, the 20th September,
he again went into the town, and after wandering
about until four in the afternoon, the thought struck
him that he would go and take leave of his sisters
before starting for Bohemia. On this occasion his
sister Walburga gave him an axe, with the request
that he would take it to the grinder at Nürnberg,
whence she would fetch it herself. At about five
o'clock, as he was going with the axe to the grinder,
he met the Schlemmers, who asked him to carry a
letter to the post for them as quickly as possible,
offering to take care of the axe in the mean time, and
to wait for him where they then stood. After putting
the letter into the post he returned to the spot, but did
not find the Schlemmers, and passed the time in walking up and down the street until about six o'clock,
when he went into Bäumler's house and drank some
red clove-brandy. At a quarter before ten, when all
the other guests were gone, the Schlemmers at length
arrived, and Bäumler greeted them as cousins. Soon
after they sent him to wait in the Caroline-strasse
for their cart, which was coming from Fürth, drawn
by two white horses. This he did; and soon after a

quarter to ten the two Schlemmers came to him, carrying a trunk between them, and one of them with a white parcel under his arm. At this moment the cart drove up with two men in it, to whom the Schlemmers said that ' they had had great luck ; they had won the great prize.' They then made him get into the cart with them. But at the gate of the town they told him that as they had had such luck they should not go into Bohemia; but that, in order to show him how kindly they felt towards him, they would give him something which might assist him in his own country. They then gave him the white parcel which one of them had under his arm, and at the same time returned the axe to him. He then went back to the suburb of St. John, and on opening the parcel found in it a greatcoat, a pair of boots, a pair of trowsers, and three bags of money."

During the whole of this examination, which with the questions and answers took up six full hours, the prisoner stood in the same position, without once sitting down on the chair which the judge offered him. The story flowed from his lips as glibly as though it had been learnt by rote, and he looked the judge full in the face the while; but when he was cross-examined about the appearance, figure, dress, &c. of the two Schlemmers, he became embarrassed, spoke more slowly, hesitated and considered, and avoided the eyes of the judge.

That no such people as the brothers Schlemmer were to be found at Hersbruck or elsewhere was of course to be expected. But that Forster had accomplices was in fact implied in this statement. This had been suspected by the judge from the very begin-

ning; and indeed it seemed scarcely credible that one
man should be able to murder two people almost at
the same moment, and in so public a street. Besides,
the mere act of killing was not all; several other arrangements and precautions were necessary to prevent interruption and discovery. At the very moment
when the maid was in all probability on her way
home, a few seconds after the murder of Bäumler, the
glass door had to be taken off, the other door to be
placed on the hinges, and the bell to be stopped,—
and then the maid was let in and murdered. The
commodes, chests, and closets up-stairs were to be
broken open and rifled. This apparently required
several pairs of hands. Moreover Forster himself had
said, while sitting in Bäumler's shop, that he was
waiting for his companion, who was gone to the play.
The maid too, when she bought the rolls, spoke of
several fellows who were still at her master's house.
One of the watchmen set to guard the waggons stated
that he saw a suspicious-looking man standing with
folded arms gazing at Bäumler's house; and Walburga, Forster's sister, declared that when her brother
gave her back the axe she saw, at a distance of fifty
paces, a person with a white apron, whom she took
for Margaret Preiss. A few days after Forster had
been confined in the fortress at Nürnberg, on the
28th September, at eleven o'clock at night, two men
were seen by the sentinel looking up at the window
of Forster's room, and on his approach they ran away.
Another time the sentinel saw two men lying under
a tree on the bank of the river close beneath the
fortress; on his calling out "Who's there?" they
only answered the challenge by a volley of stones:

the sentinel at length fired, whereupon they ran away.

The presumption that the murders and robbery were committed by several accomplices was strengthened by statements made by some of Bäumler's acquaintances, that he had at that time a sum of 1500 or 2000 florins in his house in ready money, for the purpose of purchasing a stock in trade; whereas after the murder little or no cash was found in the house, and the whole sum in Forster's possession did not amount to much more than 360 florins. All these circumstances certainly encouraged the idea that he must have had accomplices who shared the booty with him.

The judge was accordingly called upon to exert all his sagacity in endeavouring to discover Forster's accomplices, as well as in examining the evidence against the prisoner himself. An extensive correspondence was set on foot, witnesses were examined, journeys undertaken, as far even as Frankfort-on-the-Main ; the faintest shadow of suspicion was eagerly pursued; all persons of doubtful character, all who had been in any way connected with Forster or his sister Walburga, all the convicts who had been acquainted with him in prison or since his release, were examined, and many arrested. But after the court and the police had resorted to every possible means of detection, and had exhausted all their ingenuity in the pursuit of evidence, they found themselves at exactly the same point whence they had started. In most cases the innocence of the suspected persons immediately appeared upon investigation ; and all those to whom the slightest suspicion could attach proved most satisfactory alibis. In short, we are persuaded that if so much zeal and ingenuity failed in making any further discovery, it was solely because there was nothing to discover.

The remarkable coincidence between the wounds upon both corpses renders it in the highest degree probable that they were inflicted with the same hand.

The danger and difficulty of such an enterprise vanish as we become better acquainted with the character of Forster, a villain who united to great bodily strength, and a hand trained to strike, very uncommon acuteness and a determined will—one who perceived at a glance whatever opportunities offered themselves, and instantly seized them; who pursued his purpose with a clear head and a cold heart—whom no impediments could disconcert, no horrors dismay. To such a man the greater and more daring the scheme, the more inviting it would appear. But the whole can be easily explained, without supposing either the existence of accomplices, or of any very extraordinary courage in the one murderer. Forster had devoted several days to watching Bäumler's house and finding out his habits. His long stay in the shop on the evening of the murder made him thoroughly acquainted with the place, and gave him an opportunity of observing every thing, and of seizing the most favourable moment for the execution of his purpose. As soon as the maid had left the house, Forster suddenly attacked Bäumler, who was sitting upon his low seat by the stove, and felled him, dead or dying, to the ground, with one blow of the axe which he had hitherto concealed. He must then have hastened to the entrance of the shop, bent back the bell, stuffed it

with paper, taken the glass door off its hinges, shut
and locked the folding-door, and hidden himself
behind it. On Schütz's return he opened the door to
let her in, and must have struck her from behind
with his murderous weapon, as was shown by the
fracture in her skull, and then despatched her in
the corner of the shop. Bäumler's house was so
small, and every thing so conveniently placed, that
to unhinge the glass door, to fix the wooden one,
and to prepare every thing for the murder of the
maid, would scarce require more than half a minute.
Besides, Forster had so often walked up and down
the street, and so carefully examined the ground, that
he could exactly calculate the time it would take
the maid to go to and return from the baker's, and
his cool head was not disturbed by the sight of
blood. It can easily be explained why none of the
neighbours heard a scream ; the blows aimed by the
steady hand of the murderer with the heavy axe were
so sudden and so tremendous, that they must have
instantly deprived the victims of consciousness, if not
of life.

Another circumstance strongly corroborates the
opinion that only one person was concerned in the
murder and robbery : many articles of value, belonging
to Bäumler, were found in his house. Several accomplices in robbery and murder would not have left such
booty behind ; but Forster, to whom time was valuable, took only what he most wanted—money, and
such clothes as first fell into his hands. That Bäumler
had as much as 1500 or 2000 florins in the house was
a mere supposition. If even he had wanted so much
for the purchase of stores, it does not follow that he

would have kept such a sum in hard money by him. After his death, too, it appeared that common report had greatly magnified his wealth.

It was clearly proved that Forster was the only guest left in Bäumler's house after nine o'clock. Had one or more accomplices joined him then, they would have called for brandy as an excuse for staying; but on the following morning, only one glass—that out of which Forster had drunk—was found upon the table.

Moreover, Forster had been seen about Nürnberg by many persons for several days before the murder, especially in the street near Bäumler's house, and always alone. During this time no one came near him who could be in the slightest degree suspected of being his accomplice, either at Diesbeck, before he went to Nürnberg to commit the murder, or after he had returned to Diesbeck by way of Fürth, after accomplishing it. We must, indeed, except his sister, Walburga, and Margaret Preiss, but both completely proved alibis.

If he had accomplices, it is strange that all clue to them was lost, while every species of evidence accumulated against Forster.

It is true that Forster told Bäumler and the other guests that he was waiting for the return of his comrade from the play; but a stranger requires some excuse for staying from six till nine in the same tavern.

The baker's wife, from whom Anna Schütz bought the rolls, certainly understood her to say that there were still several fellows at Bäumler's house, but the poor girl was already several paces distant from the shop when she answered; and if we consider the unimportance of the question and answer, and the allow-

ances to be made for the treachery of memory, it
seems very uncertain whether the baker's wife accurately heard or remembered what the maid had said.
Moreover, she said that Anna Schütz was very angry
at being sent out so late, and anger is not apt to measure words very correctly.

The suspicious-looking fellow, whom the watchman Weismüller saw in the street opposite Bäumler's
house, at a quarter past nine, was in all probability
Forster himself, who may have made some excuse
for leaving Bäumler's shop for a moment, in order
to see whether there were many people about, or to
fetch the axe, which he may have hidden somewhere
near the house.

Walburga's statement, that on the night of the
murder she saw some one at a distance of about fifty
yards behind her brother, deserves little attention, not
only because it was dark at the time, but also because
she evidently wished to gain importance in the eyes
of the court by making interesting revelations.

The accidental circumstance of two men looking up
at the Bridewell at eleven o'clock at night, on the
28th September, could only be of consequence if it
were proved that they looked up not from mere curiosity, but with the knowledge that it was Forster's
window at which they were looking. The second
occurrence on the 31st October probably had no
connection whatever with any of the prisoners: the
two men who were then lying under the tree by the
Pegnitz were most likely a couple of drunken fellows
who amused themselves by throwing stones at the
sentinel, but who naturally ran away when he discharged his musket.

The special inquisition to which Paul Forster, his sister Walburga, and Margaret Preiss were first subjected, on the 7th November, 1820, produced nothing of importance against Forster. He underwent thirteen long examinations, in which he had to answer one thousand three hundred and thirteen questions, besides confrontations with innumerable witnesses; but no confession could be wrung from him. Animated by a spirit as powerful and enduring as his bodily frame, he often stood during his examinations for five or six hours on the same spot, and nothing ever made him flinch or waver. Once in the Bridewell he said to some of his companions, that " If ever he got into trouble again, he would persist in denial until his tongue turned black and rotted in his mouth and his body was bent double." After his discharge he said the same thing to his sister and to Wölflin. Indeed he combined in his person all the qualities which could enable him to resist truth even when most evident. He was a man whom no question could embarras and no admonition disconcert. He had considered beforehand the whole array of evidence against him as carefully as the judge himself. Thus nothing took him by surprise; there was nothing for which he was unprepared. He clung to his fable of the two hop-merchants like the shipwrecked sailor to the plank which is to convey him to shore. This tale, in which he never varied the smallest circumstance, although he admitted that unfortunately for him no one would believe it, always afforded him a loophole by which to escape from the most convincing facts or from the clearest evidence. His presence in Bäumler's house, the axe with which the murder was committed, Bäumler's clothes found upon him, did not, according to his version of the matter, criminate him, but the two hop-merchants. His confession of the murder to his sister, and the fact that his boots were bloody, rested merely on her testimony, and he positively denied both to her face. He accounted for the blood on his brown coat and that on Bäumler's green one by some incredible fiction. All means of attack recoiled from his iron soul; neither the bloody clothes nor the axe, nor confrontation with his sister and other witnesses, could shake him. If a passing flush or paleness, or a downcast eye, occasionally betrayed surprise and embarrassment, it was but for a moment, and he quickly recovered his self-possession. When the axe was produced, his changing colour and rolling eye betrayed the fearful emotion within; but his voice and his answers remained unshaken. Upon being confronted with his sister Walburga, he seemed confused, his colour fled, and his hands trembled; but he still preserved so complete a command over himself as to look her full in the face whilst he denied the most manifest truths. During the whole special inquisition, the emotions he exhibited were those of a wild beast suddenly caught in a net, vainly seeking an outlet by which to escape from the hunters who surround him. When the judge animadverted upon his changing colour or his embarrassed air, he replied with perfect truth, " It is quite possible for an innocent man to seem more embarrassed than a guilty one: the latter knows exactly what he has done; the former feels that he cannot prove his innocence." He concealed his obstinacy under an assumption of calmness, gentleness, and piety, as if humbly submitting to a fate he did not deserve. " I see plainly," said he in his last examination, " that I cannot escape unless the Schlemmers are taken. I have therefore nothing to do but to pray to God that he will enlighten my judges and enable them to distinguish between guilt and innocence, between the possible and the impossible. In this case guilt and innocence touch, and I have no means of proving my innocence." The following circumstance will give some idea of his cunning, hypocrisy, and dissimulation :—During the trial a certain John Wagner, who had formerly been in prison with him at Schwabach, was confronted with him to give evidence touching expressions which Forster had dropped concerning some scheme for future crimes. Wagner, on this occasion, accused him of stealing a pair of silk braces. Forster denied the charge, and even when the braces were produced in court and identified by Wagner, he persisted in his denial. But in the solitude of his prison he reflected that he could turn this incident to good account in giving an air of truth to his falsehoods respecting the murder. Accordingly, after an interval of two days, he requested an audience and appeared before the judge, with downcast looks and trembling hands, like one bowed down by shame and remorse, and confessed in a circumstantial manner that " he had given way to the temptations of Satan and had stolen Wagner's silk braces." This repentant confession was doubtless intended to convince the judge that one whose tender conscience could not bear even the burden of a stolen pair of braces would be still less able to endure the remorse which must follow a double murder.

Towards the close of the trial he must have seen, and indeed he acknowledged as much, that, in spite of his courage, obstinacy, and cunning, truth could not be overpowered by fables and evasions. His obstinate perseverance in denial must therefore be attributed not only to a hope of thus avoiding capital punishment, but also to pride. Impressed with a conviction of his own mental superiority, and ambitious of a character for dauntless courage and immovable strength of will, he was resolved not to allow the judge to gain the slightest advantage over his feelings or his understanding. If he must fall, at least he would fall like a hero. If he could not avoid the fate of a criminal, he would avoid the disgrace of a confession wrung from weakness or cowardice. Men might shudder at him, but his fearful crimes should excite wonder, not contempt. The murder of Bäumler and his maid was a crime which any common villain might commit; but to stand unmoved by all the dangers which followed the deed, to bid defiance to truth, to the skill of the judge,—to behold the most terrible sights with a steady gaze and without one feeling of pity; to turn a deaf ear to the admonitions of conscience; to remain firm in the dreadful solitude of the cell, as well as in the presence of the court;—this it was which raised him, in his own estimation, far above the common herd of criminals.

Forster escaped capital punishment in spite of the strong circumstantial evidence against him, as no confession could be extorted from him, and as there were no competent eye-witnesses to the murder. Sentence to this effect was accordingly passed upon him on the 22nd July, 1821 :—

" That John Paul Forster is convicted of the murder of the chandler Bäumler and of his maid-servant, on the night of the 20th September, 1820, and that he is condemned to imprisonment for life in chains."

His sister Walburga was convicted of aiding and abetting the murder committed by her brother, and sentenced to twelve months' imprisonment in the house of correction. Margaretha Preiss was acquitted.

Imprisonment in chains annihilates civil existence, as completely as death puts an end to physical life. It deprives a man for ever of his rights as a citizen, a husband, and a father; of honour, property, and freedom; nothing is left him but bare life passed in slavery and chains. Evidence of guilt strong enough to justify such a punishment ought to entail that of death. In case of error, the hardship is equally great, as it is no more possible to restore a man to civil life after the execution of this sentence, than to resuscitate him after his head has been cut off. The Bavarian code affords no means of relief for the man dead in law; how, indeed, could he recover his property from his heirs, or claim his wife then living in lawful wedlock with another? In a word, in cases in which the State hesitates to award capital punishment, it should equally refrain from inflicting this sentence of death in life.

The Bavarian law directs that the criminal be previously exposed for one hour, if possible on the spot where the crime was committed, in chains, and with a tablet on his breast specifying the nature of his offence and the sentence passed upon him. Thus a man convicted on the clearest evidence instructs the people from the pillory by the inscription on his breast, "Imprisonment for twofold Murder," that a man may be convicted of such crimes as these, and yet not have deserved death. The popular sense, utterly unable to distinguish between the niceties of legal evidence, and believing with blunt simplicity that conviction is conviction, and that guilt is guilt, must be strangely puzzled and disturbed in its faith in the justice of the laws and the impartiality of those who administer it. The most ignorant of the people are aware that the guilty occasionally escape, from want of evidence; but that a murderer publicly and solemnly denounced as guilty should escape the punishment incurred by his crime, owing to some mere technical objection, is far beyond the comprehension of the most intelligent among them, and utterly repugnant to their sense of justice.

John Paul Forster was born on the 22nd January, 1791, and professed the Lutheran faith. His father and his sisters Walburga and Catherine lived, as we have before mentioned, in the suburb of St. John's, and the whole family belonged to a sect of chosen brethren who do as little work as possible, in order that they may have more time for praying, singing hymns, and reading the Bible, and who compound with heaven for their vices by their so-called piety.

Forster has given a very circumstantial account of his own life and character, not only in his evidence before the court, but also in a MS. composed by

himself in 1817-18, during his imprisonment at
Schwabach, and entitled 'The Romance of my Life
and Loves.' In this autobiography truth and fiction
are so closely blended, that it is scarce possible to say
where the one begins and the other ends. But the
manner in which he speaks of himself, and of his real
and fictitious adventures, gives an exact picture of the
inmost workings of his mind, and serves as a key to
his character.

As a child, his quiet prudent behaviour distinguished him, as he assures us, from other boys.
While his brother was running about the streets,
playing or fighting with his companions, and often
returning home with torn clothes or a bloody nose,
Forster's delight was to sit in a neighbouring public-
house where the good burghers of the town were wont
to spend their leisure hours at the game of loto. Here
he would do them small services, by which he not only
gained many a penny, but also the "respect of the
whole company, and the name of good little Paul."
When he was in his eighth year a Prussian nobleman
came to live in a house in the garden which Forster's
father cultivated. Baron von D—— had two children
of the same age as Paul Forster, and the " good little
Paul " occasionally had the honour of associating with
these young nobles. He carried their toys, fetched
their bread and butter, and insinuated himself into
their good graces by waiting upon them "as if he had
really been their servant." He seems to have been as
proud of acting the part of a lackey to these boys as
if he had become a baron himself. " My conduct,"
says he, " pleased the noble parents so much, that they
every day renewed their invitation to me. My other

companions now began to treat me with indifference, and even with contempt. My brother Christopher looked at me coldly, and said, 'Go! I am not good enough for you now; I see you mean to be a fine gentleman, since you will not play with us any longer.' I excused myself civilly, and continued my own way of life." In his self-satisfied account of himself we trace the character of an idle effeminate boy, who prefers loitering about public-houses to the natural enjoyments of youth; a premature hypocrite, who cringes and flatters in order to worm himself into the favour of strangers, and who reckons it a high honour to be the menial slave of boys of noble birth, while he despises his own equals. The mixture of pride and meanness, of vanity and coarseness, and the desire to bask in the sunshine of nobility, even in the most servile position, still appear in the further account of his early life. When he had left school, he says that " the noble Baroness von D—— begged his father to permit the boy to enter her service." His father's consent obtained, Forster was in the seventh heaven. He was no longer called Paul, but John; and, as a reward for his attention and care, dressed in a grey livery, so that " he might accompany his noble master and mistress to balls and assemblies, and thus learn the manners of the fashionable world."

This felicity did not, however, last long. " My father," he says, " from a regard to the welfare of my soul, recalled me and endeavoured to impose upon me the task of learning the profession of a shoemaker; but my attachment to the nobility was too strong, and I threatened to run away." At last Forster chose the

trade of a gardener, because "a gardener frequently
comes into contact with gentlefolks." He speaks in
high praise of his own proficiency in gardening; and,
indeed, nothing is known to his disadvantage before
he entered the army. About this time the rector of
the parish gave him the character of being active,
industrious, and well-behaved. He himself states that
he so entirely gained the confidence of the owner of
the garden rented by his master, that after the death
of the latter it was intrusted to his management,
which he exercised for two years " with great ap-
plause," at the end of which time he was forced to
leave the place by the tender importunities of the
gardener's widow, a woman of fifty, who conceived a
violent passion for this " half-blown rosebud of seventeen." He next served as gardener in a family where
Babetta the cook "subjugated him by the charms of
her person, and still more by the graces of her mind."
The romance with Babetta was approaching its catastrophe when, in 1807, "the voice of his country summoned him to the musket of military life;" that is to
say, he was drawn on the conscription, and enrolled in
a regiment of the line.

At this time Forster seems to have entered upon
his career of vice and crime: the fact is, that he
wanted patience and fortitude to endure a life which
thwarted his inclinations and mortified his pride.
The day on which he joined his battalion was his
" first day of humiliation;" for his Babetta signified
to him that she did not consider it compatible with
her honour to associate with a common soldier. But
the worst was still to come. After his first drill, he
exclaims, "Ah, this was the real beginning of my

misery! From the earliest dawn until the close of day a merciless corporal was busied in beating military ardour into me, in twisting me about like a puppet, and making me as lank and as supple as a greyhound. He scarce allowed me time to swallow my scanty rations; and when I stretched myself at night upon my sack of straw, I felt as if I had been broken upon the wheel. Bavarian blows and Bavarian rations are an infallible remedy against love! During the first few weeks I seldom thought of my lovely Babetta, but often enough of running away. I envied every cobbler his golden leisure, and tottered through the streets at midday like a hunted stag seeking a spring of fresh water." The life of a soldier never ceased to be an intolerable burden to him. How was an effeminate libertine to endure privations and hardships, or sleep on hard boards, instead of on his mistress's bed? Was one so fond of existence to expose his person to cannon-balls? or one so vain to submit to the rude contact of a corporal's stick, and to be confounded with thousands of other men in the dress of a common soldier? His ill-regulated passions were fretted and increased by control, and his powers of dissimulation called forth by the severity of the discipline under which he was forced to bend. As his desires increased in violence, he grew more reckless as to the means by which he gratified them; and the frequency of his trials, imprisonments, and corporal punishments only taught him indifference to the penalty of his crimes.

In 1808, when his regiment was encamped at Fürth, he contrived to steal out of his tent and through all the outposts, and went to Nürnberg, where he spent the night with Babetta, and crept back early the following morning to his tent. But the same day, on parade, he was called out of the ranks and questioned as to his absence during the night. At first he denied the charge. But when he found that the proofs were strong against him, he confessed, making excuses for his conduct, " but not," he adds, " until he saw that he was clearly convicted." Twenty lashes were immediately inflicted on him.

He made the campaign in 1809 against Austria; was, according to his own account, taken prisoner, ransomed himself, and returned to Nürnberg. In 1810 he left his barracks, but returned after eighteen days' absence, and was placed under arrest. In that year he became acquainted with Margaretha Preiss, who already had an illegitimate daughter by a married man, but for whom he conceived the most violent and lasting passion. In 1811 a furlough was granted to him for an indefinite time, during which he acted as gardener and tavern-keeper at a small property near Adlitz which Margaretha rented; and he endeavoured, but without success, to obtain his discharge, in order to marry his mistress. In 1812 he was summoned to join his regiment. At Adlitz he committed several petty thefts. He stole an umbrella and a shawl from one of the guests in his garden, for which he was punished in the following year by order of his commanding officer. It is extremely probable that he committed greater thefts, as he relates that he was able to lend out at interest two sums, one of 600 florins, another of 250. In 1813 he deserted, and wandered about for eleven weeks, living chiefly in the woods : at the end of which time he went back to Margaretha, who then rented a small public-house at the suburb of St. John's at Nürnberg, where he was discovered soon after. He was condemned for desertion and theft to run the gauntlet three times backwards and forwards through one hundred and fifty men, and to six additional years of military service. On the very day of his punishment he deserted again, was again taken, and again received the same sentence. This lesson also was vain. In 1815 he was again subjected to a criminal trial for desertion, theft, and conspiracy with a younger sister of his mistress to extort money, and was drummed out of the regiment.

This long wished for dismissal from the service, disgraceful as it was, at length rewarded him for the indomitable obstinacy and indifference to disgrace which he had displayed for so many years, in a stubborn neglect of his duties.

From this time forward he led an idle and dissolute life, occasionally working as a day-labourer, but much oftener stealing and squandering the proceeds, which were considerable, with his mistress, until, in 1816, he was arrested and tried before the criminal court at Nürnberg for theft and housebreaking, and sentenced to three years and six months' imprisonment in the House of Correction. In consequence of his good conduct in confinement, he was released at the expiration of three-fourths of his term, on the 21st of August, 1820, exactly four weeks before the murder. He left this high school of iniquity firmly resolved to find the means of enjoying permanent happiness in the

undisturbed possession of his mistress, and fully convinced that no way to this object save that of crime
was open to him. He had long since broken with
virtue and honour, and Margaretha was his last remaining link with mankind. As he was to depend
upon crime for his subsistence, it was indifferent to
him what form it took. He was disposed to run any
risk in order to obtain a large sum of money, which
he might share with Margaretha. He perilled his
freedom, his life he felt sure of saving by his cunning, boldness, presence of mind, and by the fixed
determination never to confess. The wonderful
stories he had read of heroic robbers and remarkable
criminals, who escaped the vengeance of justice by
their boldness or their cunning, and of celebrated
captives who in the end obtained their liberty by
some miraculous accident, made him see his plan of
life in the light of a romance, and hope to enrol his
name in the list of those heroes whose fame he so
much envied. Filled with these hopes and schemes,
he awaited with impatience the day of his release,
and contrived by hypocritical submissiveness, repentance, and humility, to shorten the time of imprisonment. Thus resolved for the worst, he was thrown
back upon society its bitter foe; and before a month
had elapsed, he signalized himself by a deed which,
for the cruelty, cunning, and boldness with which it
was planned and executed, has few parallels in the
annals of crime.

The bare fact of writing his own life, proves how
important a personage this man considered himself.
It is true that, according to the preface, the work was
intended as a legacy for his beloved Margaretha, in

the event of his death; but it is manifestly written
with a view to other readers—nay, perhaps even to
an honourable place on the shelves of a circulating
library.

This work, allowing for several faults of spelling,
shows a degree of information, cultivation of mind,
and power of composition very unusual in Forster's
class. Several anecdotes—for instance, the account
of his childish amour with a girl of eleven, of the
name of Wilhelmine, and of his stealing out of the
camp at Fürth to visit his mistress Babette, at
Nürnberg, are told with a clearness, simplicity, and
truth, that would do credit to many a practised
pen. But by far the greater part, and especially the
long diffuse preface, is written in the pompous in-
flated style of the worst romances. In many places
he has introduced songs and poems borrowed from
the best German authors, which, according to his
own account, he sang or recited on various occasions, and which he pretends to have composed himself. His head seems to have been crammed with
sentimental phrases and romantic images, which excite disgust and horror in the mouth of such a being.
This tiger, who, with a hand reeking with the blood
of an old man, could murder an innocent and beautiful girl, can talk "of departed souls that hold constant communion with him;" of the "soft murmur
of the evening breezes, and the melting harmony of
the senses, which, after his death, would inform his
beloved Margaretha that he was near her;" of his
'name, which would die away in the shadow of the
grave, like the echo of the songs of love;" of the
" glancing of the moonbeams upon the silver stream

of the Pegnitz:" and of himself in his seventeenth
year, as "a half-blown rose on a beautiful morning in
spring." Who could have recognised the murderer
Forster in the following passages? "Ah! for one
thing I praise God," says he in his preface, apostro-
phizing Margaretha; "for this, that our child, the
first fruit of our love, sleeps the sleep of peace! When
he was torn from me I accused Heaven, and could not
understand the inscrutable ways of God, but mur-
mured against him. But now I shed tears of joy that
he is safe, and I pluck the flowers of the valley to
weave fresh garlands for his grave. Ah! do you
remember how I planted the forget-me-nots upon
his little green grave? Then my heart knew not
God, and my tears flowed in the violence of my
sorrow. I thought myself the most miserable of men.
I now understand things better." No man who really
feels thus can murder. Passages like these—and
there are many such—merely prove the utter corruption of one who, cold and hardened as he was,
could use the language of the most devout piety and
ape the most tender sensibility. The high principle and love of virtue, of which he boasts, are as
false as his sentiment. He could not have forgotten,
while writing, that he was then in prison for theft,
and yet he has the shameless effrontery to write these
words in his preface:—" Oh, Margaretha! tell our
daughter what present help in trouble is the innocence of the heart: how it inspires us with heroic
strength to support the heaviest affliction." Who
would not attribute the following phrase to a philosopher rather than to a housebreaker? " I know not
which best deserves the name of heroism, — that

courage which enables a man to conceal his woes
within his own breast, in order to spare pain and
sorrow to others; or that which induces him to sacrifice himself for the preservation of another."

Religion had no real influence on his mind. His
conviction, as he declared to a fellow-prisoner, was
that religion was necessary for the sake of public
order. He neither hoped nor wished for a future
life, for all his desires centred in the pleasures of
this world. "Had I but money and my mistress,
I should wish to remain for ever in this world, and
never think about another. The wisest philosophers
and the greatest naturalists and magicians have ever
devoted their skill and their knowledge to the art of
prolonging human life. They would not have done
this, had they thought there was a future life." This
was the confession of faith made by him to another
fellow-prisoner. Nevertheless, his knowledge of the
Bible might shame many a clergyman, and in his
autobiography he quotes passages from the sacred
volume, just as he does phrases from romances and
stanzas from love poems, but more frequently and
with greater ostentation. When he wishes to marry,
but resolves first to consider the matter more deeply,
he refers himself to the twenty-seventh and following
verses of the twenty-fifth chapter of Jesus Sirach.
When in prison, he complains with Job x. 19.
When released from gaol he exclaims with Daniel xvi.
22, "My God hath sent his angels and hath shut
the lions' mouth, that they have not hurt me: for-
asmuch as before him innocency was found in me;
and also before thee, O king, have I done no hurt."
Once, he informs us, as he was going through a wood

with a man who intended to rob him—or, as is far
more likely, whom he intended to rob—he recited
the fourth verse of the seventy-first Psalm : "Deliver
me, O my God, out of the hand of the wicked; out of
the hand of the unrighteous and cruel man." He then
suddenly called to mind the passage in the second
book of Moses, xxi. 23-25, "And if any mischief
follow, then thou shalt give life for life, eye for
eye, tooth for tooth," &c.; and encouraged thereby, he
took the initiative in attacking the robber. Two
other robbers then came to their comrade's assistance,
and began unmercifully to belabour the pious Forster
with their clubs, while he sang Luther's hymn—

> "I know not, Lord, where I may die,
> Nor where my grave may be."

But at length, though terribly bruised, he escaped,
and reached a village, where a peasant whom he entreated to give him a night's lodging, refused him
without mercy; whereupon he with the greatest civility
recommended the man to read and carefully consider
the nineteenth and following verses of the sixteenth
chapter of St. Luke.

But false as he is in everything else, his entire
devotion to Margaret Preiss cannot be doubted. She
occupies a place in the romance of his life as prominent as his own. Neither time, misfortune, absence,
disgrace, nor imprisonment was able to overcome their
mutual attachment. In spite of all impediments he
had never abandoned the intention of making this
woman his wife. He had tattooed on his breast in
red letters these words, "My heart is Margaretha's."
In the fortress of Lichtenau, where he was to pass his

life loaded with chains, he said to a fellow-prisoner, "There is but one thing I wish—to see my mistress once more, and die." In his Life he apostrophizes her as "his wife;" "his noble, true-hearted creature;" "the beloved wife of his youth;" "a pious, gentle spirit, who loved him as only angels love;" "the faithful companion of his journey through life." In his preface he longs "to be buried by her side, bedews her hair with his tears, and presses it to his parched lips."

For years Forster has borne in dogged silence the hardships of imprisonment, the misery of civil death, the burden of his chains, and the still heavier burden of a troubled conscience. This unbending obstinacy is no doubt owing partly to great want of sensibility, partly to prodigious bodily power of endurance, and partly to a cowardly clinging to life, however wretched and degraded, characteristic of the most contemptible sensualists. He may perhaps also have flattered himself with the vague hope that his punishment was only inflicted in order to extort from him a confession, and that determined silence would in the end tire out the patience of the court and procure his liberation. But what chiefly strengthened him in this resolution were his romantic ideas of the heroic greatness displayed in his own person. At Lichtenau, before his solitary cell was ready to receive him, while he was with the other prisoners, one of them exhorted him to confess; but he replied, "Steadfastness of purpose is the chief ornament of a man! He should not easily give up life: however wretched, life is a noble thing. Believe me, comrade, whenever I look upon my chains and the ball attached to them,

I feel proud to think that even on my death-bed
my last breath shall be drawn with courage. In
my earliest days, whatever I undertook, that I did.
As I said before, steadfastness and secrecy are what
adorn a man." He treated his heavy chains as a
badge of honour, and polished them in his leisure
hours till they shone like silver. During the early period of his imprisonment at Lichtenau, where the
most distinguished villains enthusiastically admired
and revered him, he condescended to amuse them
with stories of enchanted princes and princesses,
fortunate robbers, &c., to shorten their long dreary
evening hours. But one evening he suddenly declared,
"Gentlemen, from this time forward I shall tell you
no more stories : in future I will say nothing but
yea, yea, nay, nay. I see plainly that things look ill
with me, and that among the worst I am supposed to
be the worst of all." One of his fellow-prisoners asked
him whether any one had forbidden him to speak,
or whether he had taken offence ? But he answered,
"No one but my own soul, and that has never coun-
selled me amiss." Pride kept him true to his word :
from that time forward he told no more stories, and
answered only in monosyllables. Thus he stood alone,
distinguished from the common herd of malefactors.
He maintained this sullen silence for years in his
solitary cell, asking nothing, and uttering no complaint. He took what was offered to him, suffered
any thing to be taken from him, bore every thing in
sullen silence and with apparent calmness. He even
managed to give an appearance of quiet submission
to the obstinate resistance which he offered to the
orders of his superiors. Some task which was im-

posed upon him seemed to him too hard; he left it
untouched. On being asked the reason, he quietly
answered that he was unable to perform it. When
told that if it were not done they would be compelled to punish him, he replied with perfect coolness that he could not perform impossibilities, and
that they might do as they pleased with his body.
He offered his back to the lash with perfect indifference, received the severest blows without moving a
muscle or uttering a sound, returned to his cell just
as if nothing had happened, and left the work undone
as before. Exhortations and repeated chastisements
were of no avail; the authorities were at length forced
by his iron obstinacy to give him some other work
that he liked better and which he most regularly performed ever after. He frequently read the hymn-book
in prison; listened to the sermon on Sundays, though
without much appearance of interest; received the
sacrament like the other convicts, whom he far sur-
passed in religious knowledge; and, with a double
murder on his conscience, played the part of a patient,
humble, and resigned martyr to truth. He carefully avoided making any statement respecting his
crime; and whoever questioned him at all on the
subject was either civilly yet earnestly entreated to
refrain from all such inquiries, or was put off with
mysterious complaints of the terrible destiny which
forced him for ever to conceal a dark secret, on the revelation of which his innocence would instantly shine
forth like the sun at noonday. When hard pressed,
he sometimes began to relate the romance of the
Schlemmers, and accused the Nürnberg people as
the real authors of his misfortune, because the cry

of murderer! murderer! with which they assailed
him had induced him to pretend ignorance of what
had happened, which first and only falsehood had
induced his judge to disbelieve his subsequent true
narrative, and had finally brought him to these chains.
Hardened as he was, however, it appears that he did
not altogether escape from the pangs of a guilty conscience : he frequently sighed deeply ; and once, when
a lawyer well acquainted with the whole case visited
him in prison, vividly represented to him the heinous-
ness of his crime, spoke to him of the heavy burden
on his conscience, far heavier to bear in silence than
the weight of his chains—and then proceeded to describe the bloody scene of the 20th September, 1820,
and to bring before him the victims bleeding under the
axe, and trodden under his feet, the sullen countenance of the prisoner suddenly flushed scarlet, and
one present thought he saw tears in his eyes. Some
months after this visit, an organ was placed in the
chapel of the prison, and the sacrament administered
on the occasion. Forster, who had hitherto always
displayed the most callous indifference, was now
deeply affected. On approaching the altar, supporting his chains and the bullet in both arms, he trembled
in every limb, tears gushed from his eyes, and his
loud sobs filled the chapel. What he thought or felt,
whether the notes of the organ pealed in his ear like
the "Dies iræ, Dies illa," could not be discovered.
When he returned to his cell he was sullen and impe-
netrable as before.

Forster's countenance is vulgar and heavy. The
lower part of his long narrow face is of a length

strangely disproportioned to the upper; this gives a
revolting animal expression to his whole countenance,
which is singularly harsh, and so unvarying that his
head is like a marble bust, lifeless but for two large
prominent eyes, which are usually fixed on the ground,
and filled with rage and despair.

THE ANTONINI FAMILY;

OR,

THE MURDER ON A JOURNEY.

AT four o'clock in the evening of the 26th November, 1809, Joseph Antonini and his wife Theresa, both dressed as postillons d'armée in the French service, drove up to the door of the post-house at Maitingen near Augsburg, accompanied by a beautiful young woman called Dorothea Blankenfeld. They arrived in a carriage, had a French passport (*feuille de route*), and took rooms at the inn. The landlord showed them into two adjoining rooms on the first floor, one of which was occupied by Blankenfeld, the other, containing two beds, by the Antoninis. Shortly after their arrival a boy joined them, who was not, however, again seen in the house until the following morning. This was Carl Marschall, the brother of Antonini's wife.

About three or four in the morning, the postmaster and a postboy heard a piercing shriek, like that of a child. The former jumped out of bed and listened at the door, but lay down again on hearing nothing further. Soon after, the boy Carl Marschall ran hastily down the stairs, covering his face with his hands as if he were crying, and complained to the postboy that his master (Antonini) had beaten him.

At about six Antonini went into the postboy's room with a light, and requested him to make a large fire in the stove above stairs, as it was bitterly cold. His hand was stained with blood, but the postboy thought nothing of this, and merely supposed that Antonini had made the boy's nose bleed by striking him.

On the previous evening the strangers had announced their intention of starting at five in the morning. But it was past nine before they were ready to go. The postmaster, who was standing at the window, observed how busy they were; and his attention was attracted by a large strangely shaped bundle which Antonini and the boy dragged out of the house and flung into the carriage: it looked, he thought, just like the carcass of a dead dog, or of a human being. At last Antonini, the boy Carl Marschall, and Theresa Antonini, who was now dressed in women's clothes, got into the carriage and drove away. At that moment the thought struck the postmaster's son, who was already surprised by Theresa's change of dress, that the young woman who had arrived with the party on the evening before, had not got into the carriage. This alarmed the people of the house, who hastened to the two rooms which had been occupied by the strangers. The first look showed them, by the stains of blood on the floor, the wall, and the bed, that a murder had been committed. They instantly informed the local authorities of the fact, and the carriage, which had scarcely gone more than four hundred yards from the door when the discovery was made, was immediately followed, and overtaken under the gates of Augsburg. The suspicious-looking bundle wrapped in a blue cloak, which had been put inside the carriage at Maitingen, was now tied up behind it. When opened it was found to contain the body of a woman covered with wounds.

When it was shown by the police to the three prisoners, they recognised it as the body of Dorothea Blankenfeld, who had travelled with them as far as Maitingen, and on seeing it the boy at once confessed that he and his brother-in-law Antonini had murdered the woman. Antonini and his wife denied that they had any share in the crime. They said that the boy had murdered her from hatred, and without their knowledge; and that it was only out of charity to him that they had concealed the deed, but that the boy was a hardened villain, who had already attempted to kill his father and to stab his sister, and that Antonini had taken him away from Berlin in the hope of reforming him.

On inspecting the body, the hands were found much bruised and swollen, the collar-bone broken, and nine wounds, apparently inflicted with some blunt instrument, on the brow and other parts of the head—quite sufficient, in the physician's opinion, to cause death. He nevertheless asserted that the wretched woman had not died immediately of her wounds, but had perished gradually under continued violence.

The boy had openly confessed his share in the murder, but for a long time the Antoninis obstinately persisted in denial. Carl, they said, had done it all. They continued to deny everything save the concealment of the murder, of which they were con-

victed by the clearest proof. At last, after nineteen
long examinations, Theresa Antonini, on being confronted with her brother, confessed the main points of
her own share in the deed. Antonini, whose cunning
equalled his obstinacy, endeavoured, after long though
vain denial, to deceive the judge by a variety of false
confessions, till at length he was confronted with his
wife, and forced to confess the truth, though still in a
disjointed manner.

Joseph Antonini, a man about thirty years of age,
was born, according to his own account, at Messina,
where his parents carried on the trade of cloth-
weavers. He stated himself to be a barber by trade.
He related that in his eleventh or twelfth year he
sailed to Naples to be present at the feast of the Holy
Grotto, and that during this voyage he was unfortunately taken by an Algerine corsair, which was again
captured in the roads of Alexandria by a French ship
of war. He thus obtained his freedom, and was
landed in Greece. The first portion of his life was as
romantic as the rest was strange, dark, and varied.
At one time he was a drummer in the Corsican battalion under the French, then a laquais de place,
then a sutler, and lastly a French postillon d'armée.
He had been twice in prison at Berlin: once on suspicion of theft, by command of the French authorities,
who transferred him to Mayence; and a second time,
together with his wife, by order of the Berlin police,
for having in their possession various articles of which
they could give no satisfactory account. They were,
however, released after eight days' confinement; and
within a few weeks they committed this cruel murder
on the unfortunate Blankenfeld. The following cir-

cumstance, however, joined with the history of his chequered life and the character he bore before the murder of Blankenfeld, shows that in all probability this was not the first crime Antonini had committed. Whenever Antonini and his wife quarrelled, the latter always called him a thief and an incendiary, and the passionate Sicilian bore it in patient silence. He told his companions in gaol that he had once stolen three hundred louis d'or and some valuable rings, and had not only broken out of prison at Erfurt, but had also effected the escape of his fellow-prisoners. His conduct on examination, and during his imprisonment at Augsburg, showed boundless cunning and malice. To relate how by cunning, force, and bribery he endeavoured to effect his escape,—how he contrived to steal out of his cell in order to ascertain the state of the proceedings against him,—how he plotted with his fellow-prisoners to escape,—how he wrote to his wife, urging her to persist in a denial of her guilt,— and how he at length attempted to destroy himself,— all this would be beyond the scope of the present work.

Carl Marschall and Theresa Antonini, the former not quite fifteen, the latter about twenty-six, were the children of a certain John Christian Marschall, a very poor but honest workman in a manufactory at Berlin. Carl, according to the unanimous testimony of his parents, schoolmasters, and acquaintance, was a good-humoured and remarkably docile boy, always anxious to please and to do what he was bid. On the other hand, Theresa was described by her own parents as a wild, obstinate, malignant, and dissolute girl. Advice and punishment alike failed to bend her stubborn

will or to mend her morals. She showed neither
love nor honour to her parents, nor obedience or
respect to those she served. At Berlin she became
acquainted with Antonini, then a postillon d'armée in
the French service, and married him at Kustrin, in
1806. Their life is involved in mystery from that
time till 1809, when they visited Theresa's parents
and were arrested by the Berlin police for having in
their possession suspicious property. From Berlin
Antonini wished to return home to Messina with his
wife, and persuaded Carl to accompany them and
to take care of his horse during the journey. The
parents refused their permission; but the boy, thus
placed between obedience to his father and mother
and the more attractive scheme of the Italian, naturally chose the latter, and was taken from his parents
against their will and almost by force. It is worthy
of notice that the old father, when informed of
the charge against his children, wrote a touching
letter to the magistrates of Augsburg begging the life
of his poor misguided boy, and of the boy alone;
even the father's heart could find nothing to say in
favour of his daughter.

Dorothea Blankenfeld, born at Friedland, of parents
in the middle class of life, was a beautiful girl, scarce
four-and-twenty, of spotless reputation, and a kind
and gentle disposition. She left Danzig in November,
1809, on her way to Vienna to join her lover, a French
commissaire ordonnateur, to whom she was about to
be married. The secretary to the French commissaire,
Mons. Gentil, to whom she was recommended at
Dresden, had taken a room for her at the Hôtel de
Bavière, and there she waited for a convenient oppor-

tunity to continue her journey. This soon presented itself, but—for her destruction.

Two persons, giving their names as Antoine (Antonini) and Schulz, and stating themselves to be French postillons d'armée, appeared before the above-named secretary, provided with the proper recommendation from the commandant at Dresden, and demanded a passport for the army. Mons. Gentil immediately acquainted Dorothea Blankenfeld with this cheap and safe opportunity for continuing her journey, and offered to insert her name in the feuille de route. She gladly accepted the offer, and after staying three or four days at Dresden, she started in a carriage with these people.

The feuille de route named Sieur Antoine, Sieur Schulz, and Dame Blankenfeld. Meanwhile Carl, who had first assumed the name of Schulz, changed characters with his sister, who was not mentioned in the passport, and she now got into the carriage dressed in men's clothes, under the name of Schulz ; while Carl acted as a servant to the party, in which capacity he contrived to get through everywhere with the rest.

Dorothea Blankenfeld was well provided with money and property. Her trunk was full of good clothes and fine linen, and she had 2000 thalers sewed in her stays. The Antoninis did not know this at first, but Blankenfeld's fashionable dress, and the rank of her acquaintances at Dresden, led them to suspect enough to be a strong temptation to villainy.

Antonini and his wife were very ill provided with money for their journey. They wanted to reach Messina, and Antonini had but a few thalers in his pocket. It is impossible to avoid suspecting that in undertaking the journey with such utterly insufficient resources, they must have relied on obtaining money by dishonest means on the road. One cannot believe that Antonini, who had not nearly enough for himself and his wife, would have burdened himself with the additional expense of young Carl, merely for the sake of giving the boy pleasure, or for the use he might be of as a groom. Was it not far more likely that he took the boy with the intention of making him a tool and a scape-goat for his crimes? The feigned name of Schulz which was given to Carl, Theresa's disguise and subsequent change of parts with her brother, make this extremely probable. This masquerading and changing of names and persons was excellently contrived to help them through difficulties and to mislead the police. Moreover, the thought of murdering Blankenfeld seems to have struck the Antoninis so soon, and to have been so quickly resolved into a settled plan, that one can hardly resist the inference that the idea of procuring money for their journey by some crime had been all along firmly fixed in their minds, and only waited for an opportunity to be carried into execution.

They had left Dresden but a few posts behind them, when Antonini acquainted his wife with his intention of murdering Blankenfeld, in order to obtain possession of her property. Theresa, far from raising any objections, approved highly of the plan. They immediately took young Carl into their confidence, telling him in a few words that " Dorothea Blankenfeld must and should be murdered."

The docile boy had nothing to say against it, and

was ready to do their bidding in all things. Thus the main point was settled at once, and nothing remained but to determine the how, when, and where.

On so long a journey some favourable opportunity could not fail to present itself, and to that they resolved to trust. From this time forward these three people were incessantly occupied in seeking opportunities and devising means of murder and concealment of their crime. Each strove to surpass the others in zeal, activity, and ingenuity. The whole journey was one continued attempt to destroy the innocent and unsuspecting Blankenfeld. Each succeeding failure incited them to fresh attempts. Their night quarters were always selected with a view to the execution of their project; and every night, while the ill-starred girl slept unconscious of her impending fate, death threatened her in one form or another. Nothing but accident diverted the murderers from their plan, until it was executed at Maitingen.

At Hof, Antonini devised a plan for stifling Blankenfeld with smoke while she slept. But his wife raised some objections to it. She thought the idea a good one, but too uncertain. This plan, therefore, was not even attempted.

The next sleeping-place between Hof and Baireuth, probably Berneck, appeared peculiarly well suited for the execution of their scheme. The village itself lies in a hollow at the entrance of the Fichtelgebirge; the inn was lonely, out of the way, and stood just at the foot of a mountain covered with wood. Thus the deed might have been committed in security, and the dead body buried during the night on the mountain. But Theresa Antonini had appeared at Berneck in women's clothes, and not as a postilion, so that the people of the inn had seen two women arrive; and the Antoninis feared that if only one left the inn on the following morning it might excite suspicion. This excellent opportunity was thus lost.

On the following night, at Baireuth, matters became still more serious. Antonini returned to his original scheme of stifling Blankenfeld with smoke, and talked of making holes in the stove of her room, and then heating it with damp straw.* But Theresa repeated her former objection, that the result was uncertain; Blankenfeld might awake, and open her window to get rid of the smoke. It was therefore finally resolved to kill her by blows. Carl was ordered to provide himself with a good club, and to have plenty of water ready to wash away the blood. But Blankenfeld was again protected by some chance which prevented the murder.

The Antoninis had thus lost three days. Experience had taught them that the execution of their design was not so easy as they had at first imagined. They saw difficulties and dangers before them to which they did not choose to expose themselves for a trifling gain. They accordingly determined, before proceeding with their perilous undertaking, to convince themselves that their risk and trouble would be sufficiently rewarded. A little village between Baireuth and Nürnberg—most likely Leopoldstein— was selected for this purpose. Blankenfeld here ordered some negus, into which Antonini contrived to pour opium. When she was in bed and fast asleep, the keys were taken from under her pillow, and her

* The German stoves are supplied with fuel outside the room.

trunks opened and examined by Antonini and his wife. They found in them no money, but plenty of fine linen, good men's and women's clothes, and a few jewels. "At all events," said Antonini, " it is worth while to kill her." Hereupon they replaced every thing with the utmost care, locked the trunks, and put back the keys under her pillow. This was sufficient for that night.

The following day found them at Nürnberg, again debating how they might kill Blankenfeld. The many streams of water which run through the city afforded favourable opportunities for getting rid of the body; but a sentinel, who stood opposite the inn, was an insurmountable obstacle. Carl, who endeavoured to deserve the trust reposed in him, not only by obedience, but occasionally by advice and suggestion, proposed to mix pounded glass in Blankenfeld's soup, and thus to do the deed quietly. But Antonini rejected the scheme as inefficient; he had often swallowed broken glass himself in sport, with no ill effect. Blankenfeld thus escaped once more.

From Nürnberg they went to the small manufacturing town of Roth, which they reached towards nightfall. The active, watchful Theresa discovered a mattock, with three iron prongs, in the loft, and showed it to her husband and Carl with the words, " That would give a deadly blow." Carl, who was the one selected to do the deed, secretly conveyed this instrument into the bed-room, and hid it behind the stove. His sister, meanwhile, instructed him how to use it. Another sleeping-draught was administered to Blankenfeld, and nothing more was wanting but to find a place of concealment for the dead body.

Carl and Antonini went out separately to reconnoitre : the former discovered a hole in a field, which might do ; the latter chose a pool of water-in the neighbourhood. But all was again in vain. Accident had brought a number of carriers to the inn, whose eyes and ears might have been awkward witnesses : the murder was, therefore, again deferred.

They encountered similar impediments on the two following nights, which they passed at Weissenberg and Donauwörth, on the road between Roth and Maitingen.

Time now pressed, for Blankenfeld was to leave them at Augsburg, and they were to pass only one more night on the road before reaching it. Now, then, or never, the plan must be carried into execution.

During the last post before Maitingen, Antonini exercised all his ingenuity to ascertain from Blankenfeld whether she had money or valuables concealed elsewhere than in her trunk. He turned the conversation on the Tyrolese insurgents, and the dangers which she might encounter. He said that the Tyrolese had already penetrated into Swabia and Bavaria, where they committed all sorts of cruelties and murders for the sake of the most trifling booty. By these exaggerated statements, he excited the imagination of the unsuspecting girl to such a degree, that at length, losing all prudence in her terror, she put her hand to her breast and said, " Ah ! I will give the Tyrolese all this most willingly, if they will only spare my life !" Had any scruples still lurked in the minds of the Sicilian and his wife, this discovery would have dissipated them. The prospect of a rich booty determined them to run all hazards, and they arrived at Maitingen firmly resolved that their intended victim should die that night.

Antonini and his wife had calculated that if so young a lad as Carl committed the murder alone, he would relieve them of the greater part of the guilt, without incurring capital punishment himself. They hoped to secure themselves by throwing the whole blame upon him. They had accordingly drawn him into the plot from the very beginning, and the execution of the murder was now intrusted to him at Maitingen, as it had been before. At this last place they did everything in their power to inflame his young blood, and to inspire him with courage and determination. The boy, equally docile for good or for evil, blindly followed Antonini's orders, and regarded the murder of an innocent girl as a commonplace event. No feelings of compassion, no pangs of conscience, seem to have touched him in favour of one who had treated him with uniform kindness during the journey; nor had he any fear of detection or punishment. He only hesitated from fear that his strength was not equal to the undertaking; but his sister promised him all her husband's clothes as a reward for the deed, and Antonini said he would assist him, if necessary, as soon as the first blow had been struck.

Carl had discovered in the post-house a large roller weighing about four pounds, which he thought might serve their purpose, and had concealed it in Antonini's bed-room. He was then sent out to dig a hole in a dunghill, in which to conceal the body; but in this he did not succeed. Antonini secretly bought some candles, so as to have a light all night, and some brandy. After supper he persuaded her to drink some of the brandy, with which he had mixed laudanum; and at about eight o'clock she went half stupified to bed in her own room, leaving the door open between herself and the Antoninis. Warm water was then procured, under the pretence of a foot-bath, to wash away the blood, and the outer door was locked and bolted.

About midnight Carl stole into Blankenfeld's room to see how she lay. She slept heavily, but her position was by no means favourable for their purpose, as her face was turned towards the wall.

While the murderers were waiting for her to move into a more convenient posture, it struck Antonini that it would be better to kill the sleeping woman by less violent means than blows on the head, and he proposed to pour melted lead into her ears, or, as Carl suggested, into her eyes. They broke a pewter spoon into small pieces, which they melted in an iron one over the candle. But a drop which fell upon the sheet and merely scorched it, proved to the murderers that melted pewter cooled too soon for their purpose. This plan was therefore abandoned, and they determined to abide by their original intention.

At about four Carl again stole into the room, and found Blankenfeld lying on her back asleep, with her head towards him. " Now," said Antonini, " is the proper moment," and went up to the bed. Carl followed him with the heavy roller, and when urged to strike the blow he raised the murderous instrument, but hesitated, trembled, and drew back in alarm. Antonini whispered to him some words of reproach, seized his hand which clasped the weapon, gave it a proper direction over their victim's head, and the first blow fell upon the forehead of Blankenfeld, who exclaimed, "Jesus! my head!" and raised herself in bed. At this moment Antonini seized her by the shoulders, and Theresa by the feet; the unhappy girl now began to cry, and offered her murderers everything she possessed, if they would but spare her young life. Pity, fear, and horror seized upon Carl, who hastily flung the weapon upon the floor, and ran to the door to escape. But Antonini's wife rushed after him, dragged him back into the room, and, placing the roller in his hand, ordered him to complete his task. He again stepped up to the bed, and aimed a second blow at Blankenfeld's head, which struck Antonini's forehead at the same time, and Carl again threw down the roller and ran away, while the pain of the blow forced Antonini to let go Blankenfeld, who collected all her strength, jumped out of bed, and rushed towards the door of the outer room. But Antonini fiercely pursued her, and struck blow after blow on her head till she sank upon the floor, where he still continued to strike her. As she lay on the ground with the death-rattle in her throat, Antonini tore off her clothes and the stays which contained her money. He then lifted the dying woman on his shoulders, intending to carry her out into the yard and bury her in the dungheap. But the weight was too much for him, and Theresa dissuaded him. They therefore took her back into her own room. But the wretched woman still breathed, and again began to groan. "The carrion is coming to life again," exclaimed Theresa. Antonini then stood upon Blankenfeld's body and trampled on it with both feet until she was dead. The corpse was then by Theresa's advice thrust into a sack and rolled up in a coverlet. In order to be perfectly secure Antonini took the further precaution of tying a cord tightly round her neck, while Theresa was busily employed in washing away as much as she could of the bloody stains. She then prepared for the journey by taking off her postilion's dress and putting on the clothes which Blankenfeld had worn on the previous day.

This is the connected narrative of the transaction, as repeatedly and circumstantially confessed by Carl Marschall.

Theresa Antonini acknowledged the truth of Carl's statement on most points; but, when confronted with her brother, she so stoutly denied having held Blankenfeld's feet, as to make Carl hesitate and conclude himself mistaken. But on his fourteenth examination he returned to his former charge, and confidently asserted that his sister held Blankenfeld's feet; at all events, while he struck the second blow. On a second confrontation, Theresa persisted in her denial; and when Carl repeated his statement she grew violent, attempted to strike him, swore she would be revenged on him, and cursed him and her parents. We can only account for Theresa's denial of this one circumstance, on the supposition that she entertained the vulgar notion that the other charges against her, the truth of which she had confessed, would not be punished with death, provided she could prove that she had not laid hands upon the murdered woman.

Antonini himself, in all his examinations and confrontations with Carl and Theresa, never made a clear and connected confession.

In his first twelve examinations he threw the whole blame on Carl, and asserted that he himself had had no share in or even knowledge of the murder.

In his thirteenth audience, which he demanded, he unintentionally confessed something by relating the following tale : " That he had been awakened in the night by his wife, who told him there was a noise in the next room, and that she thought some one was attempting suicide. He jumped out of bed, and on entering Blankenfeld's room received a blow on the head. While in the act of parrying a second, the club with which he had been struck fell into his hand. He seized it and gave a violent blow, he knew not to whom, for the room was pitchy dark, and he was half stunned. He then struck towards the other side of the room, but encountered nothing. He shortly afterwards discovered that Blankenfeld had been murdered by Carl."

In his fourteenth examination, which he also demanded, he gave a second version totally different from the first. He said that at about five in the morning a chaise arrived at the post-house : thinking it was theirs, he awakened Carl, and told him to call Blankenfeld. Soon after he heard angry words, and then blows. He jumped out of bed and went into her room, where he found her fighting with Carl. He tried to separate them, but received a kick from Blankenfeld which sent him reeling against the bed. He called out, ' Carl, help me !' and the lad then redoubled his blows. Anger then took possession of me," said Antonini, " and I wrested the club out of Carl's hands and struck Blankenfeld three or four blows, whereupon she fell dead on the floor." It was not till afterwards that he discovered—for desire of gain was not the motive of his crime—that Blankenfeld had money concealed about her person, which however he appropriated to himself. He confirmed this confession in his fifteenth examination ; adding, that he had no intention of killing Blankenfeld ; that he had struck about him wildly, and might have hit her on the body as well as the head. This he improved into a statement that his agitation had prevented him from seeing whether he struck Carl or Blankenfeld.

In his nineteenth examination he came somewhat nearer the truth. He stated that " During the journey they had constantly quarrelled with Blankenfeld. As he had spent his own money, and had frequently paid for her, Carl suggested to him that ' As Blankenfeld had a good deal of money in her possession, why not kill her on the road ? No one would observe it, as Theresa might pass for her.' But he (Antonini) and his wife had refused to agree to this, whenever it was proposed. At Maitingen, Carl came to him during the night with the club in his hand, and awoke him, saying, ' that he was determined to kill Blankenfeld, come what might.' He (Antonini) represented to him that this was not to be done in a place where it would be sure to be discovered, and to get them all three into mischief. Hereupon he went to sleep, but was awakened by the sound of blows, and on running into Blankenfeld's room he caught hold of some one, who turned out to be Blankenfeld, and found his hands covered with her blood. Carl still continued to strike her, but he (Antonini) exclaimed, ' My God ! my God ! Carl ! and, let go Blankenfeld.' He then wrested the weapon out of Carl's hands, and struck Blankenfeld three blows more, which felled her to the ground, but did not intentionally strike her on the head. He must, however, confess that during the journey he had thought of killing her, in order to possess himself of her money; but his wife had always dissuaded him, and that he certainly should not have killed her had not Carl struck the first blow. He added, that on his entrance into Blankenfeld's room, he had stumbled; and, half stunned by that, and by a knock he received on the head when he quitted his hold of Blankenfeld, he only discovered, after giving the third blow, that it was Blankenfeld whom he had struck. It was not until after she was dead that he knew anything of the money concealed about her person."

The twentieth examination elicited from him the following circumstance : — That at Maitingen, immediately before the deed, Carl represented to him their wretched condition, and again urged him to kill Blankenfeld, and take her money. When he objected from fear of discovery, Carl proposed to him to pour melted pewter into Blankenfeld's ears. He agreed; but on attempting to hold the spoon over the candle, his hand shook so violently that the spoon fell upon the ground, and he told Carl that he never could do such a deed. He then repeated much the same version of the murder as before.

Neither the subsequent examinations nor repeated confrontation with Carl, produced a clearer confession. It was only on being brought face to face with his wife, who coaxed him to confess the truth, that he conceded some few points: but he never made a complete and repentant confession.

Joseph Antonini and his wife Maria Theresa were sentenced by the court at Nürnberg to death by the sword. Carl Franz Ludwig Marschall, in consideration of his youth, was condemned to ten years' imprisonment with hard labour.

Antonini escaped his well-deserved punishment by dying in prison; but his wife mounted the scaffold, and died as she had lived, bold, hardened, and unrepentant.

RIEMBAUER,

THE TARTUFFE OF REAL LIFE.

———○———

FRANCIS SALESIUS RIEMBAUER was born on the 27th
January, 1770, in the market-town of Langquaid
(circuit of Pfaffenberg). He was the son of a poor
day-labourer, and began life as a shepherd-boy: he
early displayed considerable talents and a strong
desire for knowledge, and soon conceived the ambi-
tion of studying for the church. In his thirteenth
year he fell upon his knees before the priest of his
parish, whom he implored to give him the instruction
required to prepare him for the gymnasium of the
town. The boy made such rapid progress that within
the year he was received into that school. After remaining there a short time he was admitted into the
gymnasium of Ratisbon. Here his good behaviour,
diligence, and rapid progress, gained him the character of an admirable student who would one day
do honour to the church and to himself. His knowledge of ecclesiastical law and history was considerable. He chiefly devoted himself to the study of
dialectics and casuistry, in which ne seiected as his
guide the works of P. Benedict Stattler. In 1795
he took holy orders at Ratisbon, and for many years
served different parish churches in succession. At

Christmas, 1815, he was translated to Pirkwang, where he had charge of the Filial Church at Ober-Lauterbach. He remained there for two years; and in 1807 passed his examination, as candidate for a cure, with great honour at Munich, and was appointed parish-priest at Priel on the 18th March, 1808, from whence, two years later, he was translated to Nandelstadt.

From the commencement of his ecclesiastical career, he was so remarkable for his talents and virtues as to be held up as a model to other priests. His stately figure and handsome face, his persuasive eloquence and insinuating manners, gained him general good will. He performed his clerical duties with punctuality, dignity, and grace, and his outward demeanour was decorum itself. His leisure hours—at least until his removal to Pirkwang, where the purchase of a small property involved him in agricultural pursuits—were passed in reading and study. And when those priests to whom he was attached as chaplain, expressed their admiration of his zeal for learning, he replied that this was the proper calling of the clergy, who ought not to concern themselves with worldly affairs. His preaching was distinguished for fire and unction, and out of church, as well as in it, he declaimed against the corruptions of the world : his soft words and gentle manners seemed those of a saint living in communion with God, and in charity with his neighbour. He always walked out of church smiling, with his head on one side, his eyes half closed and fixed upon the ground, and his hands folded. Even those who felt a personal dislike to him, or distrusted his character, praised his merits as a priest, and his eloquence in the pulpit. " He was," said one Niedermeyer, " really a most charming preacher, and would have converted us all to righteousness, had he stayed longer at Hofkirchen : he cast his eyes towards heaven, and preached most powerful doctrine." Besides this, the common people believed,—and he encouraged the idea,—that he stood in close and constant communication with the invisible world. The dead came from purgatory to visit him in his chamber, and entreat him to say a mass for the repose of their souls, and when this was done they were released. Even before the mass was over, he saw the beatified spirit fly towards heaven in the form of a white dove. When his spiritual duties called him abroad by night, the distressed souls of the departed flitted before him in the shape of small flames, probably to obtain his benediction, and followed the direction of his hallowed finger as he pointed to the right or to the left. For some time he was honoured almost as a saint by the people, and many would eagerly rush to seat themselves upon the chair he had just left, in the hopes of feeling something of his holy influence.

Some of his clerical brethren, indeed, beheld in him a hypocrite and a pharisee. It was whispered at Hirnheim that the parish priest had received a letter from his brother priest at Hofkirchen, where Riembauer had acted as chaplain, warning him against the new comer as a wolf in sheep's clothing ; and telling him that he had obtained his removal on this account. Nor did all his penitents implicitly believe in the piety and virtue of this holy man : some of them privately doubted whether a man, who flattered all alike, and looked no one in the face, were not a very great hypocrite. There were many good, prudent fathers of families, who, while they felt highly honoured in receiving the pious young ecclesiastic in their houses, nevertheless took especial precautions for the security of their daughters, to whom Riembauer invariably paid particular attention, whenever he passed the night under their roofs.

It was not until many years later, when other far more important discoveries had been made, that the following circumstances in the life of this holy man became public. While he was chaplain at Hofkirchen, he seduced the priest's cookmaid, Maria H—, and afterwards gave her the means of retiring to Landshut, where, in 1801, she was delivered of a son, who died soon after. During his residence at Hirnheim as chaplain, he lived with Anna Eichstädter, the kitchen-maid at the manse, and in 1803 he had a daughter by her, which was born and christened at Ratisbon, both parents giving false names. While he was chaplain at Pfarrkofen, in 1803, he seduced a sempstress, Walburga R—, who bore him a daughter, named Theresa, who also was alive at the time of the trial. It was also rumoured that the cookmaid of the parish priest of Pfarrkofen was in the same state by him. He was then chaplain at Pondorf in 1804, where, according to his own account, he received great offence from the wickedness of the world, and the corruption of the young clergy; for some of the other chaplains paid particular attention to the youthful cousin of the parish priest, to which she did not appear insensible. He was hereby compelled to procure his removal to some other curacy. He was translated to Pirkwang; and at Lauterbach, a small village within his cure, he selected as his mistress a farmer's daughter, named Magdalena Frauenknecht, whose history we shall have to relate hereafter. After the death of this mistress, he lived with his last cookmaid, Anna Weninger, by whom he had no less than three children.

In order to quiet the conscience and secure the fidelity of those concubines with whom he intended to live for any length of time, Riembauer used to perform the marriage service over them, uniting in his own person the characters of priest and bridegroom. Catherine Frauenknecht asserted that, hidden behind Riembauer's bed, she witnessed the strange espousals of her sister Magdalena; that Riembauer repeated all the usual prayers and exhortations, and placed a gold wedding-ring on her sister's finger. Anna Weninger said that the same thing took place at her union with him, but was not sure whether the priestly bridegroom performed the ceremony clad in his stole and with burning candles, or not. He himself denied having thus profaned his sacred functions, but confessed that he had instructed his mistresses in the duties of the married state, and then given and received a formal promise. He was very earnest in persuading his female penitents that they might safely permit themselves certain sins with the saints of the Lord. Many other charges were proved against him which we will pass over in silence, the more so as we want nothing further to convince us that the whole of

his ecclesiastical career was a perfect illustration of
the well-known and popular maxim—

> Le mal n'est jamais que dans l'éclat qu'on fait.
> Le scandale du monde est ce qui fait l'offense,
> Et ce n'est pas pécher que pécher en silence.*

Without having read Molière, Riembauer thoroughly
understood not only how to sin in secret, and to
appear before the world as a saint, but also how
to keep an amicable account with heaven for sins
already committed, or to be committed hereafter.

> Le Ciel défend, de vrai, certains contentements ;
> Mais on trouve avec lui des accommodements.
> Selon divers besoins, il est une science
> D'étendre les liens de notre conscience,
> Et de rectifier le mal de l'action
> Avec la pureté de notre intention.†

These errors and frailties were not his sins,
but the sins of celibacy ; and casuistry furnished
him with arguments to prove that in procreating
illegitimate children he was instrumental in ex-
tending the kingdom of God ; that, therefore, this
conduct, far from being reprehensible, was praise-
worthy, and agreeable in the sight of heaven. " I
considered," these are his words, " 1st, That reason
tells us that it cannot be unlawful to beget a child ;
for to call into existence an immortal and rational
being is a good deed. It is thus that a man becomes
in a peculiar manner the image of God, with whom
he co-operates in the creation of a human being, as is
said by Saint Clement of Alexandria ; 2nd, That it
cannot be contrary to God's ordinances, for thus it is
that the number of the elect is increased ; 3rd,

* Le Tartuffe.   † Ibid.

Neither is it against the decrees of the Church, if the child be educated in the Christian faith ; 4th, Nor against the interests of the State, provided this member of it receive moral and civil instruction, so as to become a good citizen and faithful subject, and provided the mother of the child be not forsaken. I frequently considered all these arguments, which were supported by the history of the church,* and by my own experience. My conscience was thus made easy under these errors of celibacy."

Riembauer, impelled by feelings of duty and kindness, or by prudential motives, did everything in his power to provide for his children and to keep their mothers quiet and contented, so that they might do nothing to injure his reputation.

The child of Anna Eichstädter was educated at his expense at Ratisbon, and he kept up a constant and friendly intercourse with the mother, who served in various places as housemaid or waiting-maid. He corresponded with her, and provided her with linen, money, &c.; occasionally visited her, and held out hopes of taking her to live with him permanently as his cook, whenever he should have a parsonage of his own. Anna Eichstädter, the daughter of a carpenter at Fürth, was a well-shaped, tall, strong, broad-shouldered woman, remarkable, among other things (which is important in the sequel), for two rows of most beautiful teeth. The intimate and friendly connexion subsisting between her and Riembauer received a con-

---

* It is probable that the learned Riembauer refers to those portions of ecclesiastical history which treat of the lives of Sergius III., John XII., Innocent II. and VII., John XXIII., Alexander VI., Julius II., &c.

siderable shock about a year after his removal as chaplain to Pirkwang : this shock eventually caused her cruel death.

Riembauer, as we have already said, had the charge of the church at Ober Lauterbach, where the Frauenknecht family lived at a farm called the Thomashof. The Frauenknechts, by their industry and frugality, their benevolent and Christian spirit, and their pious conduct, had gained the respect and love of all their neighbours. When Riembauer began his ministry there at Christmas, 1805, the family consisted of the father, who died two years after, his wife and two daughters—the eldest of whom, Magdalena, was born in 1788 ; the second, Catherine, in 1796. The former was described by all who knew her, both high and low, as a most pious, gentle, amiable girl ; and, until Riembauer came near her, of spotless reputation. The latter, who was then but a child, was generally said to be a frank and honest girl, with an understanding beyond her years.

Riembauer's cupidity was soon excited by this family, and he determined to possess not only the daughter, Magdalena, but likewise the property of these simple-hearted people. He obtained their entire confidence, not only by his air of sanctity and the superiority of his education and profession, but also by laying aside in his intercourse with them the outward honours of his station, and becoming, in pure Christian humility, their equal. Whenever his duties or his pleasure took him to Ober Lauterbach, he assisted the Frauenknecht family in their husbandry, doing for them, to the astonishment of the neighbours, the work of a common day-labourer.

He who could find in his theological code a triumphant apology for every action, frequently quoted the decrees of the Council of Carthage, the testimony of Saint Epiphanius, and the example of many bishops and priests of ancient times, who united the offices of preachers arrd common labourers, to prove that an ecclesiastic forfeited none of the dignity of his sacred calling by following the plough or carting dung. Without having any money, he bought the farm called the Thomashof from the Frauenknecht family in December, 1806, for 4000 florins, fraudulently inserting into the contract a recital that 2000 florins had already been paid : and after the death of old Frauenknecht he presented to the widow a false bill of expenses, amounting to 2000 more, which she, in her good-natured simplicity, admitted. After thus gaining possession of the Thomashof, where, however, the Frauenknecht family continued to reside, he removed to Lauterbach, and lived there, dividing his time between his professional duties and agricultural labour. This conduct procured for him the reputation of a patriarch among some of his neighbours of the higher class; but the peasants, whose good common sense was shocked by the impropriety of this proceeding, called him the farmer of Thomashof.

Soon after the fraudulent purchase of the farm, the eldest daughter, Magdalena, found herself about to become a mother by this reverend patriarch, and was sent by him to Munich, nominally to learn cooking, but in reality to conceal her pregnancy. There she served for six or seven months in the house of the Registrar Y——, and was afterwards delivered of a son in June 1807, while living in the same house with Riembauer—at the very time when he passed his examination for priest's orders with great honour. The expenses of Magdalena's stay at Munich—which was entirely owing to Riembauer—were put down by him at 500 florins, and deducted, with other charges of a similar nature, from the sum owing to the widow Frauenknecht for the Thomashof.

During Riembauer's stay at Munich, from about the 9th to the 15th June, Anna Eichstädter, who was then in service at Ratisbon, came to Lauterbach to extract from her lover the money for her child, which Riembauer's embarrassments had prevented him from paying as heretofore; and possibly also to take him to task about his connexion with Magdalena, and to compel him to fulfil his promise of taking her as his cook. When she learnt from Catherine Frauenknecht that Riembauer was absent, she demanded the key of his room, saying that she was his cousin. Here she acted as if she were mistress of the house, ransacked all the chests and drawers in her search for money. On finding none, or at any rate not enough, she wrote him a threatening letter, which she left; and after sleeping at Thomashof she returned to Ratisbon. After Riembauer's return from Munich he received a second and still more angry letter from her, threatening him with legal proceedings if he did not fulfil his engagements towards her.

Shortly after, Riembauer went to visit Anna Eichstädter at Ratisbon, and satisfied her for the present. On his departure she accompanied him with her child as far as Kumpfmühl, and urged him to break off his connexion with Magdalena, and not to forsake herself. She sat on the bank by the road-side with her child, and implored him, with uplifted hands and tears in her eyes, to keep the promises he had made her. But the pious priest raised his stick with a threatening gesture, struck it angrily upon the ground, and—went his way.

Anna Eichstädter had lived hitherto with a horse-dealer at Ratisbon, but in October, 1807, she quitted his service for that of the parish priest at P——. On the 1st of November she went to the house of her new master, but requested permission to visit her relations before entering upon her duties as cook. As a pledge of her promise of service she left with her master her silver necklace, and several other articles of value. As it was raining, he lent her a green cotton umbrella, on the handle of which were engraved his initials, J. O. Several days passed, and she did not return. Her master, who had reason to suspect that she had gone to Riembauer, wrote to him, requesting him to tell Anna Eichstädter, if she did not like to enter his service, at any rate to return his umbrella. Riembauer answered that he was unable to give any information about her, as he had neither seen her nor the umbrella. Anna Eichstädter never appeared again from the 1st of November, the day she left her master's house ; she neither returned to Ratisbon, nor went to her native town, Fürth. Her relations and friends could not discover her place of abode, or whether she were alive or dead. It was supposed either that she was drowned, or had fallen into the hands of a notorious robber, who was executed in the

following year; and, at length, nobody thought any
more about her.

Some months after the disappearance of Anna
Eichstädter in 1808, Riembauer was appointed to the
living of Priel. Hereupon he sold at a profit the ill-
gotten farm of Thomashof, and the widow Frauenknecht and her two daughters accompanied him
to his new home, where Magdalena served him as
cook. But in the following year both she and her
mother were seized with a sudden illness and died,
the daughter on the 16th, the mother on the 21st
June, 1809.

The younger daughter, Catherine, had quitted the
parsonage some time before her mother's and sister's
death, partly on account of quarrels with her sister,
partly from confirmed dislike to Riembauer. She
first went into service at his brother's house, after
which she lived with different masters. Wherever
she went, though generally even-tempered and cheerful, she was subject to fits of terror and despondency.
Solitude filled her with horror ; she was afraid to
sleep alone: she seemed to be haunted by fearful
visions, and her terrors increased with her years.
Some dreadful secret appeared to weigh upon her mind.
Occasionally she let fall expressions about some woman, whose image pursued her wherever she went.
She once told a certain Catherine Schmid, with
whom she slept at Ratisbon, of a horrid murder committed by the priest Riembauer. Afterwards, when
she was in service at D——, she told the same story
to her mistress, who advised her to open her heart to
a confessor. She accordingly applied to a priest, to

whom she related that Riembauer, by whom her family had been defrauded of 2000 florins, and she herself deprived of her home, had cut the throat of a woman who visited him at Lauterbach in November, 1807; that he had also destroyed her mother and sister by poison, on account of their knowledge of the murder; and, lastly, that he had endeavoured to get her into his power, doubtless with the intention of putting out of the world the only living witness of his crime. The confessor dissuaded her from laying any information against Riembauer in a court of justice, and advised her to leave him, if he were guilty, to the judgment of God. He afterwards assured her that he had secretly consulted several other ecclesiastics on this case, and that this advice had been approved by them all. Another priest, Co-operator S——, to whom Catherine subsequently told the same tale, also recommended silence, but took the opportunity of endeavouring to serve both her and Riembauer, by writing to the latter an anonymous Latin letter, threatening him with the revelation of some terrible secret if he did not satisfy the person knowing it by a full restitution of her property.* The co-operator had previously asked advice upon this *casum conscientiæ* of the parish priest, who was of opinion that the affair should certainly be laid before the proper tribunal, but approved the generosity of the motives which had dictated the threatening letter.

* The letter which Riembauer afterwards repeated from memory was as follows:—"Habeo casum mihi propositum, quem tantummodo tu solvere potes. Vir quidam, quem tu bene noscis, debet alicui personæ 3000 florenorum circiter. Si conscientia tua vigilat, solve hoc debitum. Nisi intra quatuor hebdomedas respondeas, horrenda patefaciet ista persona. *Hannibal ante portas!*"

At length, in 1813, Catherine Frauenknecht laid a formal accusation against Riembauer, first at Ober Lauterbach, and afterwards at a criminal court at Landshut, specially held for this case. The evidence she gave was nearly as follows, and she repeated it upon oath in the following year, when she became of age.

"During the summer of 1807, while my sister Magdalena and the reverend Mr. Riembauer were at Munich—the former to learn cooking, the latter to pass his examination—a woman of about twenty-two, tall, handsome, with an oval face, and light brown hair, in a peasant's dress, with a gold cap on her head, came to our house; my mother was at work in the field. She told me that she was a cousin of Riembauer's, and on hearing that he was at Munich for his examination, she requested me to give her the key of his room, which I refused. But when my mother returned home she obtained it from her, went into Riembauer's room, and searched it thoroughly, just as though she were in her own house. She remained with us that night, and said that she had found no money, and had therefore left a letter for the priest, sealed up in a cover. In about a week Mr. Riembauer returned from Munich. I told him what had happened, and he said, ' that she was a cousin of his, to whom he owed some money.'

"In the November of the same year, I do not know exactly on what day (it was afterwards discovered to have been All Souls' Day, the 2nd of November), the same cousin came again to Thomashof, just as Riembauer had carted home turnips from the field. My sister was at home with him, but my mother and I came in from work somewhat later. As we drew near the house we heard a voice upstairs in the priest's room—whether crying or laughing we could not at first distinguish—but we soon perceived that it was wailing. The moment we reached the threshold of our house, my sister ran towards us, all in tears, and hastily told us, ' that a strange woman, who called herself his cousin, had come to see the reverend gentleman ; that Mr. Riembauer had taken her up into his own room, and had there told her that he was going to fetch some beer : that under this pretext he had come down stairs, fetched his razor, and gone up stairs again with it in his hand : that he had then approached the woman, who was sitting on a chair (as Magdalena, who had crept up-stairs after him, saw through the key-hole), and catching hold of her neck, as if to kiss her, had pressed her head down towards the floor, and cut her throat.'

" While my sister was telling us this on the door-step, we still heard the wailing noise, and Mr. Riembauer's voice saying, ' Nanny ! make a clean breast, for you must die.' We then heard a moaning voice saying, ' Franzel ! don't do it ! only spare my life, and I will never again come to you for money.'*

" My mother and sister instantly went into the room below, but from curiosity I ran up-stairs, and distinctly saw, through the key-hole, Mr. Riembauer

---

* An attempt was afterwards made to impugn the credit of Catherine's evidence on this point. It was said that if Riembauer had already cut the woman's throat before Magdalena had come down stairs, it was impossible she should speak loud enough to be heard on the door-step. But Von Walther gives it as his opinion that even when the windpipe is cut, it is possible for a person to speak with the head bent forward.

sitting or kneeling upon the body of the woman, who lay upon the floor kicking and struggling. He held her head and throat with both hands while the blood gushed from her.

"I then went down stairs, and told what I had seen to my weeping mother and sister, who still hesitated whether they should not call for help. When I went out again into the passage I met Mr. Riembauer coming down stairs, dressed in his usual brown jacket and a white apron; his hands and the apron were covered with blood, and in his right hand he held the bloody razor, which he laid upon the small chest by the door; he then went into the room where my mother and sister were. I listened at the door, and heard him tell them ' that this woman had had a child by him ; and was always plaguing him for money ; that she had now asked him for between 100 and 200 florins, and had threatened him with an action if he refused ; and that, as he could not raise the money, he had cut her throat to get rid of her.'

"I afterwards slipt into Mr. Riembauer's room, and there I saw the same person who had been at our house the previous summer, stretched on the floor, in a pool of blood, with her throat cut through, her hair dishevelled, and her clothes torn. I screamed and let fall the candle from fright.

" When I came down stairs again, I saw the reverend gentleman washing the blood from his hands, and told him that I had seen the person who had come in the summer lying dead in his room. He then coaxed me, told me I was mistaken, and promised me quantities of fine clothes if I would not mention what I had seen or heard to any one. My mother still continued to weep, and to declare that she must inform against him. But Mr. Riembauer threw himself at her feet, and entreated her not to betray him. My mother still insisted, adding that her silence would be of no avail, as the neighbours must have seen the stranger and heard the noise. Mr. Riembauer at last said that nothing then was left for him but to destroy himself.

" He then put on his coat, fetched a rope out of the outhouse, and ran with it towards the wood. My mother and sister, who followed him at a distance, saw that he was really in earnest, and thinking that it would only make matters worse if Mr. Riembauer were to hang himself, they ran after him, and by promises of secrecy prevailed upon him to relinquish his design.

" When he had returned home with my mother and sister, he debated in my presence about a safe place where he might bury the body, and chose for the purpose the little room on the left hand in the newly built outhouse. He quieted my relations by assuring them that he would bury the body himself, and that nothing would be discovered if only I, then a child of twelve, could be prevented from talking.

" At midnight, between twelve and one, he took a lantern and a spade, and went into the closet in the outhouse, where he dug a hole. After a time I heard a noise overhead, opened our room-door, and saw a light near the cellar-door, and Mr. Riembauer dragging the body, which was completely dressed, down-stairs by the shoulders, so that the head hung down backwards. A shudder came over me, and I cannot tell how he then conveyed the body into the outhouse. But I afterwards went thither, and looking in at the open door, my mother and sister and I saw that the reverend gentleman had already put the murdered woman into the hole, and was covering her over with earth.

" He washed away the blood which stained the ground from the house to the outhouse the same night, and on the following morning he cleansed the house with his own hands, first using cold, then hot water.

" But in his own room the blood was already dry, and washing was of no use; I was therefore sent to borrow a plane from our nearest neighbour, Michael the carpenter; with this Mr. Riembauer planed the floor till the stains disappeared, and threw the shavings into the grate.

" On the morning after the murder, as I was going to school, I saw our dog dragging a woman's bloody shoe about the yard. I mentioned this to Riembauer, and he told me to carry it into the room down-stairs. I took it up on a stick, as it made my blood run cold, and threw it on the floor of our room: I do not know what became of it afterwards.

" When our neighbours inquired what had happened in our house to cause such disturbance and crying, we answered, as the reverend gentleman had instructed us, that we had wept about our father's death and the loss of the 2000 florins which Mr. Riembauer had squeezed out of us, as all the village knew.

" The murdered woman had brought with her a green umbrella belonging to the priest at P——.

Mr. Riembauer kept it, and still had it when he was parish priest of Priel.

" About fourteen days after the body was buried there was a dreadful stench in the outhouse. The women who were threshing complained of this to Mr. Riembauer, who told them he could not conceive the reason. Soon after, one of the women, who had gone into the little side-room, stumbled against something in the dark, and called for a light, that she might see what it was, as she was sure that it could not be a stone. Mr. Riembauer prevented her, and instantly fetched a padlock out of his own room, and fastened the door, which until then had always stood open. He told us all this down-stairs, adding that it was one of Nanny's feet sticking out of the earth. That same evening he fetched more sand, and covered the grave over with it."

Catherine then proceeded to give an account of the sickness and sudden death of her mother and sister in June, 1809, when she was at the vicarage, having been fetched from school at Ratisbon to take charge of the kitchen during her sister's illness. She confidently asserted that Mr. Riembauer had poisoned her mother and sister, and added that they had frequently quarrelled with him, and that her sister had even threatened to leave his service, for which reason Riembauer lived in constant dread of discovery. That during their illness he did not allow them any medical or religious attendance, and himself gave her sister medicines, which he got from a barber-surgeon, and even forced her to take them. She herself was sent to fetch some drugs from the barber, which Riembauer gave next morning to her sister, who shortly after swooned and died. "The body of my sister," said Catherine, "was exceedingly swollen and covered with spots; blood ran from her nose and mouth. The barber supposed her to have been with child; the village people said the same, and pointed out Riembauer as the father. All wondered that my mother and sister should both have died so suddenly."

Lastly Catherine maintained that Riembauer had several times expressed an intention of killing her also. Her sister once warned her that he had said that he would not mind giving two or three hundred florins to any one who would put her out of the way: adding, " the girl is growing taller and more sensible every day, and at last no dowry will be large enough to keep her silent." After her sister's death he begged her not to leave him, and promised to give her eight thousand florins as her marriage-portion if she would but stay. But after four weeks she left his house, and because he appropriated to himself all her sister's money, clothes, and letters, she said to him as she went away, "Reverend sir, I do not forget the past;" whereupon he answered, " It will go harder with you than with me : I have made up my mind what to say; your mother and sister are dead, and can tell no tales, and I shall say it was they who murdered the woman." But he did not lose sight of her, and several times afterwards attempted to get her into his service, or rather into his power.

This accusation, brought by a girl of seventeen against a clergyman of high consideration, was so strange in its details, so improbable and extravagant, that at first it was regarded as the invention of a dis-

eased imagination. But the narrative was so consistent, so circumstantial and so clear, and the girl
showed so much sense, and was so unembarrassed and
confident, that it was impossible to let the matter rest.
The farm-house of Thomashof, in which the event
was said to have taken place, and the body of Anna
Eichstädter to be buried, had fortunately passed into
other hands, and the accused priest was living at
a distance. It thus was possible without exciting attention to make the necessary investigations on the
spot.

Directions were accordingly given at Lauterbach
to examine the Thomashof. The new outhouse described by Catherine was found, and within it on the
left hand a small closet. On digging, they found,
very near the surface, one shoe and a female skeleton,
the skull of which contained two rows of beautiful
white teeth. On the floor of the room formerly inhabited by Riembauer stains were found, which, on
being wetted with warm water, clearly showed themselves to be marks of blood; several of the boards bore
traces of having been planed by an unskilful hand,
evidently for the purpose of effacing similar spots.
The carpenter Michael remembered that the Frauenknecht family had borrowed a plane of him some six
years before.

Upon this Riembauer was apprehended and conveyed to Landshut. He showed but little surprise,
and indeed seemed fully prepared for the occurrence.
At the first examination, of the 27th October,
1813, he did not affect ignorance of the cause of his
apprehension, but immediately mentioned Anna Eichstädter. He said he had made acquaintance with

her at Hirnheim, but that nothing improper had
passed between them : that she had had the greatest
confidence in him, had intrusted to his care 50 florins
of her savings, and had begged him to take her as his
cook, which he promised to do, on condition of her
future good conduct. That since he had left Hirnheim
he had heard nothing more of her, excepting at
Pirkwang, where she had twice sent or written to him
for part of the 50 florins. That during the summer
of 1807, while he was at Munich for his examination,
she had come to Lauterbach to see him, and had told
the Frauenknecht family, to their great annoyance,
that he had promised to take her as his cook.

"It was," said Riembauer, "about the 3rd, 4th, or
5th November, 1807 (he purposely misstated the
day), that I returned from celebrating a funeral
at Pirkwang to Thomashof, the farm which I had
lately bought. It was just twilight. I went straight
up to my own room, and found the door open and a
person lying upon the floor. ˙I imagined it to be one
of the women belonging to the house, and called out
'How now—what is the matter?' On receiving no
answer, I touched her, and found, to my horror,
that she was dead. I ran down stairs in utter
dismay, and in the room below I found the mother
and her daughter Catherine clinging to each other
and trembling like aspen-leaves. Upon asking them
what had happened, they seized my hands and implored me amid tears and lamentations to keep everything secret. I then learnt that Anna Eichstädter,
who had been to see me once before, while I was at
Munich, had arrived at Thomashof that afternoon,
and had insisted upon going up into my room ; that

both mother and daughter had quarrelled violently with this woman, who had attempted to stab them, and that Magdalena had seized my razor and cut her throat. The dispute which led to such terrible results had been caused by Eichstädter's assertion that she was come to be my cook, and that the Frauenknechts would be forced to leave the house.

" I afterwards lighted a candle, and in the person lying in my room recognised Anna Eichstädter.

" I wished to quit Thomashof immediately, and told the Frauenknechts that I could no longer stay with them. But they held me by both hands, imploring me with tears and groans, by all that was most sacred, to stay, that they would give me anything I might ask, and deduct as much as I pleased from the purchase-money which I still owed them for the farm. At last I suffered myself to be persuaded to stay, brought my bed down into the passage, and slept there.

" I went out early the next morning, leaving the dead body in my room. When I returned in the evening, it was lying on a litter, and the Frauenknechts told me that they wished to bury it in the left-hand room in the outhouse. I told them that they might do as they pleased, that I could not assist them.

" Between eight and nine at night, the mother and daughter carried the body on a litter into the little closet and covered it with the earth, which had already been dug out.

" The following morning I went to the spot myself, and found the earth loosely heaped over the body. Upon calling their attention to this, and remarking that should any man or beast enter the outhouse, the thing must be discovered, they took some sand and rubbish and covered the grave with it.

" I continued to sleep down stairs in the passage some few nights longer, and then returned to my own room after it had been cleaned."

These were the chief points of a statement by which he attempted to prove that he had, at his own peril, consigned this horrible event to the keeping of his priestly conscience, out of compassion for the criminals, whose spiritual director he was, and because that which was done could not be undone, and the women deeply repented of their crime.

Unlike meaner criminals, who usually deny everything, Riembauer pursued the highest line of policy, freely admitting all the facts which were already proved, but endeavouring to arrange them in such an order that the certainty of their truth need not bring with it a conviction of his own guilt. Upon this system Riembauer repeated the statement made against him, the tenor of which he could easily guess, almost word for word as Catherine had related it, with this one important difference, that he changed the persons, accusing Magdalena and her mother of the crime, and assuming for himself the part of spectator, which had belonged to Catherine. That which he really did, he pretended only to have seen; and to have concealed, from christian charity, that which in fact Magdalena and her mother had concealed for him.

This change of persons at once converted the account of the murder at Thomashof—the main facts of which were acknowledged by the accused to be true—from a fearful romance into a manifest absurdity. Who could imagine such a deed possible to a gentle kind-hearted woman, who, as Riembauer said, had the soul of an angel? What circumstances could be strange enough, what excitement sufficiently strong, suddenly to transform a woman so sweet-tempered, and at the same time so timid and nervous, as Magdalena is represented to have been, into a bloodthirsty fury? Eichstädter was tall, strong, broad-shouldered, and powerfully made; Magdalena, on the contrary, was small, thin, and weak: how could it have been possible for her to cut Eichstädter's throat? In a contest, such as that described by Riembauer, a few wounds might have been inflicted; but it is impossible thus to cut the throat of a person having the free use of her limbs.

Thus by admitting the fact of the murder, Riembauer confirmed the truth of the accusation against himself,—indirectly, it is true, but still conclusively.

His conduct in prison afforded convincing proofs of his guilt. He began by bribing his gaolers. He wrote long letters to a number of persons of his acquaintance, directing them what evidence to give in his favour; especially to affirm that the deceased, Magdalena Frauenknecht, had confessed to them that she had murdered the woman.* He gave especial orders to his mistress, Anna Weninger, to get rid of the green umbrella as speedily as possible. Some of these letters reached their destination, among others that

* In one letter, addressed to a priest of his acquaintance, he endeavoured to induce him to give such evidence :—1. In consideration of our brotherly love ; 2. For the sake of the worthy Nanny (his cookmaid Weninger) ; 3. On account of our friends, who are grieved for me ; 4. On account of the clergy, who are thereby cast into the shade ; 5. On account of the faithful, who are offended.

addressed to Anna Weninger, who punctually executed his commission. Riembauer went so far in his system of corruption as to endeavour, though without success, to gain a sight of the documents, or at any rate to ascertain the precise charge brought against him.

Hereupon his gaolers were changed, and himself removed to another prison, whence he inferred that his letters had been intercepted. He therefore endeavoured to weaken the presumption which his conduct might have raised against him, by informing the judge that he had a disclosure to make, namely, that distress had thrown him into a state of temporary madness, during which he had written without consciousness or design letters which might appear like the production of a sane and guilty mind. He then endeavoured to explain to his judge, according to some jesuitical theory, the difference between the human *sensus externus*, *internus*, and *intimus*; and that this very bribery, &c. proved that he possessed the *sensus externus* and *internus*, but that the *sensus intimus*, upon which everything in fact depended, was totally wanting to him when ·he wrote the letters in question.

Notwithstanding the absurdity of his first statement, it remained for four years—during which he underwent ninety-nine examinations, besides countless confrontations with witnesses—the theme to which, with few variations, he constantly adhered. He persisted in the assertion that he was not the murderer of Anna Eichstädter; that the day of the murder was the 3rd, not the 2nd of November; that Magdalena Frauenknecht committed the crime from jealousy and

anger, and that he had nothing to accuse himself of
but an error in judgment in suffering himself to be
led by christian charity and a mistaken sense of duty
as a priest, to conceal her horrid deed. This, he
said, was the truth, from which he could not depart,
even though, like Saint Bartholomew, he were flayed
alive; and which, even on the scaffold, and surrounded by a thousand devils, he would still proclaim
to the world with his latest breath.

During most of the examinations he affected the
resignation of a martyr, and usually answered the
judges with a sweet smile. If occasionally assuming an air of injured innocence and honour, he
burst forth in vehement words or gestures, he suddenly stopped short and "with bated breath and
whispering humbleness" begged pardon for this
warmth, intelligible in one who saw the most manifest truths always contradicted, who was like "a de-
fenceless sheep worried by savage dogs." When
closely pressed, he sometimes attempted to overawe
the judge by the assumption of a pulpit style; at
other times he burst into a laugh at the " unheard-
of lies which the devil invented against him;" and
then he would strain his face into an appearance
of sorrow and dejection, and vainly strive to shed
tears. All the endeavours of the judge to overcome
the obstinacy of the accused by representing to him
the improbability and the absurdity of his tale, were
foiled by his matchless self-possession and his dialectic
skill. He had a solution for every difficulty; an hypo-
thesis for every conflicting statement; there was nothing, however impossible, which he did not attempt
by dint of his psychological and metaphysical learn-

ing to demonstrate into probability. When it was urged how incredible it was that Magdalena, whom he represented as remarkable for kindness and gentleness, should commit such an action, he launched out into a disquisition upon the influence of jealousy and anger in general, and upon the excitability of the female sex in particular, under the influence of which Magdalena, hardly conscious of what she was about, might have done the deed. If his attention was called to the physical impossibility of the action as narrated by him, he was ready with the suggestion that Magdalena's mother might have come to her assistance, or, with his habitual smile, he bared his own throat, and showed upon it how easily the operation might have been performed. When it was objected that the weak and unpractised hand of a woman could not, under any circumstances, inflict so deep a wound with a razor, he brought out of his store of metaphysical learning the theory of a certain *motus primo primus*, by which, when once the razor was set in motion, it acquired unusual force in a particular direction.

He left no means untried to cast suspicion upon Catherine's character and evidence. The testimony of others who proved the falsehood of many particulars of his statement was seldom able to shake his confidence or to induce him to retract any of his assertions. When confronted with witnesses, he always gave them to understand what he wished them to say, and endeavoured to work upon their feelings of compassion or of reverence. Sometimes he would try to overawe them by eloquence, and by the dignity of his spiritual character, or to confuse and lead them into contradictions by candidly and eloquently reminding them how easily man may be so deceived by the imperfection of his nature, delusion of the senses, or want of memory, as in all honesty to mistake falsehood for truth. When these wiles had, as usual, failed, he accused the witnesses of gross error or of impudent deceit, invoked all the persons of the Godhead and all the saints in Heaven to testify that he had spoken truth; or, in holy wrath at the corrupt nature of man, he called down upon their heads the just vengeance of offended Heaven. Once, when clearly convicted of a falsehood by the evidence of several witnesses, he exclaimed with flashing eyes, " *Quis contra torrentem?* If thirty thousand men stood there, and said the devil is white, I would ever maintain him to be black, and in the same manner I must still affirm," &c. Occasionally, but very seldom, he altered his course, and confessed the truth of some fact, which, for months and in spite of all proof, he had obstinately denied ; but then either the action of melancholy on the *sensus intimus,* or some innocent confusion of his ideas—an involuntary deception caused by the *associatio idearum*—had to bear the blame of his former assertions, which were instantly replaced by others equally false. He was inexhaustible in hypocritical figures of speech, by which he endeavoured to persuade the judge of his innocence. He assured him " that his heart was like that of a dove, without gall;" " that he wished him a magic mirror in which he might behold the purity of his soul." That he had hitherto invariably shown himself to be one of the most goodnatured of men ; how therefore could any one suspect him of so horrible an action ? *cum nemo* *repente fiat pessimus.* "My heart shudders," says he, "at the bare accusation. In order that you may perceive how improbable it is, I beg of you to consider my priestly character. You know, 1, that by committing murder a priest becomes *irregularis ;* 2, *excommunicationem majorem ipso facto illatam incurrere ;** 3, that though David did severe penance for the murder of Uriah, he was no longer worthy to build the Temple. How then could it be possible for me to forget my God, my future happiness, eternal and temporal punishment, and, with hands still reeking with innocent blood, to grasp God's image, administer the sacred mysteries of religion, and thus cast myself headlong from one abyss to another?"

As Riembauer could not be moved by admonition, exhortation, argument, or evidence, the judge attempted to find a way to his conscience through his

* Riembauer is perfectly correct in his canon law; but this knowledge only made his character appear still more atrocious when he subsequently confessed the murder. Since the 2nd November, 1807, he had become *irregularis, i. e.* incapable of administering any sacred function, and still he continued to do so (Van Espen, 'Jus Eccl. Un.,' tom. II. p. ii. tit. 10, c. i. and vii.; Rieger, 'Instit. Jurisprud. Ecclesiasticæ,' p. ii. § 125-144). No fasting, no penitence, can remove irregularity on account of murder; and he who, conscious of this irregularity, continues to administer the sacraments, is guilty of deadly sin ('Add. Silvestri ad Van Espen,' I. c. 7). A dispensation from the pope was alone able to remove it, upon which one learned in the Catholic canon law (Pyrrhus Corradus) remarks:—" *Pontifex in dispensationibus hujus modi concedendis, non parum difficilem se reddit; cum abominabile sit, quod effundens sanguinem humanum, offerat sanguinem Christi et hostiam immaculatam, vel officium Deo ad altaris ministerium præstet.*" What a priest, then, was Riembauer, and what a man! Moreover, he afterwards owned that he had never confessed his crime to any other priest, but, as he expressed it, referred the whole matter to God alone.

imagination. The trial had now lasted two whole years, when the judge appointed All Souls' Day in 1815, the eighth anniversary of the murder, for a new examination, the eighty-eighth in number. It commenced at 4 P.M., and was intended to convince him, by the overwhelming mass of evidence collected against him, of the inutility of further denial, and to work upon his feelings more powerfully than usual, by admonition and appeal to his recollections. But he remained unmoved as ever. At midnight the judge, after addressing the accused in most moving language, suddenly raised a cloth, under which lay a skull upon a black cushion. " This," said the judge, " is the skull of Anna Eichstädter, which you may easily recognise by the beautiful teeth." Riembauer started from his seat, stared wildly at the judge, then smiled in his usual manner, and stepped aside to avoid looking straight into the empty sockets of the eyes, but quickly recovered himself, and said, pointing to the skull, " Could this skull speak, it would say, ' Riembauer was my friend, not my murderer!' " He added, " I am calm, and can breathe freely, but I am pained by being exposed to such scenes, and by the charge brought against me. To-morrow" (for Riembauer still asserted that the murder took place on the 3rd November) " is the anniversary of the day on which, some years ago, at my return from Pirkwang, I found the whole body lying dead in my room, as now I find this skull. As a citizen I ever stand in need of the king's mercy, but not as a criminal." When the report had been read and signed, the judge again led him up to the skull, which he held before his eyes while he exhorted him to confess. Riembauer betrayed some emotion, but with his usual hypocritical smile thus addressed the skull in a solemn tone, " Oh ! if thou couldst but speak, thou wouldst confirm the truth of my assertions !"

After a long series of examinations, during which the documents had swelled to a bulk of forty-two folio volumes, on the 13th October, 1817, the prisoner requested an interview, in which he stated to the judge " that he had reflected more deeply on the subject, and had besought the Holy Ghost to assist his memory, whereupon it had become clear to him that he had made a mistake in his former statement." He then withdrew the assertion, which he had maintained for four years, that Anna Eichstädter had been murdered by Magdalena Frauenknecht, and affirmed that he had heard one day from Madame W. that a certain Catherine Schmidt had told her that she had been told by Magdalena Frauenknecht that it was not she who had murdered the woman, but her mother. This new story gave rise to fresh judicial proceedings.

It so happened that on the 20th November, 1817, a Jew called Lammfromm was executed at Landshut for murder. Riembauer saw him led out to execution, and was struck by the tranquillity and cheerfulness with which this man went toward his bloody end. On expressing his wonder that this man, a murderer, and moreover a Jew, should meet death with so much composure, he was told that ever since Lammfromm had eased his conscience by confessing his crime, he had been in a most happy frame of mind, in which he continued till his death. From that moment the Christian priest grew more and more restless and anxious, ate and drank less, and on

the 26th requested another interview, " as he thought
he was suffering from a diseased conscience, the pangs
of which might be eased by a full confession." In
this interview, which was the hundredth, he fell upon
his knees, begged that the trial might be brought to
end, said that he was weary of life, and talked of all
manner of phantasms—how he received visits from
strangers and from persons whom he knew; and how
for the last three nights, after the Ave Maria, he had
heard the sad and solemn roll of a funeral drum.
Even now he could not at first resolve upon making
a full confession. When the judge observed that his
distress of mind was entirely owing to his guilt, he
replied that " he was exhausted by sleepless nights,
but that he had told the story as he knew it and as
it occurred." The judge once more recapitulated all
the falsehoods, improbabilities, and contradictions
contained in his statement, animadverted upon his
strangely pusillanimous and confused demeanour, and
concluded with the remark that his feelings seemed
deeply touched, and that he had better, by a free and
full confession of the truth, endeavour to obtain some
peace of mind. Upon this the criminal at last exclaimed,—" Yes! I feel deeply shaken ; my health is
broken; and you, Sir, are perfectly right when you
say that I cannot do better than make a repentant
confession. But before I take the decisive step, let
me implore the royal protection for my innocent children, and for my last cook, Anna Weninger." He
then gave directions for the disposal of his property.
" And now receive my sincere confession : Catherine
has spoken falsely on many points, but her assertions

are in the main true, for it was I who deprived Anna Eichstädter of life."

After this the criminal gave, in thirteen several examinations, a narrative of the whole transaction. His motive to the crime was the dread lest Anna Eichstädter should unmask him before the world, rob him of his honour and good name, and ruin his prospect of preferment. Anna declared, said Riembauer, " when I met her at Ratisbon, that she would not part from me. I represented to her most strongly that it was impossible for me to take her, but all in vain. My position, my reputation, everything that was sacred and dear to me, would be endangered by her coming to Lauterbach. I thought within myself, ' What is to be done should she come ?' and I suddenly remembered the maxim laid down by Father Benedict Stattler in his *Ethica Christiana*,* accord-

---

* The chief passages from which Riembauer selected his *dictamen practicum* are the 1889th, 1891st, and 1893rd paragraphs of this truly antichristian *Ethica Christiana*, which appeared in 1789, in six thick volumes. In the above-named paragraphs a christian is allowed to prevent a " *contumelia gravis certo provisa, aut perquam dolore molesta, aut magnopere ignominiosa*" or a " *calumnia*," by the murder of the " *injusti aggressoris*," or " *injusti calumniatoris.*" This species of morality would clearly justify a man in secretly murdering any one who might be suspected of designing a secret attack on his honour. This is further proved by the 1893rd paragraph, in which a man is permitted to rid himself of an enemy :—
" *Si non ipsa occisione injusti calumniatoris tantundem periculi infamiæ incurramus, quantum vitare declinatione calumniæ intendimus :*" also " *Si tantundem periculi nobis ex occisione calumniatoris immineat, profecto utile remedium occisio esse non potest, ac proinde nec licitum,*"—that is, the murder should only take place when it can be committed with secrecy and security. There is nothing, however infamous, for which Father Stattler's christian ethics do not afford a justification. The 1894th paragraph permits

ing to which it is lawful to deprive another of life, when honour and reputation cannot be otherwise maintained; for honour is of higher value than life, and the law of necessity holds good against those who attack our honour, as much as against robbers. I thought over this maxim, which Professor St——— used formerly to explain to us young ecclesiastics in his lectures; and finding that it exactly applied to my own predicament, I took it as my *dictamen practicum*. My honour, thought I, will be lost, should this wicked woman come to Lauterbach and carry her threat into execution. I shall be suspended by the consistory, my property will be forfeited, and my name will become a reproach and a byeword throughout the diocese. Although I had considered this maxim of Stattler's for some time past, and applied it to my own position, still it was but an idea, and I had not yet formed any plan for putting it in practice."

While he was engaged in these meditations, the month of November, 1807, found him in arrear with his payments to Anna Eichstädter for the support of her child; and as he had no ready money, he lived in daily dread lest she should come or write to Lauterbach.

On All Souls' day, the 2nd of November, towards

---

calumny to be met by calumny: *Licet certam gravem calumniam quæ nullo alio remedio, hoc uno autem certo et efficaciter, de pelli potest, enervare imponendo calumniatori falsum crimen præcise tale, nec majus quam necesse sit, et sufficiat ad elidendam calumniatoris auctoritatem ac fidem, et famam propriam dependendam!* Riembauer, of course, reckoned Anna Eichstädter among his *injustos aggressores.* Father Stattler's book is printed *cum permissu superiorum,* and is still used in several places as a manual for ecclesiastics!

evening, as he was carting home turnips, accompanied by Magdalena Frauenknecht, he recognised, to his utter dismay, Anna Eichstädter entering the house at Thomashof.

He found her in the lower room, and after a short conversation took her with him up stairs. " I at first intended," said he, " to hide her in the loft, so that Magdalena might not see her. But it was already too dark, and we turned back half way. I must confess that for a moment I thought of throwing her down the stairs, and I don't exactly know why I did not; I was filled with terror, and perhaps I thought within myself that she might only break a limb in the fall, and that then matters would be worse than before."

In his room Eichstädter told him that she was resolved to know what she had to expect, and insisted on his taking her as his cook, and getting rid of Magdalena. Riembauer endeavoured to pacify her by explaining the nature of his connexion with the Frauenknechts, and the impossibility of complying with her demands, but in vain.

He then left her, under pretence of fetching her some beer, went down stairs—where, he asserts, contrary to all probability, that Magdalena persuaded him to murder Eichstädter—took a bread-knife and his razor, and returned to Eichstädter, who reiterated her demands with great violence and many threats of denouncing him to justice and before the consistory, and of publishing his true character everywhere. At this critical moment Father Stattler's maxim again recurred to his mind, and he seized the bread-knife and stabbed Eichstädter with it on the right side of her throat; but finding the knife too blunt, he dropped it, and she endeavoured to defend herself; he then held her by the throat, gave her a heavy blow on the back of her head, thrust his fingers into her mouth, and tried to choke her, exhorting her in the mean time to repentance and confession, as she must die. She replied by earnestly entreating him to spare her life; "then," said he, " I took the razor out of my pocket, embraced her from behind, and with my right hand put the blade to her throat, while with my left I forced it into her windpipe. I instantly perceived by her sobs that I had made a deep incision, and I dropped the razor. She remained standing for three or four minutes, during which I said to her, ' Mariandel, I pray to God and to you for pardon : you would have it so. Pray to God for forgiveness of your sins, and I will give you absolution.' I accordingly gave it her, as it was *in casu necessitatis*. She then tottered, as if her knees were failing under her; and I took her under the arms, and let her down gently ; for a few minutes longer I gave her religious consolation as she lay on the floor, until she began to kick and struggle, and presently breathed her last."

After the murder, he went down stairs to the Frauenknechts, upon whom he enjoined silence, and washed the blood from his hands; but all at once he heard a noise of trampling and scuffling overhead. " One of the Frauenknechts," continued the prisoner, " cried out, ' Jesus and Mary! the woman is come to life again;' and I hastened up stairs in continued evil disposition, firmly resolved on no account to suffer Eichstädter to return to life, as she would be still more formidable to me after this catastrophe; so I drew her neckerchief tighter, partly to hasten her death and partly to shorten her sufferings: whether she then moved, I cannot determine."

He maintained, in direct contradiction to Catherine's statement, that the corpse lay the whole of the next day in his room, and that it was not until the night of the 3rd November that he buried it in the closet in the outhouse. He owned that he himself had dug the hole, but asserted that Magdalena and her mother had helped him to carry the body down the stairs and into the outhouse, and to bury it there; this scene we will describe in Riembauer's own words:—" The grave which I had dug was too short and too shallow, so that the head and the arms, which had stiffened in an attitude of entreaty, projected far above the sand. I therefore stamped with both feet, and with the whole weight of my body, upon the corpse, in which I heard a strange rumbling noise. I then covered it with more sand, and some time afterwards with brick rubbish, because a woman who had come to thresh stumbled over one of the hands which protruded from the earth."

He afterwards confessed that in carrying Eich-städter's body down the stairs one of her shoes fell off, which he chopped in pieces and threw upon the dung-hill; likewise that he appropriated to himself her silver buckle, her purse containing about two florins, and the green umbrella belonging to the priest at P——, and that he effaced the bloody stains partly by washing them with warm water and partly by planing the boards. "And now," he continued, " I have nothing further to tell about this sad story, save my silent grief and sorrow, and that I have applied* frequent masses for the soul of Anna Eichstädter."

Even after confessing every circumstance of the crime, he showed no true repentance; but continued to exert his skill in casuistry to justify or extenuate the murder. Sometimes he would maintain that his hands had been impelled by terror, fear, and sudden impulse, and that the gash had thus been inflicted without the consent of his reason. When it was objected to him that this excuse stood in direct contradiction to his assertion of having acted upon the maxim of Father Stattler, he attempted to prove that his reasoning powers were lulled to sleep by the maxim in question, while horror and dread rendered all further action merely mechanical. Another time he would quote the doctrine that all means are justified by the end, and would prove that his purpose being noble, his action could not be criminal. " I had no object but that of preventing the many evils and sins arising from public scandal, and of upholding the honour of the clergy and the reverence due to my sacred calling. Had I not stood in such high consideration with the people, I might more readily have submitted to the disgrace. But I foresaw that the discovery of my crime would bring with it a train of evils; that many men would henceforth think all sins permitted; some would cease to believe in God, others would no longer hold anything sacred." Thus Riembauer not only committed murder *ad ma-*

* An expression which shows the estimation in which this priest held the holy offices of his church : he talks of applying a mass as an apothecary would of applying a blister.

jorem Dei gloriam, but for the same cause persevered for four long years in denying his crime. " It was," said he, " only in order to preserve the honour of the clergy in my person that I pined so many years in captivity without confessing my crime. But as soon as I perceived that it was the will of God that I should reveal the deed, I made a full confession." So utterly perverted and corrupt was the mind of this Tartuffe, that he actually boasted that he had deserved well of the State by his deceit and hypocrisy. " I have openly confessed," says he, " my manner of life, and I think myself entitled to some indulgence for so governing my conduct as to cause no public scandal."

With regard to the alleged poisoning of Magdalena Frauenknecht and her mother, no proof was forthcoming. The bodies were exhumed in 1813, but no trace of poison was discovered, and everything led to the conclusion that they died of a nervous fever which at that time raged in the district of the Danube, and which killed many persons in the neighbourhood, among others an Austrian soldier, who, from charity, was taken into the manse, and nursed by Magdalena herself. Riembauer denied having any hand in the death of these two women.

Several other circumstances appeared during the course of inquiry; among others, a charge of forging a document for 635 florins, in which the grounds of suspicion were very strong against the prisoner, although he did not confess. In his 107th examination, he related that once when the innkeeper of Grafentraubach refused him a loan of money, he had meditated burning his house down. This was to prove that sinful thoughts are not crimes. He also

said, in another examination, in order to show his
sincerity, that he had once fervently prayed to God to
destroy some man who was hateful to him, and that
the man had died, probably from the effect of his
prayers.

However, the murder of Anna Eichstädter was the
chief point under consideration of the court.

So long as Riembauer denied his guilt, the whole
force of the examination was directed to cumulate
evidence against him. Catherine's testimony was on
some points defective. Riembauer's confession removed all difficulties, and changed the whole posture
of affairs.

It was confirmed beyond doubt by the evidence of
Riembauer's own brother, who up to this time had
resolutely denied, in the face of several witnesses, all
knowledge of his brother's crime. He now made the
following statement:—

" I am indeed in a most terrible position : Riembauer is not only my brother, but has also been my
constant benefactor ; gratitude and fraternal love have
induced me hitherto to deny all knowledge of the
murder of Eichstädter, but now that my brother has
himself confessed the dreadful deed, I may speak
without incurring the reproach of ingratitude. I once
visited my brother at his parsonage at Priel, and
stayed there three or four weeks : one evening his
cookmaid, Magdalena Frauenknecht, a good quiet
girl, came to my bedside, and began to weep bitterly.
I asked her why she cried, and she answered, ' Ah!
brother, if you knew what I know, you would cry
too ! ' "

Riembauer's brother then repeated Magdalena's

statement, which exactly coincided with that of
Catherine, save only that she admitted that she herself was present at the murder, and helped her master
to carry the body into the outhouse, and to bury it
there. Her reason for confiding the story to Riembauer's brother was, that the farmer who had bought
Thomashof of him was then digging in the outhouse, and she was afraid lest the body might be
discovered. " I knew not what to say," continued
his brother, " save my horror of the crime, and that
I could advise her nothing, but to let things take their
course."

Riembauer's confession is complete, consistent in
all its parts, and legally sufficient. It tallied with a
number of facts which were proved by other witnesses. It was certain that Anna Eichstädter had a
child by Riembauer, that she pressed him for money,
and that at the time of the murder he had none to
give to her. It was further proved that Eichstädter
had left Priel on All Souls' day, 1807, and might
easily have reached Lauterbach the same day, and
that she was never after seen alive. On the very spot
described by Riembauer himself the skeleton of a
woman was found, which was recognised by the teeth
as that of Anna Eichstädter. Six years after the
murder there were spots of blood upon the floor of
Riembauer's room, as well as marks of the plane, evidently made in endeavouring to obliterate the traces
of the murder. Only one shoe was found—Riembauer mentioned having chopped the other in pieces.

According to the common law of Germany, the
proof of a murder having been committed, confirmed
by the confession of the murderer, justifies sentence

of death ;* and in Riembauer's case the fact had been fully proved and the confession made ; nor were there any extenuating circumstances which should mitigate the severity of the usual punishment.

Nevertheless, on the 1st August, 1818, the court passed the following sentence on the criminal :—

" Francis Salesius Riembauer is found guilty of murder, and is condemned to imprisonment of the severest kind in a fortress for life."

The reasons assigned for so lenient a sentence were, first, that the fact of the murder was not clearly proved, as the skeleton, which had lain six years in the damp earth, bore no marks of violence ;† and secondly, that Riembauer's character was not notoriously bad.‡

* Stübel über den That bestand der Verbrechen.

† Art. 271 of the Bavarian code.

‡ When the fact of a murder having been committed rests chiefly on the murderer's confession, the Bavarian penal code (art. 269, § 2) requires that " the accused should be either a notorious criminal, or one proved by the clearest circumstantial evidence to be a person from whom a crime such as that of which he is accused may be expected." Feuerbach adduces several excellent but obvious arguments against this law, and states his opinion that in this particular case every condition required by law was fulfilled, and every defect in the evidence supplied by the confession.

THE UNKNOWN MURDERER;

In the year 1817 there lived in the town of M——
a goldsmith of the name of Christopher Rupprecht.
He was between the ages of sixty and sixty-five, and
in easy circumstances. He had been twelve years a
widower, and had but one child living, a daughter,
married to a furrier named Bieringer, a brother and
two sisters. Rupprecht could neither read nor write,
and therefore kept no accounts either of his trade or of
the money he lent out at interest, but trusted entirely
to his memory and to the assistance he occasionally received from others in arranging and drawing up his bills.
He was a man of vulgar mind and coarse habits, fond
of associating with people of the very lowest class, and
of frequenting alehouses, where his chief delight was
in slang and abuse, and where he suffered himself to
be made the butt of the roughest jokes and the most
vulgar witticisms. His ruling passion was avarice,
and his favourite business the lending money at
usurious interest. Though rich, he deprived himself
of necessaries, and was glad when his sister or his
daughter sent him a dinner; and for a long time
after his wife's death he kept no servant, in order
to save food and wages. Two days before the occur-

rence which caused the present inquiry, he had taken one into his service. Hard, morose, and repulsive, as a miser is apt to be, and at the same time crotchety, violent, and ready on the most trifling occasion to use abusive language, he kept most of his family at a distance. His daughter and his sister Clara visited him regularly, but his brother, with whom he had a law-suit, and his other sister, avoided his company; he had also quarrelled with his son-in-law several months before, and had ceased to see him from that time. He was cross-grained and quarrelsome, continually at law with his neighbours, and on bad terms with a number of people, though no one could be pointed out as his declared enemy.

For about a year he had been in the daily habit of frequenting a small beer-shop, commonly called the Hell. To this place, which was scarce fifty yards distant from his own house, Rupprecht went on the 7th February, at half-past eight in the evening, in his dressing-gown and with a leathern cap on his head. The party assembled there consisted of eleven respectable burghers, who sat talking and drinking together till about half-past ten, when Rupprecht called for another glass of beer, and the host left the upper parlour where his guests were assembled, and went down into the tap to fetch it. As he was going up stairs with the beer, and had almost reached the top, he heard the bell over the street-door, and on asking what was wanted, he was answered in a strange voice by the inquiry whether Mr. Rupprecht was there. Without looking round, the host answered that he was, and the stranger requested him to desire Rupprecht to step down to him for a moment. The host delivered the message to his guest, who instantly rose and left the room. Scarcely a minute had elapsed, when the other guests were alarmed by hearing loud groans like those of a person in a fit of apoplexy. They all hastened down stairs, and found Rupprecht lying just within the door, covered with blood which was pouring out of a large wound on his head. About a foot and a half from the body lay his cap, cut evidently by a sharp instrument. He was only able to mutter the words "Wicked rogue! wicked rogue! with the axe!" When asked whether he knew who had done it, he made an effort to speak, but no one could understand what he said. The guests carried him into the parlour, where he began to moan and mutter unintelligibly. Excited by the questions of one of the guests as to whether he knew the man, he distinctly said "My daughter! my daughter!" which was understood to mean that he wished to see Madame Bieringer: she was accordingly informed of what had happened, and brought to the house by one of those present; but Rupprecht apparently did not recognise her; he was insensible, and lay moaning like one in a fit, with his head drooping upon his breast and his limbs paralysed.

The physician and surgeon attached to the Criminal Court were sent for, and found a wound four inches long, which had penetrated the skull. This they attributed to a blow from some sharp heavy instrument—according to all appearances a large sabre, wielded by a practised hand.

The Hell Tavern stands in the end of a narrow dark alley, from which there is no outlet. The side on which is the door forms an angle with the opposite house, so deep that no light falls into it by night. Two stone steps lead up to the house-door, of which one wing only opens, and is provided with a bell. Outside the door, on the left of these steps, is a stone bench. The hall within is small, narrow, and little more than six feet high; the wound could not therefore have been inflicted upon Rupprecht in the hall, as space and height were required to give force to the blow. It would moreover have been madness to attempt the deed in a passage which was lighted by an oil-lamp, which, though dim, would have enabled the victim or a passer by to recognise the murderer. In the hall, too, Rupprecht coming down the stairs would have met his enemy face to face, and must have seen him prepare for the attack, from which he might easily have escaped by running to the rooms above.

Supposing the wound—which slanted downward, and had evidently been inflicted from behind—to have been given during Rupprecht's flight up the stairs, those who ran down on hearing his screams would have found the wounded man on the staircase, or at any rate close to the foot of it. But he was found just within the house-door, and it is far more likely that, after receiving the wound outside, he tottered back into the hall and fell there, than that he should have attempted to reach the house-door after being wounded in endeavouring to escape up the stairs.

Again, the wound was on the left side of the head, and the dark corner we have before mentioned is on the left hand of any one leaving the tavern. The probability therefore is that Rupprecht received the wound on the very door-step. In this case he had

but to totter one step back to fall on the spot where
he was found. It would have been scarcely possible
for one in Rupprecht's condition to retain sufficient
strength to crawl up the steps from the street into
the hall.

On the other hand, it would have been impossible
for the murderer, standing in the street, to have struck
Rupprecht from behind, while he stood on the door-
steps. This difficulty is, however, completely removed
by the stone bench on the left of the door, which we
have already mentioned.

Thus all circumstances combine to make us conclude that the occurrence took place as follows :—As
soon as the murderer had requested the landlord to
send Rupprecht down to him, he went into the dark
corner on the left, mounted the stone bench near the
door-steps, and stood there in readiness to strike.
Rupprecht went down stairs, expecting to find some
one who wanted to speak to him on business, and
seeing no one in the passage, went outside the door
and turned to look down the street after the man who
had sent for him, when he was struck a well-aimed
heavy blow from the stone bench behind him.

Nothing was found on or near the spot that could
throw the slightest suspicion on any one, nor could
any person present form a conjecture as to the author
or the motive of the deed.

Something, it was hoped, would be learnt from
the wounded man himself when he should have recovered consciousness. On the evening of the following
day, the 8th of February, the judge and two other
officers of the court accordingly visited him, and
found him sensible. He frequently said " Oh, dear !

Oh, dear!" and when he wished for something to drink, he pronounced the word beer plainly enough. Conceiving him to be in a fit state to give information, the judge asked him the following questions, which were thus answered by the wounded man:—Who struck you the blow?—"Schmidt." What Schmidt? —"Woodcutter." Where does he live?—"In the Most." With what did he strike you?—"Hatchet." How did you recognise him?—"By his voice." Does Schmidt owe you money?—He shook his head. What then could have induced Schmidt to do such a thing? —"Quarrel." As Rupprecht was unable to speak connectedly, no questions were asked about the nature of this quarrel. But when the first and second questions were again put to him, he distinctly repeated the words "Schmidt—woodcutter." The judge ordered that an officer of the court should be in constant attendance on the wounded man, in order to gather every word that might fall from his lips. In this man's presence Rupprecht continually repeated "Schmidt—woodcutter," whenever any one, his maid-servant, his daughter, his sister, or his son-in-law asked him who the murderer was. Only when his sister Clara asked him if he knew who had struck the blow, he muttered something apparently in the negative.

The first though not the sole object of the judge now was to discover the Schmidt of whom Rupprecht was thinking. But in this town, as everywhere else, there were a vast number of people called Schmidt, several of whom were woodcutters. Three of these especially engaged the attention of the court: the first was a certain Abraham Schmidt, who lived in the

Hohes Pflaster, and who, it was rumoured, had once been taken up with a band of robbers and been sent to the House of Correction. The second was one John Gabriel Schmidt, commonly known as "big Schmidt," who lived in a street called the Walch, and had formerly been on friendly terms with Rupprecht, whose favour he had lately lost by some evidence which he gave against him in an action for defamation. The third was big Schmidt's half-brother, distinguished from him by the name of "little Schmidt:" he also lived in the Walch, and was one of Rupprecht's acquaintance.

This seemed to point out the direction in which investigation should be made. On the 10th February the physician announced that Rupprecht had been trepanned the day before and was now sensible, and a commission of inquiry with two witnesses accordingly went to his house. The judge seated himself beside the bed and greeted Rupprecht, who opened his eyes, looked about him, and distinctly answered "Yes" to the judge's question whether he knew him. The judge, convinced by this and other appearances that the wounded man was in the possession of his faculties, desired him to remember that, when asked about his wound, he had always mentioned a name in connection with it, told him that the commission was now come to take down his deposition in the presence of witnesses, and adjured him to reflect upon the danger in which he lay, the infinite knowledge and justice of God, and the awful consequences of every false word. Then came the following questions and answers. "Do you know who struck the blow?" Rupprecht repeatedly moved his right hand, imitating

the motion of striking, and answered "Schmidt."
"Have I understood you aright? did you say
Schmidt?" "Yes." "Who is this Schmidt?"
"Woodcutter." "How do you know that it was
Schmidt, since it was dark?" Rupprecht endeavoured
to speak, but could not utter a sound: he then moved
his right arm with increased vehemence. "But there
are several of that name; can you tell me whether
you mean the big or the little Schmidt?" Rupprecht
made vain attempts to answer this and the question
where the Schmidt lived to whom he referred. When
asked whether he lived in the Walch, the Schütt, or
the Most, Rupprecht was silent. At last, when asked
whether Schmidt lived on the Hohes Pflaster, he distinctly answered "Yes." Hereupon he sunk into a
state of stupor, and the inquiry had to be postponed.

As equal suspicion attached to the three Schmidts
above named, Abraham, as well as the big and the
little Schmidt, were arrested that evening; and notwithstanding the alarming condition of the wounded
man, they were severally taken to his bed-side on the
chance that the murderer might be recognised by
Rupprecht, or that fresh cause for suspicion might
appear against him on the occasion. Rupprecht appeared sensible, but could not open his eyes, so that
the main object entirely failed. Both the big and
the little Schmidt appeared perfectly unembarrassed:
the former exclaimed several times, "Poor Christopher! how ill you have been served—poor fellow,
many's the good jest we have had together. He must
have owed you a powerful grudge who could serve
you so." He likewise called to him repeatedly,

"Christopher! Christopher! your Hans is here," &c. Abraham Schmidt behaved far differently: when asked whether he knew the man in bed, he at first answered "I do not know him," but immediately added, "That is Mr. Rupprecht, I know him well; what is the matter with him?" When asked why he at first said he did not know him, he answered, "Because that is Mr. Rupprecht." He was then desired to give a proper answer, but only exclaimed, "I can give no answer; I did not do it; ah! good Lord! I did not do it; I am not the man; as I hope for mercy, I am innocent. I am a poor woodcutter. You may ask my neighbours, my wife, and my mother. On Friday night I was cutting pegs at the house of my mother-in-law till eleven o'clock, and on Saturday and Sunday I was at home." On being asked at what hour he had gone home on Friday night, he said, "I stayed until past nine with my mother-in-law." When the manifest contradiction in his statement was pointed out to him, he only repeated "From nine to eleven." These strange contradictory answers and the agitation and confusion exhibited by the prisoner, together with the circumstance that Rupprecht had that morning mentioned Schmidt on the Hohes Pflaster, seemed to point suspicion towards Abraham Schmidt, who was accordingly placed in arrest.

The following morning, at about five o'clock (the 11th February), Rupprecht died, without having recovered his speech or consciousness.

Meanwhile suspicion strengthened against Abraham Schmidt. The police handed the hatchets be-

longing to the three suspected men 'into court, and
that of Abraham Schmidt was spotted apparently
with blood.

On his examination he stated that he was about
six-and-thirty, a Lutheran, and the son of a nail-
maker, and that he had at first learnt the trade of
pinmaking, but that finding it insufficient for his support, he had become a woodcutter. He had been
married five years, and had had two children, of which
one, a boy a year and a half old, was living. He had
once been in prison, about twelve or fifteen years
before, for carting some stolen vegetables into the
town for other people. He asserted that he was perfectly innocent of the murder of Rupprecht, whom he
had neither known nor seen. Hereupon he was reminded that when the wounded man was shown to
him, he had at first said that he did not know him, but
had immediately after recognised him as Rupprecht:
how was this? He then replied, " I do not know why
I said that, and I said it was Rupprecht directly, but
I never saw him in my life before." He was asked
how then he had recognised him, and answered that
" every one was talking of the murder, and that he
had heard of it at the public-house." Whenever he
was questioned as to where he was on Friday evening
at the time of the murder, he invariably involved
himself in contradictions. The judge questioned
him as follows :—" Where were you last Friday ?"
" I went to the house of my mother-in-law at nine
o'clock in the morning, to help her to cut pegs. I
dined with her, and did not leave her house till nine
o'clock at night, when I took my little boy home,

went to bed directly, and did not get up again until seven o'clock on Saturday morning." "When did your wife leave her mother's house?" "At ten o'clock." "Why did you not go together?" "Because she was still at work, and as the boy would not go to sleep, she asked me to take him home, which I did." "At what o'clock then did you go home on Friday?" "At nine o'clock." "Yesterday you said it was at eleven; how is that?" After some hesitation, "I don't know what you want of me; I went home with my wife at eleven." "Just now you asserted that you went home at nine?" "All my neighbours can testify that I always come home at nine." "That answer will not suffice; first you say nine, and then eleven: which is the truth?" "At nine o'clock, with my wife and my child. No, my wife stayed a little longer with her mother." "Who took the child home?" "I took him home with me at nine o'clock." "When did your wife come home?" "After ten o'clock." "How do you know that?" "Because she always comes home at that time; I was asleep when she came, and can't tell exactly when it was. I did not wake, though I sleep in the same bed with her and the child." "Have you a key of the house?" "Yes, but my mother has got it." "How then did your wife get in?" "My wife took the key with her." "You said at first that your mother had the key the whole night through?" "Yes, it lay upon the table." "Then your wife could not have used it to let herself into the house?" "So I said, for my wife went home with me and put the boy to bed, and then she took the house-door key and went back to her mother." "How long did she stay

there?" "Till eleven." "You said before that she
came home at ten?" "I was asleep, I can't tell whether it was ten or eleven when she came home."

At first the accused did not seem embarrassed, and
answered readily, but appeared anxious to avoid
entering into details; and on being told that he
contradicted himself, he grew impatient, hesitated,
coughed, and stamped. He did not encounter the
searching gaze of the judge, but looked down or on
one side.

The same evening Rupprecht's dead body was
shown to him, and he was asked whether he recognised it. "This," he answered, "is Mr. Rupprecht.
I can swear to you by my conscience and my honour,
and to Almighty God by my hope of salvation, that
I never injured this man; for I never saw him before
in all my life." "You say you never saw him before
now; how then do you know him?" "I heard of
him from the people here and in the public-house,
besides I saw him yesterday. My heart and my soul
are free from guilt: I never harmed this man. I am
in your power, and you may do with me what you
will. I am a child of innocence." When the accused
first entered the room, he appeared much oppressed
and overcome, but while asserting his innocence his
firmness soon returned.

The person of the prisoner had been carefully
examined when he was first taken to prison, but no
stain of blood was found upon his body or his clothes.
His house, and that of his step-mother, were rigidly
searched, and in them were found tokens of great
poverty, but not of crime.

He accounted for the blood on his hatchet by

saying that his hand was chapped with the cold, and had bled the day before, and that this might have caused the stains. But these stains were close to the blade, and it was his right hand which was chapped, whereas in chopping wood the left hand would naturally be nearest to the blade of the axe, while the right hand grasped the handle. On further inquiry, however, the accused was found to be left-handed, which solved the difficulty.

A comparison of the axe with the wound and the cut in the leathern cap rendered it, to say the least, very doubtful whether such a weapon could have been the one employed: the edge of the axe was only three inches and one-third in length, while the wound measured four inches, and the cut in the cap nearly four inches and a half; and an axe cannot be drawn in striking.

As the murderer had called to the landlord of the tavern to send Rupprecht down to him, the trial was made whether Abraham Schmidt could be recognised by his voice as the assassin. The landlord at first doubted the possibility of such a recognition, as he had paid no particular attention to the voice at the time, and the subsequent fright had driven all recollection of it out of his head—the experiment could, however, do no harm. The judge sent for Schmidt into the audience-chamber, while the landlord was placed in an adjoining room, where he could hear, but not see, the prisoner. He declared without hesitation that Schmidt's voice was much rougher than that of the person who came to his house on the night of the 7th February, which was like the voice of a woman.

The witnesses who were examined as to where the prisoner was when the murder took place, in great part removed the suspicion which he had raised against himself by his confused and contradictory statements. His mother-in-law, Barbara Lang, said that " Schmidt, with his wife and child, had come to her at half-past seven in the morning, as they usually did when he had no chopping to do, in order to save fuel and candles. They stayed all day, and at half-past nine or a quarter to ten he went away with his little child and his wife, who lighted him home. The latter returned and stayed with her another hour or hour and a half, making pegs." The wife's account did not exactly tally with this in point of time, as she said that they left Barbara Lang's house at a quarter to nine; but in other respects her statement agreed with her mother's, with the further addition that " when they got home she waited while her husband undressed and went to bed with the child, as she wanted the lantern to light her to her mother's house and back again home. When she returned, at about ten, she found her husband asleep, and woke him, as he took up too much room in the bed. He asked what o'clock it was, and she told him it was ten. He certainly did not leave her side after that." She added, " This is as true as that my poor child is now at my breast"—she had brought the child into court with her. The woman in whose house the Schmidts lodged confirmed this statement in every particular.

The discrepancy between the assertions of the several witnesses as to the time when Schmidt and his wife returned to their lodgings is easily accounted for, when we consider that they were poor people who had no clocks or watches, and that it was in the month of February. It is true that there was an interval of about an hour between the time of Schmidt's coming home and his wife's return. But the distance from the Hohes Pflaster to the Hell Tavern is' above a mile, and a murder requires some preparation. Here, however, was a commonplace good sort of man, who passed the whole evening with his old mother-in-law, employed with his wife in cutting pegs to earn a crust of bread — returned home with his child in his arms, his wife carrying a lantern, and went to bed with his child—whom we must then suppose to have jumped out of bed the moment his wife's back was turned, to have seized an axe, and leaving his child, to have hastened to the spot where he committed a murder remarkable for cunning and cruelty, hurried back into bed, where he was found shortly afterwards by his wife, fast asleep. All this, too, without any one in the house hearing any noise, and without leaving a trace of the murder on his person. The only way to account for this would be to suppose the wife to be an accomplice, a supposition for which there was not the slightest foundation.

The evidence of one Anna Keinitz, an old woman of seventy-eight, proved that on the 8th of February Abraham Schmidt was in all probability ignorant of the murder committed on the previous evening. Returning from market she passed Rupprecht's house, where she heard the news. On her way home she stepped in at neighbour Barbara Lang's to warm herself, and found Schmidt and his wife were cutting pegs, as he had no chopping to do. Anna Keinitz related what she had heard. Schmidt asked her who this Rupprecht was? She answered that he lived near the butchers' stalls; and the mother-in-law added, "It is Rupprecht who so often comes to the tavern—do not you know him?" Schmidt replied carelessly, "I do not."

On the 9th February, Schmidt was at a tavern called the Sow, where several guests were discussing the murder. Schmidt said nothing, and showed no embarrassment; his manner was, as usual, quiet and reserved.

The evidence of the two men who by turns watched the dying man, completely overthrew one of the chief causes of suspicion against Schmidt. They stated that when the maid or Rupprecht's daughter asked the wounded man where Schmidt lived, he answered indifferently, "On the Hohes Pflaster," or "In the Walch."

Schmidt's bad repute, owing to a vague recollection of some former transgression which vulgar exaggeration had magnified into a great crime, disappeared on further inquiry. All who were questioned about Abraham Schmidt's conduct—his landlord, his neighbours, and the superintendent of police of the district—described him as a very poor, hard-working, peaceable, good-natured man, and a good husband and father.

His strange conduct in the presence of the dying man, and his contradictory statements, were thus accounted for. According to his mother's testimony, he was hard of hearing, timid, and awkward. The smallest trifle made him lose all presence of mind, and he was often so confused as to say the very opposite of what he meant about things the most

familiar to him. "I believe," said the magistrate of
his district, "that there is not any one in my whole
district who is so blundering. For instance, he seldom
calls any one by his right name; and when he does
not understand what is said to him, or cannot express
his meaning, he is apt to be angry." And this poor
blockhead—he knew not why or wherefore—was suddenly dragged into the presence of a dying man,
whom he found himself accused of having murdered,
and, while agitated and dismayed by a scene so strange,
solemn and terrible, questions were put to him about
the most minute and trifling circumstances—questions
the drift of which he was too stupid and confused to
understand.

The contradictory statements which he made concerning many important details, were manifestly the
result of the prisoner's habitual confusion of ideas and
defective memory. His recognition of Rupprecht,
joined to his declaration that he did not know him,
would have appeared perfectly consistent had he possessed the power of expressing himself intelligibly.
Without having ever seen Rupprecht he must have
guessed that the wounded man lying before him could
have been none other than the Rupprecht whose accident was in every one's mouth.

Nothing now remained which could throw any suspicion on Abraham Schmidt, and the court endeavoured
to follow out the slight traces of suspicion against John
Gabriel Schmidt and his half-brother Erhard Düringer.
The former, commonly called big Schmidt, was a married man of forty, with one child; the latter, generally
known as little Schmidt, was twenty-seven, also married and had two children. Both were woodcutters,

and lived together on excellent terms in the same house. Both were boon companions of Rupprecht's, who was much in their company, particularly in that of John Gabriel, whom he familiarly called his Hans, and with whom he amused himself with all sorts of vulgar pranks and coarse jokes. This intercourse had, however, been interrupted a few months before Rupprecht's death by a dispute between the quarrelsome jeweller and the overseers of the district, Friedmann and Götz. The last-named men were accordingly arrested on the suspicion that if they did not actually murder him themselves, they might have induced one of these woodcutters to become the instrument of their vengeance. The quarrel had arisen one evening when Friedmann, the two Schmidts, and several other persons were sitting together in a tavern, on which occasion Rupprecht used some very offensive expressions with regard to the other overseer Götz, accusing him of gross partiality and injustice in the administration of his office. Friedmann and Götz complained to the police, and the two Schmidts were summoned as witnesses. Rupprecht was condemned to an imprisonment of eight and forty hours on bread and water, and to make an apology to Götz. He endeavoured to revenge himself by bringing an action for defamation against Friedmann and Götz, which was still pending when Rupprecht was murdered.

But on examination these suspicions melted away, and Rupprecht appeared to have acted the part of a revengeful, angry, insulting foe, and the others that of quiet peaceable citizens. No one had perceived any bitter feeling in either Friedmann or Götz; on the contrary, they both expressed regret and indignation when they heard the manner of his death. Götz had been from eight till eleven on the evening of the murder at a tavern, where his manner was grave and quiet, as usual ; and both he and Friedmann were well known as just and upright men, incapable of committing any bad action, much less a crime of this magnitude. Finally, Rupprecht himself, when asked on the morning after his accident whether he did not suspect one of the district overseers of the deed, had distinctly answered " No."

John Gabriel Schmidt and his half-brother Erhard Düringer had the reputation of well-conducted, hard-working men, of spotless integrity, who only visited the tavern on certain days in the week, and then only for a few hours. Kunigunda Pfann gave evidence on oath that Erhard Düringer could not have been at the Hell Tavern on the evening of the 7th February, as she had stayed with him and his wife from half-past eight till ten, and had only left their room as they were preparing to go to bed. This evidence was confirmed by the mistress of the house in which they lived, who inhabited the rooms above them. She stated that although she had not been in Düringer's room she was satisfied that he had remained at home, as Friday was not the day on which he and his half-brother went to the tavern. With regard to John Gabriel Schmidt she said, " As I live up one pair of stairs, and he just above me, and I heard no one come down stairs after eight o'clock, and all was quiet in their room, I feel convinced that after that hour they were in bed. Besides, she was stirring till eleven, and even later, and she heard no suspicious knocking or ringing at the door." Kunigunda Pfann, whose room was near the Schmidts', said that as she was returning home at about half-past eight, she looked up at their window and saw no light; moreover the key had been taken out of the door, as was their custom when they went to bed; neither had she heard any noise during the night. Martin Haas, the landlord, confirmed these statements, adding, " I take it for granted that the Schmidts were at home on Friday, as they never go out on that day."

In order to leave nothing untried, two other wood-cutters, whose names were Schmidt, were examined : they did not live in either of the streets mentioned by Rupprecht, nor even in the town, but in the suburbs. These two men, John and Godfrey, were nearly con-nected, and generally came to Nürnberg for work : and one of them was usually employed by Rup-precht's son-in-law. But in this case also the inquiry led to the same result.

Thus, when every woodcutter of the name of Schmidt in the town and neighbourhood had been examined, it became evident that the court, by trust-ing to the unconnected words of the dying man, had suffered itself to be led in a totally false direction. His disjointed exclamations were but the expression of his vague, confused suspicions, or perhaps even mere *ægri somnia*, engendered in his shattered brain by delirium. A man so severely wounded in the head as almost entirely to lose the power of speech cannot be supposed to be in the true possession of his faculties even when consciousness appears for a moment to re-turn. It is not difficult to explain how his fancied suspicions were directed against the Schmidts, when

we consider that so deep a gash, even if inflicted with
a sabre, would feel as if it were made with an axe.
The mere association of ideas would naturally connect
a woodcutter with the axe, and every throb of the
wound would recall to Rupprecht's disordered imagination the image of the Schmidts, with whom he had
lately quarrelled.

The judge, while carrying on the inquiry with the
utmost zeal in a direction which eventually proved to
be a wrong one, had not in the mean time neglected
to follow up all other indications. He had from the
first kept his eye upon John Bieringer and his wife,
who was Rupprecht's own daughter.

Rupprecht, soon after he was wounded, had exclaimed, " My daughter! my daughter!" which those
who were present had interpreted as the expression of
a natural desire on his part to see her; but which
might have referred to the same event as the words
he used shortly before—"The wicked rogue! with
the axe!" This supposition received weight from the
circumstance that Rupprecht usually called his son-
in-law " the wicked rogue."

One of those who were present went, after fetching
a surgeon, to Bieringer's house and informed him of
what had happened, and of Rupprecht's wish to see
his daughter. Hereupon Bieringer, with extraordinary coolness, said to his wife, " You must go to the
Hell Tavern directly; something has happened to
your father; one really has nothing but trouble with
him."

When Rupprecht's daughter saw him lying wounded, she wept, and lamented: but several witnesses
thought that she did not show so much interest and

sympathy for him as might have been expected from a daughter on such an occasion.

One witness asserted that soon after she had seen her father, disfigured as he was with blood and wounds, she asked for his keys, and said "she would look whether they were in his pocket, or whether the murderer had taken them to open her father's lodging and rob it." As soon as she recovered his keys, she went on before to his lodging.

The same witness further said, "When her wounded father lay in his own house, the daughter appeared not only composed, but even careless. When I went to see him on the following day, I observed that she showed great indifference to her father's fate; she ate up, in my presence, a whole basin of soup which would have more than satisfied most people."

Meanwhile she manifested the greatest anxiety to fix suspicion on John Gabriel Schmidt, and on the district overseer Götz. On the 8th February she suddenly exclaimed, that her father had named Schmidt as the murderer; adding, that it was likely enough, as this man was an intimate friend of Götz's, who had been involved in a lawsuit with her father. This she repeated so often and so loudly, that the officer appointed to note down every expression that fell from the dying man, was forced to order her to be silent.

She further stated, at her examination on the 9th February, that her father, on coming to himself, had accused the woodcutter Schmidt of the deed; and added that, on her repeatedly asking who had struck him, her father had answered, "He was a big fellow." As no one else had heard Rupprecht say this, it looked as if she had invented it in order to avert suspicion from her husband, who was of small stature.

On the following day, the 10th February, when the three woodcutters of the name of Schmidt were brought into the presence of the wounded man, she pressed the judge, when it came to John Gabriel's turn, to allow her to be present, and to speak to him ; saying, " This John Gabriel Schmidt was the man whom she alluded to in her yesterday's examination ; and that she wished to speak to him, and to remind him of the omniscience of God, as he might then, perhaps, confess. The others, she was sure, were innocent.

Bieringer, a well-bred and well educated man, of about five-and-thirty, was perfectly composed and unconstrained during examination ; only once he started from his seat, complained of illness, and walked up and down ; he then sat down again and quietly continued to answer the questions put to him.

The principal ground for suspicion against him was, the terms on which he lived with his wife and his father-in-law.

Bieringer's domestic quarrels had occasionally been so violent as to draw together a crowd before his house; and his wife had once been sent to prison for eight and forty hours, in consequence of a complaint laid by her husband before the police. Bieringer accused her of violence of temper and love of finery ; and her father of always supporting her against her husband. The imprisonment, it is true, had produced a wholesome effect, and Bieringer's domestic peace had remained unbroken for some time. But the quarrel between Rupprecht and his son-in-law was irreconcilable. Rupprecht would not see him; and on the very day before his death he had said to his maid, "Bieringer is a cursed rogue, who shall never come into my presence." Rupprecht thought him a careless fellow, who worked less and spent more than he ought; and who, moreover, did not show him sufficient respect. He had long intended to make a will leaving his whole property to his daughter, and placing it entirely out of the reach of her husband. He had mentioned this plan to his daughter some months before. He had also told his fellow-lodger Högner, who was more in his confidence than any one else, that " he would make a will, in which he would not forget his good friends, and would settle his money in such manner upon his daughter that his rascally son-in-law should not be able to touch it, so that his daughter might have something to live upon in case of a separation." On Friday the 7th February, at about 3 P.M., only a few hours before he was murdered, he sent to his familiar friend Högner, and requested him to " look out from among his papers some acknowledgments of debts, amounting to 1200 florins, as he must take them directly to the magistrate's office. The search took up some time, as his papers were in disorder, and he requested me to come on the following Sunday, and sort them for him, as he wished to alter and arrange several matters, and to make a will. His maid was in the room at the time." Had Bieringer been aware of this, he would undoubtedly have had the greatest interest in preventing Rupprecht from executing his intentions; and the circumstance that Rupprecht was murdered at ten o'clock at night of the same day on which he had talked about making his will, would no longer appear merely as a strange coincidence.

But here again everything which at first appeared suspicious was explained away.

The hostess of the tavern proved that Rupprecht's words, "My daughter, my daughter," undoubtedly expressed his desire to see her. She stated that on seeing his dangerous condition, she cried out " Fetch his daughter," whereupon Rupprecht repeated the words " My daughter." Furthermore his sister Clara and his familiar friend Högner testified that it was Rupprecht's custom to send for his daughter every time he had even a pain in his finger.

This habit again accounted for Bieringer's cool impatience when he told his wife to go to her father: he very naturally thought that matters were not so bad as they afterwards turned out.

The small sympathy which the daughter apparently felt with the fate of her father proves but little; not to mention that several other witnesses who had ample opportunity of observing her conduct stated the very reverse, and asserted that she showed great feeling.

The taking possession of her father's keys was no more than what any other daughter would have done under the circumstances. They were essential to prepare for his reception in his own house. Moreover it afterwards appeared that she only took the keys at the suggestion of the physician, who suspected that some one might attempt ·to rob the house, in consequence of which suspicion, and at her request, two police officers accompanied her to her father's house.

Her loud and eager announcement that her father had named the woodcutter Schmidt as his murderer,

and her endeavours to fix the guilt on the so-called
big Schmidt, would certainly have been suspicious,
had not old Rupprecht really named him. But her
anxiety to force the man whom her imagination represented to her as the only possible murderer to
confess his guilt, cannot surely be construed as evidence of her participation in the murder. Nor need
we conclude that she put expressions into her father's
mouth about the murderer being a tall fellow in order
to shield her husband; it is very possible that her
father may have used them during the absence of
other witnesses.

It is quite obvious that it was not her interest, while
living on bad terms with her husband, to get rid of
her father, who hated his son-in-law, and was her
constant refuge and support against him, at the very
moment, too, when she knew that her father was about
to make a will which should secure her independence
of her husband. Rupprecht's dying intestate was as
great a loss to his daughter as it was a gain to his son-
in-law.

On further examination, everything was cleared up
in Bieringer's favour also.

Bieringer's comparatively polished manners rendered him most unsuitable to his coarse father-in-law,
whose avarice and meanness were shocked by his son-
in-law's more generous manner of living. Bieringer
was considered by his fellow-citizens as a well-conducted and upright man, who loved society, without
neglecting his business, and was not addicted to drinking or gaming. The chief cause of dissension between
him and his wife was rather her love of dress and
quarrelsome disposition than any fault of his. All

who were acquainted with him said that they knew of no stain upon his honour or good name.

Even if Rupprecht's intention to deprive Bieringer of all power over his daughter's fortune appeared a sufficient motive for the murder of his father-in-law, it remained to be proved that Bieringer was aware of the project. But on examination it appeared the old man confided his thoughts to none but his friend and his daughter, who certainly could have no interest in betraying the secret to her husband. Neither his brother nor his sisters knew anything whatever of the matter. It is true that on the day he was murdered his maid was present when he talked of making his will, but he mentioned it quite vaguely without entering into any particulars.

It was proved beyond doubt that Bieringer could not have committed the murder himself. On the evening of the 7th February he was at a tavern called the Golden Fish, distant full ten minutes' walk from that frequented by Rupprecht. He was dressed as usual, and carried no weapon, not even a stick. Here he remained till a quarter past ten o'clock at night, and at half-past ten he came home and took off his clothes. He was found undressed by the man who went to his house in order to fetch his wife to her father. It was therefore impossible that he could have stayed at the Golden Fish until a quarter past ten o'clock, have murdered his father-in-law at a tavern some distance off, and be back in his own house, which was distant at least a mile from the scene of the murder, by half-past ten.

At the commencement of the inquiry the judge had endeavoured to discover with whom Rupprecht had dealings, and more especially who had been with him on the 7th February. The evidence given by Rupprecht's maid seemed important. She stated that among others three trumpeters belonging to the regiment quartered in the town had been with Rupprecht on business on the very day of the murder, and had been told by him to call again on the following day : they did not return, having probably heard what had occurred. These three men were immediately arrested and examined. Although their depositions agreed on every point, and each one separately stated where they had been at the time of the murder, it nevertheless appeared as if one of these three trumpeters must be the murderer. One of them owed Rupprecht money, which he had no means of paying, and his two comrades had accompanied him to Rupprecht's house, nobody exactly knew why. On the same evening Rupprecht received a deadly blow, and the wound presented the appearance of a sabre-cut inflicted by a practised hand.

But this was "like the lightning, which doth cease to be ere you can say it lightens." Alibis were most clearly proved : two of them had been at their barracks, and the third had been sitting from eight till eleven in some tavern, whence he went straight to the hospital.

One means of detection, however, seems to have been forgotten. The physicians stated that the wound was to all appearance inflicted by a sabre, and it is probable that some discovery might have been made, had the arms of the garrison, and of the burgher guard, been examined on the morning after the murder. But when the court began the inquiry, it was already too late to

hope for any results, even had this suggestion, made
by the judge, been attended to.   His colleagues were
so completely possessed by the idea that the murderous
blow had been inflicted by an axe wielded by a woodcutter, that they negatived a proposal founded on the
supposition that Rupprecht had been killed by a sabre-
cut.

Meanwhile two men, whose names were unknown,
became the subject of inquiry.   On the day after the
murder, Rupprecht's confidant and fellow-lodger,
Högner, laid information before the court as follows:—
" At about half-past five in the afternoon of the fatal
Friday, Rupprecht came to me and requested me to
allow his maid to spend the evening in my rooms, as
two gentlemen were coming to him, with whom he
wished to be alone.   The maid came and stayed
about an hour and a half, when Rupprecht returned
and gave her the key of his rooms, saying that
he was going to the tavern."   The maid confirmed
this statement, adding that as she went down stairs to
fetch her supper she had seen through the window
which looks from the kitchen into Rupprecht's room
two young men, who were busied with something on
the table.   But this mysterious affair was soon cleared
up : the two gentlemen were the regimental tailor
and a shoemaker, the former of whom borrowed of
Rupprecht the sum of 600 florins for three months,
giving a bill for 650 florins, and leaving a large
quantity of cloth as a pledge in Rupprecht's hands.
His friend the shoemaker merely acted as a witness in
the transaction.

Several other men were arrested on divers suspicions, but all brought forward witnesses who com-

pletely disculpated them. The court was therefore
forced to rest content after releasing Abraham Schmidt
from his provisory arrest, and to close the proceedings
until fresh suspicions should arise.

Ten years, writes Feuerbach in 1828, have since
passed, and the manner of Rupprecht's death is still
involved in mystery.

Most likely the old usurer was murdered out of
revenge or hatred by some disappointed suitor for a
loan, or by a debtor who thought this the easiest way
of paying his debt, and whose name was never known
owing to Rupprecht's habit of keeping no regular accounts and trusting chiefly to his memory. Not one
even of his nearest relations knew the exact state of
the old man's affairs; even Högner was only admitted
to his confidence in cases of absolute necessity, when
he wanted to have a note of hand looked out from
among his papers, or to get them put in order. Thus
probably the only clue to the discovery of Rupprecht's
murderer was buried with him.

In the year 1807 a widow, nearly fifty years of age, calling herself Nanette Schönleben, lived at Pegnitz in the territory of Baireuth, supporting herself by knitting. Her conduct gained her a reputation which induced Justice Wolfgang Glaser, who was then living at Rosendorf separated from his wife, to take her as his housekeeper, on the 5th March, 1808. On the 22nd of the following July Glaser was reconciled to his wife, who had been living with her relations at Grieshaber near Augsburg. Soon after her return to her husband's house, though a strong healthy woman, she was suddenly seized with violent vomiting, diarrhœa, &c., and on the 26th August, a month after the reconciliation, she died.

Anna Schönleben now left Glaser's service, and on the 25th September she went to live as housekeeper with Justice Grohmann at Sanspareil. Her new master, who was unmarried, was thirty-eight years of age, and though a large and powerful man, had suffered from gout for several years, and was often confined to his bed. On these occasions Anna Schönleben always nursed him with the utmost care. In the spring of 1809 he was seized with an illness more violent than any he had had before, and accompanied by entirely new symptoms,—violent vomiting, pains in the stomach, diarrhœa, heat and dryness of the skin, inflammation of the mouth and throat, insatiable thirst, and excessive weakness and pains in the limbs. He died on the 8th May, after an illness of eleven days, and his housekeeper appeared inconsolable for his loss. Every one, the medical men included, took it for granted that Grohmann, who had long been ailing, had died a natural death.

Anna Schönleben was once more out of place, but her reputation for kindness, activity, attention and skill as a sick-nurse soon procured her a new home. At the time of Grohmann's death the wife of the magistrate Gebhard was just expecting to be brought to bed, and asked Anna Schönleben to attend her as nurse and housekeeper during her lying-in. Anna Schönleben, always willing to oblige, readily agreed, and from the day of the confinement she resided in Gebhard's house, dividing her time between the care of the household and of the child. Madame Gebhard was confined on the 13th May, 1809, and both the mother and the child were doing very well until the third day, which the mother fell ill. Her illness became more alarming every day; she was seized with violent vomiting, nervous agitation, distressing heat in the intestines, inflammation in the throat, &c.; and on the 20th May, seven days after her confinement, she died, exclaiming in her agony, "Merciful Heaven! you have given me poison!" As Madame Gebhard had always been sickly, and moreover had died in childbirth, her death excited no suspicion, and, like Madame Glaser and Grohmann, she was buried without more ado. The widower, embarrassed by his

household and the infant which was left upon his
hands, thought that he could do nothing better than
to keep Anna Schönleben as his housekeeper. Several
persons endeavoured to change his resolution. They
said that this woman carried death with her wherever
she went ; that three young persons whom she had
served, had died one after the other within a very
short time. No one made the smallest accusation
against her ; their warnings arose from a mere superstitious dread of an unfortunate sympathetic influence
exercised by her upon those with whom she lived :
her obliging deportment, her piety, and her air of
honesty, humility and kindness, protected her from
every breath of suspicion. Thus she remained for
several months in Gebhard's service unsuspected and
unaccused.

During her residence in Gebhard's house various
suspicious events occurred, without, however, exciting
attention. On the 25th August, 1809, a certain
Beck, and the widow Alberti, dined with Gebhard.
Soon after dinner they were both seized with violent
vomiting, colic, spasms, &c., which lasted until late
at night. About the same time she gave the messenger Rosenhauer a glass of white wine, and not long
after he had swallowed it he was attacked in precisely
the same manner, and was so ill as to be forced to go to
bed. On the very same day she took Rosenhauer's
porter, a lad of nineteen named Johann Kraus, into
the cellar and gave him a glass of brandy. After
drinking a small quantity he perceived a sort of white
sediment in it, and therefore left the rest, but in a
short time he felt very sick. During the last week
of August, one of Gebhard's maid-servants, Barbara

Waldmann, with whom Anna Schönleben had had several trifling disputes, was taken ill after drinking a cup of coffee, and vomited every half-hour during the whole day. The most remarkable occurrence, however, took place on the 1st September. Gebhard, while playing at skittles with a party of his friends, sent for a few pitchers of beer from his own cellar. He and five other persons drank some of the beer, and were seized soon after with sickness and internal pains; some of the party, among whom was Gebhard, were so ill as to require medical aid.

This first inspired distrust and dislike of Anna Schönleben. On the following day, chiefly at the instigation of one of his fellow-sufferers at the skittle-ground, Gebhard dismissed her from his service, but gave her a written character for honesty and fidelity.

She was to leave Sanspareil for Baireuth on the next day—3rd September. She expressed her surprise at so sudden a dismissal, but was civil and obliging as usual, and busied herself during the whole evening in various domestic arrangements. Among other things she took the salt-box out of the kitchen (which was no part of her usual duty), and filled it from a barrel of salt which stood in Gebhard's bedroom. When the maid-servant Waldmann commented upon this, Anna Schönleben said, in a jesting manner, that she must do so, for that if those who were going away filled the salt-box, the other servants would keep their places the longer. On the morning of her departure she affected the greatest friendship for the two maid-servants, Hazin and Waldmann, and gave each of them a cup of coffee sweetened with sugar which she took out of a piece of paper. While the carriage was waiting for her at the door she took Gebhard's child, an infant five months old, in her arms, gave it a biscuit soaked in milk to eat, then let it drink the milk, and finally parted from it with the most tender caresses, and got into the carriage which was to convey her to Baireuth, and which Gebhard paid for, besides giving her a crown dollar and some chocolate.

She had been gone scarce half an hour when the child became alarmingly ill and vomited terribly, and in a few hours more the two maid-servants were attacked in the same manner; and now, for the first time, suspicion was excited. On hearing from his servants how Anna Schönleben had busied herself, Gebhard had the contents of the kitchen salt-box analyzed by a chemist, and a large quantity of arsenic was found among it. The salt-barrel was likewise found at the trial to contain thirty grains of arsenic to every three pounds of salt.

To these facts were now added a number of hitherto unnoticed reports of persons who had been taken ill immediately after eating or drinking at Glaser's and Grohmann's houses, whilst Anna Schönleben was in their service. Moreover it came out that Schönleben was only her maiden name, and that she was in fact the widow of a notary called Zwanziger, who had lived at Nürnberg.

It is strange that after all these discoveries it was not till the 29th September that Gebhard laid information against her at the criminal court of Baireuth, which immediately appointed chief magistrate Brater to conduct the inquiry. He went at once to the spot, where the charges against her of various cases of poisoning were confirmed, and increased in number.

The most important point was to discover the causes of the sudden and unexpected deaths of those three persons whom Anna Schönleben had served in succession since 1808. The body of Madame Glaser was dug up on the 23rd October, in the churchyard at Rasendorf. It presented in a very remarkable manner all those appearances which the discoveries of modern science have taught us to regard as the peculiar symptoms of death from arsenic. Although the body had been buried for fourteen months, it was very little decomposed, dried up and hardened like a mummy, and the skin was the colour of mahogany. The abdomen was rather swollen and gave a peculiar hollow sound when struck. The coats and muscles of the stomach were converted into a substance resembling cheese in appearance and smell, and the whole body emitted the same peculiar odour. On the following day the body of Madame Gebhard and that of Grohmann, which had lain in the earth for nearly six months, were disinterred in the churchyard at Wonsers, and presented exactly the same appearances as that of Glaser's wife. On investigation the intestines of the two female corpses were found to contain arsenic. In those of Grohmann the presence of the poison was not discovered, although his body exhibited every symptom of it.

Meanwhile, Anna Schönleben, or, as we will henceforth call her, Zwanziger, felt perfectly secure. On quitting Gebhard's service she had left a letter for him in which she reproached him with exaggerated sensi-

bility for the ingratitude with which he had repaid
her care of him, and her devotion to his child.
" If," says she, " the child should be restless and
unhappy, my guardian angel will say to you, ' Why
didst thou take from her that which she held most
dear ?' If, six weeks hence, you should ask for me,
you will hear 'She is no more,' and then woe to your
heart, for it will break; woe to those who have calum-
niated me to you." She then prays God to reward
him for his kindness, begs him to continue his friendship to her, and promises to write to him every fortnight. This promise she faithfully kept; and both
from Baireuth, where she actually quartered herself
for a month upon the mother of Gebhard's dead wife,
and afterwards from Nürnberg, she sent him several
letters, in which she tells him the state of her health,
how well she was received, and how soon she hoped
to get a place, and then recommends herself to the
" kind recollection of her revered master;" or talks
about " her darling child," sends it kisses, and asks
after its health. It is clear that she hoped no less
than to be recalled by Gebhard, and that the true
purpose of her letters was to put this into his head
by every means in her power as frequently as possible. She was equally lavish of her letters to
several other persons. Among others she wrote to
Glaser and offered him her services again as housekeeper. After waiting in vain both at Baireuth and
at Nürnberg for a recall, she went to Mainbernheim
in Franconia, where she hoped to be received by her
son-in-law, a bookbinder called Sauer. But he had
meanwhile divorced her daughter, who was in the
house of correction for stealing and swindling, and

was celebrating his second marriage on the very
day on which his former mother-in-law arrived at his
house. This disagreeable coincidence soon caused
her to leave Mainbernheim, and return to Nürnberg,
where she was immediately arrested on the 18th
October, 1809. On searching her person two packets
of tartar emetic and one of arsenic were found in her
pocket.

We will postpone for the present the history of her
life, which came out on her examination at Culmbach
and at Nürnberg, though only piecemeal and in very
general terms. Neither would it answer our purpose
to follow the long course of examination, as it would
be impossible to describe the cunning and adroitness
with which the criminal contrived to evade all questions and remonstrances, or the patience, prudence,
and skill with which the judge enclosed her within
narrow and narrower circles, until she was no longer
able to resist the truth. From the 19th October, 1809,
till the 16th April, 1810, she resolutely denied every
accusation connected with the charge of poisoning.
On the last-named day she appeared before her judge
with perfect composure, believing that all the evidence
against her was exhausted, when he opened the proceedings with the unexpected announcement that
the body of Glaser's wife had been dug up; that upon
minute investigation she was found to have been
poisoned with arsenic, and that there was the strongest
ground for suspicion that the poison had been administered by the prisoner. After the judge had represented this to her in various forms during two whole
hours, her courage at length gave way. She wept,
wrung her hands, protested her innocence, and en-

deavoured to mislead the judge in broken and unconnected sentences which she uttered with great rapidity and in evident terror, and at length confessed that she had twice given poison to Glaser's wife, at the same time interweaving with her confession an atrocious calumny. The words had scarcely passed her lips when she fell as if struck by lightning, rolled upon the floor in strong convulsions, and had to be carried out of court.

The poisonings which Anna Zwanziger partly confessed and partly was proved to have committed, were as follows :—

Justice Glaser, a man upwards of fifty, had lived for several years separate from his wife, from no fault of his own, when, on the 25th March, 1808, he took Anna Zwanziger into his service, at the recommendation of his son. She soon contrived to ingratiate herself with her master, and to place herself upon a footing almost of equality with him. She had not been long in his service before she began to be very officious in endeavouring to effect a reconciliation between him and his wife, partly indeed without Glaser's knowledge or consent. Not satisfied with using all her powers of persuasion to induce Glaser to take back his wife, she opened a secret correspondence with the latter, who was living with her brother at Grieshaber, wrote to several friends of the family in order to induce them to assist in the work of reconciliation, among others to the neighbouring Catholic priest at Holfeld, enclosing a piece of money, with the request, Protestant as she was, that a mass might be read for the success of her undertaking.

She at length succeeded in persuading the wife to

return, and the husband to receive her. Madame Glaser left Grieshaber, and, a few days before her arrival in Kasendorf, she wrote to one of her relations to announce that on the following Wednesday a formal reconciliation would take place between her husband and herself.

On the 22nd July, 1808, Glaser went to meet his wife at Holfeld, and on returning with her to Kasendorf he was met by a brilliant reception which had been prepared by Anna Zwanziger to celebrate the reconciliation. All Kasendorf was in commotion : the floors of the house were strewn with flowers, and the doorposts and walls hung with garlands ; the bed was decorated with wreaths, and on it was pinned an ornamental sheet of paper with the words—

> The widow's hand
> Hath joined this band.

The poetry and the writing were Anna Zwanziger's.

The real motive for her uncalled-for interference in this affair is obvious. In spite of her age and ugliness, she expected no less than that Glaser would marry her in the event of his wife's death, and she herself confessed that she hoped by this murder to secure a provision for her old age.

Thus she acted the pious part of a peacemaker merely with the view of getting Glaser's wife into her power, and welcomed and caressed her victim in order the more quickly and safely to sacrifice her.

Madame Glaser had been only a few weeks in the house of her husband, who treated her with the greatest kindness and affection, when Anna Zwanziger began to put her scheme into execution. On the 13th or 14th August, she put, as she declared, half a teaspoonful of arsenic into some tea which stood at the fire, and gave it to Madame Glaser, who drank it, and soon after was seized with vomiting. "When I gave her the arsenic in the tea," said Zwanziger, "I said to myself, I must make my old age comfortable, and if the poison does not do her business this time, why I will give it her again till it does." And accordingly a few days afterwards, on the 15th August, between four and five in the afternoon, she dissolved a large dessert spoonful of tartar emetic in a cup of coffee, and invited Madame Glaser into her room to drink it. She did so, and drank her death. That night she was seized with vomiting and pains in the intestines, which increased in violence, and in ten days she was a corpse. "When," said Zwanziger, "I had mixed the poison in the cup, and saw how thick it was, I said to myself, Lord Jesus! this time she must surely die."

It is highly characteristic of Zwanziger that in her confession she endeavoured to implicate Justice Glaser in crime; she accused him of having instigated her to murder his wife, of being privy to the attempt with the tea, and of having given her the tartar emetic to put in the coffee, with the words—"There, do you give it to her; such carrion is no loss." In consequence of this statement, Justice Glaser was arrested and involved in the examination, which, however, terminated in his complete acquittal.

About a week before the first attempt on Glaser's wife, a certain Wagenholz, with his wife and son, came to call on the Glasers, and stopped to supper. Soon after, the whole party were taken ill with sickness and vomiting. Next day Zwanziger gave the remains of the food to the son of Harbach, the watchman, and he too was so sick as to be confined to his bed for some time. It is uncertain whether her object was merely to try the effect of her poison preparatory to her more important scheme, or whether the guests were unwelcome to her and she wished to punish them for coming uninvited, and her master and mistress for receiving them too graciously. However this may be, she denied the charge altogether, at the same time taking the opportunity of throwing fresh suspicion upon Glaser. " He was," said she, " as savage as Satan himself against Wagenholz and his wife, and I thought at the time that he must have put something into the food, for I was very sick and ill myself."

After Madame Glaser's death, on the 25th September of the same year, 1808, she was taken into Justice Grohmann's service. Here her envy and jealousy were immediately excited by the two messengers Lawrence and Johann Dorsch, who, besides their official duties, rendered various domestic services to Grohmann. Moreover she asserted that they constantly teazed and laughed at her, and it vexed her that they drank too much beer. " I determined," said the prisoner, " to spoil their appetite, and took four pitchers of beer, two of which I mixed with tartar emetic, and the other two with a larger dose of arsenic ; my intention was to give them the contents of these pitchers by degrees, not in order to kill them, but only to make them sick. I once set one of these poisoned pitchers before them, but they did not like the taste of the beer, and drank very little of it, after which they emptied another pitcher, which contained no poison."

The two Dorschs felt no bad effect whatever, and Zwanziger never repeated the attempt, probably because her attention was speedily directed to a more important object.

In the spring of 1809 Justice Christopher Hoffmann, of Wiesenfels, visited Grohmann, who was then ill in bed. A few glasses of beer, which tasted flat and unpleasant, were given to him, but he cannot remember by whom, and immediately after he went to see Gebhard. Scarce had he arrived at Gebhard's house, when he felt very sick and went out into the air, whereupon he was seized with violent vomiting. The prisoner denied having poisoned him intentionally, but said that she put the pitchers which she had mixed with poison for the Dorschs into the cellar with the rest of the beer without marking them, and that she was unable to distinguish the poisoned from the unpoisoned beer. "Thus then," said she, "it is possible that he may have drunk some of the poisoned beer by accident, but it certainly was never my intention even to make him sick, for he was a very respectable and excellent man, for whom I had a great regard, and who had always shown me every respect, as also had his wife."

One day Madame Schell and her husband went to see Grohmann, and she drank a cup of coffee. During the course of her visit at Grohmann's she fainted and vomited—the prisoner denied having given her any poison, and there was room for doubt, as Madame Schell did not remember distinctly whether she was taken ill before drinking the coffee or after.

It was not juridically proved that Grohmann died by poison, but the unusual symptoms that appeared during his last illness, the traces of arsenic found in the exhumed corpse, and the opinion of the physicians attached to the court, rendered it not only possible, but highly probable. A probability, amounting almost to certainty, pointed out Anna Zwanziger as the poisoner. A person who had already poisoned one woman, who was in the constant habit of dealing with poisons, and who kept a large store of poisoned drink ready in Grohmann's house, which she had, according to her own confession, already used to the injury of two persons on the very slightest provocation,— such a person would look upon such a deed as a commonplace occurrence. Moreover she was constantly about her master while suffering from gout; sought to keep away those who wished to wait upon him, and was angry when others gave him his medicines. These suspicions were strengthened by her violent demonstration of grief at Grohmann's death, and the cries and lamentations with which she made the whole house resound, more especially whenever any stranger came into the room. Nor are her motives for murdering him difficult to guess. Ill as he was, Grohmann intended to marry the daughter of the neighbouring Justice Herrgott, at Dachsbach. Grohmann's courtship and the prospect of his marriage were highly distasteful to Anna Zwanziger, and she showed this in various ways. Every letter that went to or came from Dachsbach was watched, waylaid, and examined. Grohmann once told Madame Schell that he was by no means satisfied with his housekeeper; that " she imagined every letter he received contained some offer of marriage, and that, old as she was, she had actually taken it into her head that he would marry her." John Dorsch also said, "Whenever I went to the house, and asked after the health of her master, her constant answer was, 'Why, he is always ill, and yet, to be sure, he wants to marry." She talked in the same strain to Grohmann's sister : "Your brother's intended is accustomed to a merry life, and will never be happy in such a quiet place as Sanspariel, with nothing to do but to be always mixing draughts." At length there was a report in Grohmann's house that the banns had actually been published, and that the bride was expected in eight days ; this threw Zwanziger's tongue and temper into a state of extraordinary excitement. Just at this time Grohmann was taken ill, and in a few days he died. If we consider these circumstances and the woman's character, the following explanation appears extremely probable :—That she, who never entered any man's service without reckoning upon him as her future husband, indulged like hopes of Grohmann. But when, spite of all the flattery and subservience by which she had hoped to worm herself into his good graces, she found herself disappointed, anger against her master, envy of the young girl whose good fortune she envied, hatred of them both, and of the marriage which she foresaw would cost her her place—these were sufficient to induce a person of her disposition to resolve upon punishing Grohmann by death, and his intended bride by depriving her of her bridegroom—and thus to avenge her jealous fury upon them both. The most charitable interpretation of which her conduct admits, is, that she administered the poison to him with the object of keeping him continually so ill as to prevent the marriage, and by making herself necessary to him as a nurse, of securing the permanence of her situation. She denied having poisoned Grohmann intentionally, but admitted that he accidentally drank some of the poisoned beer which she kept ready for the Dorschs. When she set the poisoned pitcher before them, they refused to touch it, and placed it on a table with the other pitchers intended for Grohmann and his visitors. " The three remaining poisoned pitchers," she continued, " I placed in the cellar with those containing the sound beer, and, as I had not marked them distinctly, the pitchers got mixed, so that I could no longer distinguish between those which were poisoned and those which were not. It is therefore very possible that Grohmann may have drunk some of the poisoned beer, in the same manner as Hoffmann also did. I cannot deny that he vomited very often. But Grohmann was much too valuable to me that I should injure him purposely ; he was all in all to me ; and what he ate, that 1 ate too. He was my best friend, and never offended me, so that I had nothing to revenge upon him."

According to the strict letter of the law, the intentional poisoning was not clearly proved, but no unprejudiced person could entertain any doubt of it. How improbable is the statement by which she attempted to explain away her crime! Grohmann is " her all in all ; her best friend ;" and yet she leaves a pitcher of poisoned beer in his way ; she knows that the pitchers of poisoned and sound beer are mixed together in the cellar, and yet, regardless of the consequences, she places those which may possibly be poisoned before her sick and " highly treasured best friend !"

On the 24th May, 1810, the body of Madame Gebhard was again disinterred and shown to Zwanziger, in the churchyard at Wonsers. She touched the right hand, saying, ' Peace be with your ashes! I wish I lay in the grave by your side; I should there be freed from my woes!" She was then led to Grohmann's grave. " Yes," said she, " this is the grave of Justice Grohmann! With his death, as with Madame Gebhard's, I had nothing to do." Madame Gebhard, however, was, as she afterwards confessed, actually poisoned by her. She therefore probably had as much to do with Grohmann's death as with Madame Gebhard's; and her asseverations at his grave may be considered as a sort of veiled and half ironical admission that she was as innocent of his murder as of Madame Gebhard's. In Gebhard's house, which she entered on the 13th May, 1809, as housekeeper and monthly nurse, her career of guilt was still more rapid.

Scarce had she been in the house four days before she selected the lying-in woman as her victim. " Because," said the prisoner, " Madame Gebhard was very cross, treated me roughly, and scolded me for having, as she said, neglected the housekeeping, I resolved to poison her." On Wednesday the 17th May, Zwanziger accordingly went into the cellar, where she poisoned two pitchers of beer, one with as much tartar emetic as she could take up between the fingers of her right hand, and the other with a still stronger dose of arsenic. On the same day a glass jug was filled out of the first pitcher for the lying-in woman; and Gebhard himself, unconscious of what he was doing, repeatedly handed the poisonous

draught to his wife. On Friday the 19th May, the day
before her death, the contents of the second pitcher
were placed before the sick woman, who drank but
little. "I did not give her the poison to kill her,"
said Zwanziger, "but only to plague her by making
her sick, because she had plagued me. I knew very
well that the beer could do her no harm. Had I
thought that Madame Gebhard died by my fault, I
would have laid myself in the grave beside her; for
she had always been fond of me; she was my best
friend, and always helped me by word and deed; she
praised me wherever she went, and was invariably kind
to me. We were like two sisters; we constantly met
and talked about economical matters." The malice
and duplicity exhibited in this statement surpass all
one can believe of human depravity, and it presents a
very remarkable parallel to her declarations about
Grohmann. She confessed that she intentionally gave
poison to her "best friend—her sister—her friend in
word and deed,"—Madame Gebhard; and on the
other hand she asked, how could she have wished to
poison Grohmann, who was her "best friend—her all
in all."

No one can doubt that her assertion that she did not
give Madame Gebhard poison with the intention of
causing her death, was a mere lie. Why, if she did not
want to destroy her, did she, after the first pitcher was
exhausted, give to her mistress—already dangerously
ill—the beer containing a still larger dose of poison?
Nor does her assertion that she did it to revenge insult
and unkindness at all agree with any other part of the
evidence. It was completely proved by the evidence of
a number of witnesses, and by several passages in

letters found in her commode, that she had conceived
the same wishes and formed the same scheme with
regard to Gebhard as she had already done with
regard to Glaser and Grohmann; and although she
had no ground for hope that Gebhard would marry
her, still there was always the possibility that if left a
widower he might be induced to do so; and to a person of her character this was sufficient reason for
putting his wife out of the way.

Towards the end of August, as we have already
stated, Beck, a shopman, and the widow of the secretary Alberti, dined with Gebhard, and were poisoned.
The prisoner confessed this charge. She said that
Beck had occasionally teased and laughed at her, and
that she gave him some beer mixed with arsenic out
of the same pitcher from which Madame Gebhard had
been poisoned, and which, when half empty, she had
merely filled up with fresh beer. She declared that
it was never her intention to kill him, but only to
punish him for laughing at her. "I must confess,"
said she, "that it was good fun to see people who had
teased me made very sick." She also acknowledged
that Madame Alberti drank out of the same pitcher,
but added, that it was not her intention that she
should do so, for that she dissuaded her from it, and
gave her a cordial and some coffee after she had been
made sick by the poisoned beer.

She denied having poisoned the messenger Rosenhauer with wine, but confessed having done so with
beer. She said that she had an antipathy to Rosenhauer because he told tales against her, and that she
gave him some of the same beer that she gave to Beck
a few days later, in order to punish him; adding that

on both occasions she did no more than fill up
the pitcher from which Madame Gebhard had been
poisoned.

With regard to the charge of poisoning Rosenhauer's lad, she did not deny the deed, but only the
means alleged. She said that "it was contrary to
common sense to suppose that any one could be
poisoned in brandy, which is so clear that the least
grain of dust could be seen in it; but that as Kraus
had always been very rude to her, she gave him a
glass of the poisoned beer to make him sick." Her
statement is in direct contradiction to the fact that
Kraus was taken ill after drinking some muddy-
looking brandy given him by Zwanziger; whereas
he affirmed that she had frequently given him beer,
from which he had never perceived any ill effects.

It is likewise proved that on the 1st September,
Gebhard, Beck, his brother, who had been poisoned by
Zwanziger only a few days before, the burghermaster
Petz and the clerk Scherber, who were assembled on
the skittle-ground, were all taken ill after drinking
some beer which was sent by Zwanziger, at her
master's desire, and out of his cellar. Zwanziger
resolutely denied any criminal intention; she asserted
that she did not know how it happened; "that perhaps
some sediment might have remained in the bottom of
the two pitchers originally prepared for Madame
Gebhard, that they may have been filled up afresh,
and that she may have sent them by accident."
Nothing can be more improbable than this statement
and nothing more certain than her guilt, according to
all the rules of experience and common sense. She,
to whom, according to her own confession, it was

" great fun " to watch the torments of the people whom she had poisoned, might think it vastly droll to spoil the sport of a whole party and be entertained by the mere thought of their pains, contortions, and wry faces; not to mention that among them was Beck, whom she hated, and on whom she had played the same trick only a few days before.

Nor is her statement that she did all this with the same two pitchers, into which she had put poison on the 17th May, without adding any fresh arsenic to the old sediment, at all more credible; if it were true, they must have strangely resembled the widow's cruse of oil. First, Madame Gebhard was destroyed by their contents ; next Beck and Madame Alberti each drank several glasses, after which they were both violently ill; then Rosenhauer and Kraus; and finally a party of five persons, who were all taken ill, and most of whom felt the effects of the poison for months. The following circumstance gives the key to a far more probable explanation :—On the evening before her departure from Gebhard's house, after he had taken the keys from her, she went into the cellar with Scherber, the clerk, in order to show him, what he could easily have found without her, the place where the candles were kept. As Scherber was going out again with the candles, she took up a little earthen jar, saying that she would take it with her, for that it had stood there for a long time past. She then gave it to the housemaid, and told her to wash it; and in doing so the latter perceived a hard white deposit, about one-eighth of an inch thick, in the bottom of the jar. This was in all probability the vessel in which she prepared the poison for the beer as often as she wanted it. She denied any concern with the sickness which attacked the two maid-servants, Hazin and Waldman, after drinking the coffee. On the other hand, she confessed that she put poison into the salt-box in the kitchen on the evening before she left Gebhard's house. " I must confess," these are her own words, " that on the evening before my departure I mixed the contents of the salt-box which is used in the kitchen with arsenic, in order that after I was gone everybody who stayed in the house might get some of it, and also in order to get the maid into trouble. I took a pinch of arsenic out of my pocket, went with it from my bed-room into the kitchen, whence I carried the salt-box into the servants' hall, and dropped the arsenic into it while I stirred the salt three times, and made some joke about it."

Now the store of salt in the barrel was likewise found to contain a considerable admixture of arsenic, and out of this very barrel Zwanziger had with her own hands filled the kitchen salt-box. There is scarce room for doubt that she who put poison into the one put it into the other; and yet she asserted her innocence in the face of all this evidence. " I can only suppose," said she, "that several persons have conspired to destroy me."

With regard to Gebhard's child, an infant six months old, "her darling," as she called it, to which she was accused of having administered arsenic in a biscuit and some milk, under pretence of affection, she stated that she did not give it anything in the biscuit, but that she put " just the least bit of tartar emetic" into a coffee-cup full of milk, of which she gave the child a few spoonfuls, and then threw away the rest, on perceiving that the tartar was not entirely dissolved. She says that she had no design upon the child's life, but only wanted to make it feel sick, so that it might cry and be uneasy, and thus induce Gebhard to send for her back from Baireuth to quiet it: she then adds, that she waited in this hope at Baireuth for four weeks. That her account of the motives which led her to commit this crime is in the main true, is proved by various passages in several of her letters to Gebhard; but her endeavour to extenuate her guilt is as evident in this instance as in all the preceding ones; for the maid-servant Hazin states that Zwanziger gave the child a biscuit soaked in the poisoned milk, which filled not quite half a coffee-cup, instead of a whole one, and which she let the child drink right off, instead of, as she said, giving a few teaspoonfuls.

It appears strange that this woman, after confessing, as she well knew, more than enough to ensure her sentence of death, should have endeavoured till the very last to explain away and gloss over her chief crimes, and, in the face of the most complete evidence, have altogether denied her lesser offences. It seemed impossible to her false and distorted nature to be quite sincere, or to utter a truth without associating with it a lie.

When Anna Zwanziger fell into the hands of justice, she had already reached her fiftieth year; she was of small stature, thin and deformed, her sallow and meagre face was deeply furrowed by passion as well as by age, and bore no trace of former beauty. Her eyes were expressive of envy and malice, and her brow was perpetually clouded, even when her lips moved to smile. Her manner was cringing, servile, and affected, and age and ugliness had not diminished her craving for admiration. Even in prison and under sentence of death, her imagination was still occupied with the pleasures of her youth. One day when her judge visited her in prison, she begged him not to infer what she had been from what she then was, for " that she was once beautiful, exceedingly beautiful."

The following story of her life is founded partly on the testimony of witnesses, and partly on her autobiography, which filled eighteen closely-written folio sheets.

Anna Schönleben was born at Nürnberg, on the 7th August, 1760, at the sign of the Black Cross, an inn belonging to her father, whose name was Schönleben. He died only a year and a half after her birth, and before she was five years old she lost her mother and her only brother. After her mother's death she was put to board with an old maid at Nürnberg, and two or three years later she went to live with an aunt at Feucht, who, she says, was a second mother to her; at the end of two years more she was sent back to Nürnberg to live with the widow of a clergyman. At last, when she was about ten years old, her guardian, a rich merchant, took her into his house, where she received a very good religious education, and learnt writing, reading, arithmetic, and the rudiments of the French language, besides all kinds of needlework, in which she acquired extraordinary skill.

She had scarcely completed her fifteenth year when her guardian determined to marry her to a notary named Zwanziger. She did not like her future husband, who was already past thirty, and for a long time she avoided him and rejected all his offers. At length,

however, her guardian's persuasions subdued her resistance, and in the nineteenth year of her age she
became Zwanziger's wife.

Married to a man whom she feared and disliked, and
who moreover was always engaged either in business or in drinking, leaving her to lead a life of
solitude and monotony, which contrasted most dis-
agreeably with the gaiety of her guardian's house,
she endeavoured to divert her melancholy by reading
novels. " My first novel," said she, " was the 'Sorrows of Werther,' and it affected me so much that I
did nothing but weep ; if I had had a pistol, I should
have shot myself too. After this I read ' Pamela' and
' Emilia Galeotti.' " Thus uncultivated and frigid
natures excite their imaginations to represent as really
felt emotions they are incapable of feeling. Such
natures strive to deceive themselves as well as others
by a mere grimace of sensibility, till at last it becomes
so habitual to them, that they are really incapable of
distinguishing truth from falsehood, and end by poisoning the very source of truth, the natural feelings.
Hypocrisy, falsehood, and malice are fruits easily
produced, and fearfully soon matured in a soul
accustomed to disguise its real feelings under assumed ones ; and thus it is that sentimentality is
perfectly consistent with total hardness of heart, and
even with cruelty. `

The pleasures of sensibility were soon superseded
by enjoyments more congenial to her character ; she
came of age, and her property was delivered into the
hands of her husband, who spent it in amusements,
in which, as was but fair, he permitted his wife to
take part. They gave dinners, concerts, balls, and

fêtes champêtres, and spent their days and nights in a constant round of dissipation.

A few years of this kind of life exhausted her fortune. She now had two children to support, and her husband was a confirmed drunkard, who often drank ten bottles of wine a day, and always wanted to be at the tavern; he was as irritable and tyrannical when money for this purpose was not forthcoming, as he was obliging and indulgent when he got it. The admirer of 'Pamela,' she who had wept over the 'Sorrows of Werther,' now offered her person for hire. "But," said she, "I always had the delicacy to admit none but men of rank and discretion; for from my youth upwards my principle has ever been to stick to those who could advance my fortunes; and thus, I had the good luck to receive a great deal of assistance from many distinguished men."

After about two years, Zwanziger contrived a scheme for a lottery of watches, which for a time restored their fortunes. This improvement in their circumstances immediately brought with it a return to habits of dissipation; the course of life which Zwanziger had entered from want and for money, she now pursued from habit and inclination. A scandalous and expensive connection with a Lieutenant von B—— gave rise to a violent domestic quarrel. Zwanziger left her husband, and went to her lover's sister at Vienna, but soon returned to Nürnberg in consequence of her husband's representations, where, at her lover's instigation, she commenced an action for divorce against her husband, and obtained it after a short suit. On the very day after the proclamation of the divorce she remarried him, and, according to her own statement, lived with him very contentedly till the day of his death. She says that she ended by being positively attached to him, for that on several occasions he had shown "a very noble way of thinking, and a susceptible heart."

On the 20th January, 1796, Anna Zwanziger was left a widow, after eighteen years of marriage. Her husband died after a short illness, and she was suspected of having poisoned him, but this suspicion was not confirmed on investigation.

Ever since her husband's death Zwanziger's life was one tissue of misfortunes, follies, vices, and, finally, crimes. Her patrimony was consumed, and every other source of income dried up. She was unable to collect in all more than 400 florins. With this sum she went to Vienna, as she gave out, to establish herself as a confectioner. Failing in this, she became housekeeper in several considerable families. She then grew intimate with a clerk in the Hungarian exchequer, " of very fine sensibilities," by whom she had an illegitimate child, which she put into the foundling hospital, where it died soon after. She returned to Nürnberg after an absence of a year and a half.

She had at first no intention of remaining long in her paternal city. But one day a certain Freiherr von W—— called upon her, and offered his protection, his friendship, and his love. She perceived, as she said, that in the Freiherr she had found a " very noble man," and thereupon hired a private lodging. Here she was constantly visited by her protector, who provided her with money ; but, according to her own account, respected her virtue. She added to her means by making dolls.

This connection lasted about three months, when the place of housekeeper to one of the ministers resident at Frankfürt was offered to her. Her noble protector at Nürnberg was so generous as not to stand in the way of her promotion, and she set out for the place of her destination with 100 florins, which he gave her. She did not, however, remain in this situation above two or three months, chiefly owing to her dirty habits and want of skill in cookery. According to her own statement, indeed, she stayed there a year and a half, and left her place for quite different reasons.

She then hired an apartment over a hairdresser's shop at Frankfürt, for a month : entered the service of a troop of equestrian performers, whom she quitted at the end of eight days, as they were going to Bamberg, and returned to the hairdresser at Frankfürt, where a merchant took her for a short time into his family as nursemaid—all this within the space of a few months. So many misfortunes in succession, added to the insupportable thought of having fallen from her station as mistress of a house and family to the condition of a servant, worked so strongly on her feelings as to cause her to behave like a mad woman. She wept, laughed, and prayed by turns. She received her mistress's orders with a laugh, and went obediently away, but never executed them.

In her extreme need she applied by letter to her noble friend the Freiherr, who accordingly again offered her his protection, and on her arrival at Nürnberg received her with open arms. " But, to her astonishment "—so she would have it believed—" she now found a great alteration in his manners. He, a married man, grew free in speech and conduct, and at last so far forgot his dignity " as to cause her to have the prospect of becoming a mother." * As soon as her protector was informed of this fact, his manner became colder and his visits less frequent, and she soon ascertained that he paid far greater attention to an actress of considerable reputation in Germany, who was then at Nürnberg. This shock, as she pretended, brought on a miscarriage; and not content with this, on the following day she borrowed a lancet from the people of the house and opened a vein in each arm, but, as she said, "was stopped in the execution of her purpose, and lost only a teacupful of blood." The owner of the lodging called upon Freiherr von W——, told him what had happened, and showing him the fatal lancet, induced him to visit this female Werther on the following day. The Freiherr appeared, but not as a penitent. When the teacupful of blood was shown to him, he laughed at her folly, and after a scene of violent reproaches on her side he turned his back upon her, and never saw her again. Burning for revenge, she collected his letters and sent them to his wife. She then went with Siegwart in her pocket, and accompanied by her maid, to the Pegnitz, resolved, as she asserted, to drown herself. She seated herself on the bank of the river, and read Siegwart, till she came to the song " Mein leben ist so traurig," &c., whereupon she jumped into the stream. Two fishermen who were near at hand rescued her, with no other injury than a thorough wetting. A change of clothes was immediately brought her, and the wet ones were carried to the Freiherr as evidence of her second attempt at suicide.

* This was probably a mere pretext to attach her lover to her more firmly.

The maid who conveyed them received from the Freiherr 25 florins, with the recommendation to her
mistress to quit Nürnberg as soon as possible. She
accordingly went to Ratisbon that very night, without
even returning to her lodging.

It is evident that the object of these two attempts at
self-destruction was the same. She let herself blood
with no intention to bleed to death ; and jumped into
the water merely that she might be pulled out again.
Nevertheless she ascribed, and no doubt truly, her
hatred of mankind to the faithless and hard-hearted
conduct of her protector. She said in one of her
examinations, " It is all Freiherr von W——'s fault
that my heart is so hard. When I opened my veins
and he saw my blood, he only laughed. And when I
reproached him with having once before ruined a poor
girl who drowned herself and her child by him, he
laughed again. My feelings were terrible, and when
I afterwards did anything wicked, I said to myself,
No one ever pitied me, and therefore I will show no
pity to others."

At Ratisbon she lay ill for three weeks of a fever ;
she then went to Vienna, thence back to Nürnberg,
and finally into Thuringia, where in 1804 she entered the service of Kammerherr von S—— at Weimar, as housemaid. According to her account all
the servants in the house were hard worked and ill
paid, for which reason she soon got tired of it and
resolved to leave it secretly without giving warning,
and to carry away something "to make herself
amends." " My plan," says she, "succeeded admirably. One day while my master and mistress were at
dinner, I was told to play with the child to keep

it quiet. I accordingly went with it into the drawing-
room, where there was a small round table with a
drawer, in which were a diamond ring, a number
of pearls, earrings, jewels, and other such trinkets.
Where, thought I, such things as these are left for a
child to play with, it is clear that they are not much
valued; if they were, they would be locked up. At
that moment the child was playing with a ring-
case, and, after rolling it to and fro, put it into my
hand; I opened it, and on seeing the ring I felt
as if some one stood beside me and said 'Keep it!'
I obeyed the inspiration, put the child to sleep, and
quitted the house and the town before my master and
mistress had left the dinner-table." This ingenious
romance, in which she ascribes a deed which she had
unguardedly owned to be premeditated, to the sudden
inspiration of an evil spirit, and which is moreover
calculated to give an unfavourable idea of the habits
of order and care of her mistress, is utterly inconsistent
with the very prosaic account of the affair given by
the latter, who declares that the ring was taken out
of a locked escritoire, the key of which was kept in
her own work-basket.

Having escaped from Weimar with her booty,
Zwanziger took refuge with her son-in-law Sauer,
a bookbinder, at Mainbernheim. Scarcely, however,
had she been three days in his house, when a
newspaper fell into his hands containing an advertisement from Weimar for the apprehension of his
mother-in-law on the charge of having stolen a diamond ring. He immediately turned her out of his
house, and on the same day she went to Würzburg,
whence she had the audacity to write to the master

whom she had robbed, reproaching him for bringing her into misfortune by this public advertisement. And indeed it had fallen upon her like a thunderbolt; her name was dishonoured, she was outlawed and civilly dead; and in order to be tolerated among men she was forced as it were to cease to exist in her own person, and from this time forward she exchanged the name of Zwanziger for her maiden name of Schönleben.

She wandered about Franconia for some time, staying now in one place and now in another, and finding temporary shelter and assistance chiefly among people of rank and education. At length, in the year 1805, she found a provision in the little town of Neumarkt, in the upper Palatinate. She established herself there to teach needlework to young girls, got a number of pupils, besides earning a good deal by sewing, and, according to the testimony of the magistrates, won universal good will by her industry and her decorous behaviour. But her fate, or rather her restless discontented spirit, would not suffer her to remain quiet. Unhappily for her, old General N. came to stay a while at Neumarkt. She contrived to insinuate herself into the old gentleman's favour, who descended to the closest familiarity with her, and on one occasion promised to provide for her. She was again filled with the memory of bygone days, in which she enjoyed the protection of " distinguished noblemen," and fancied that, old as she was, those days were now about to return. She already dreamed of going to Munich as the mistress of " his Excellency." She indulged these visions with feelings of perfect security, as she had "always heard that the Catholics

nearly always kept their word." General N. left
Neumarkt, and soon after she wrote to him, but received no answer. Some time after she wrote again,
and falsely told him that she was with child. But
instead of an answer, she received, through the hands
of a clergyman, a trifling sum of money to stop
her importunities. Not yet discouraged, she left
Neumarkt, where she had found peace and support
for a whole year, and went to Munich to present herself in person before his Excellency, but was refused
admission. She wrote a letter to him from the inn,
but received a verbal answer through a secretary or
servant to the effect that she was no longer to trouble
his Excellency with her foolish impertinence ; he
also sent her a small sum of money for her travelling
expenses.

Thus forced to leave Munich, she went to several
different places in succession till her destiny led her to
Pegnitz in 1807, and from thence to Kasendorf and
Sansparcil, the scene of her greater crimes.

In her youth this woman showed herself irresolute,
coquettish, superficially accomplished, and perverted
by reading sentimental novels. Always the slave of
circumstances, she at first gave herself up to folly
and dissipation, until she gradually sunk into vice,
and at last sold her person for money ; and thus,
with honour and self-respect, she lost her last social
restraint and support.

Her vanity, which she dignified with the name
of delicate sensibility, drew her towards the higher
classes ; she was often compelled to please and attract
men whom she did not like, to assume a cheerful
countenance among strangers by whom she was re-

pulsed and humbled, and to smother the passions
which were raging within her. She was too restless to live honestly by the work of her hands in
quiet and retirement, and too proud to be satisfied
as a mere domestic servant; she therefore affected
great zeal in the service of her various masters, and
endeavoured to place herself upon such a confidential
footing with them as to preclude all exercise of authority on their part. Thus, always acting a part,
and forced to appear different to what she really
was, she learnt the art of accommodating herself to
those with whom she lived, and lost what little truth
and honesty was still left in her. She became false,
cunning, smooth-tongued, and hypocritical. There
was a smile upon her lips, while within there was
burning hatred; her mouth spoke of God, while her
heart took counsel of Satan; she sowed hatred, while
she spoke the words of conciliation; her praises were
calumnies, and her calumny was concealed in praise;
when forced to speak the truth, she invariably coupled
with it a lie. But she was not yet prepared to become a
poisoner, and a compounder of poisons, as she showed
herself at Kasendorf and Sanspareil. With no worse
a character she might still belong to the world; with
these vices a man may command a distinguished
place in the best society, as they frequently form the
basis of what in fashionable life is called knowledge
of the world.

But Zwanziger thought herself unfortunate, and
in her this feeling severed all the ties of human
sympathy. Persecuted by destiny, or rather by the
consequences of her own faults and vices, her ever
ready self-love led her to ascribe every hope deceived,

and every evil that befel her, to the malice or the cruelty of mankind. With such dispositions as these, is it surprising that her heart should soon be filled with envy and mischief?

After being for twenty years a wanderer on the face of the earth, nearly fifty years of age, and still homeless, friendless, and only endured among men by concealing her real name, she now anxiously sought a resting-place and a provision, and that not as the maid-servant she now was, but as the mistress of a house which she had formerly been. She could no longer endure to belong always to others, and never to herself; continually to cringe and flatter, and to affect zeal in the service of those whom in her heart she hated; to be always dependent and subservient, while her soul was filled with the recollection of bygone days, in which she was the object of attention and flattery. She was resolved to escape from this position, or at all events to find some compensation for it.

But no means of acquiring independence presented itself to her within the pale of social order, till at length she discovered the secret of a hidden power, by the exercise of which she might not only emancipate herself from restraint, but also rule unseen and uncontrolled. This secret power was poison.

As Zwanziger never made a complete and sincere confession, we have no means of knowing at what time and on what inducement the idea first occurred to her—whether suddenly or by slow degrees—whether she at once formed a systematic plan, or whether it developed itself little by little and almost unconsciously in her mind. Her confession almost always leaves us in the dark with regard to the secret springs which guided her actions, but the actions themselves are so numerous and so clear, that we may trace them to their source with perhaps as much certainty as the most open confession could do for us.

Thus much is clearly proved by her whole course of action,—that we cannot attribute it, as in the case of ordinary criminals, to any one ruling passion, or to one especial motive. Her attachment to poison was based upon the proud consciousness of possessing a power which enabled her to break through every restraint, to attain every object, to gratify every inclination, and to determine the very existence of others. Poison was the magic wand with which she ruled those whom she outwardly obeyed, and opened the way to her fondest hopes. Poison enabled her to deal out death, sickness, and torture to all who offended her or stood in her way—it punished every slight—it prevented the return of unwelcome guests—it disturbed those social pleasures which it galled her not to share—it afforded her amusement by the contortions of the victims, and an opportunity of ingratiating herself by affected sympathy with their sufferings—it was the means of throwing suspicion upon innocent persons, and of getting fellow-servants into trouble. If she flattered herself with the prospect of marrying an already married man, at her will wives descended into the grave, and left their husbands free for her. She grudged the bride her bridegroom, and the wedding-feast was held in vain. In time mixing and giving poison became her constant occupation; she practised it in jest and in earnest, and at last with real passion for poison itself, without reference to the object for which it was given. She grew to love it from long habit and from gratitude for its faithful services, she looked upon it as her truest friend, and made it her constant companion. At her apprehension arsenic was found in her pocket, and when it was laid before her at Culmbach to be identified, she seemed to tremble with pleasure, and gazed upon the white powder with eyes beaming with rapture. This love for poison may perhaps in some degree explain why she, who had confessed the most atrocious crimes and was under sentence of death, in her written memoirs speaks of her deeds as " slight errors," accuses of cruelty and injustice those who could bring destruction upon her for the sake of such " trifling offences," and boasts of her " piety" as only " too great," and as the origin of all her misfortunes. So true is it that habit reconciles us to everything, and that we are inclined to excuse the most atrocious crimes when they are committed by one we love.

On the 7th of July, 1811, the court at Bamberg sentenced Anna Margaret Zwanziger to have her head cut off by the sword, and her body to be afterwards laid upon the wheel.

The sentence of death received the royal confirmation, accompanied by the command that the exposure of the body on the wheel be omitted.

Zwanziger received her sentence without any perceptible emotion, and signed the papers presented to her with a firm hand. She passed the three days which remained to her of life with perfect composure. She confessed to her judge that her death was fortunate for mankind, for that it would have been impossible to her to discontinue her trade of poisoning. On the day before her execution she wrote, in the presence of the judge, a farewell letter to one of her friends at Nürnberg, in which she thanks her in measured terms for the friendship she had shown her, begs her forgiveness and sympathy, sends her love to other persons, and concludes thus:—" I must now end; the hour will soon strike at which my woes will cease. Pray for me. The 17th of September is the day fixed for my death, on which I shall receive from God the reward of my actions. I have already ceased to belong to this world." She wished to prove to the judge her sense of the kindness he had shown to her by the strange request that he would allow her, if it were possible, to appear to him after her death, and to give him ocular demonstration of the immortality of the soul. She remained constant to her character on the day of her execution. She listened to her sentence with the greatest composure, and without shedding a tear. While it was read she held her handkerchief before her face, as the crowd put her to shame; and when the wand was broken over her,* she took courteous leave of the judge and officers of the court, as of some every-day company.

A short time before her execution, the judge appealed to her conscience to confess the innocence of Justice Glaser; but she persisted in her slanderous accusation that he had participated in her first murder, and with this lie upon her soul she laid her guilty head upon the block.

* " Breaking the wand " in Germany answers to " putting on the black cap" in England.— *Trans.*

JAMES THALREUTER;

OR,

THE FALSE PRINCE.

JAMES THALREUTER was the illegitimate son of Lieut.-
Colonel von Rescher and Barbara Thalreuter, the
daughter of an exciseman : he was born at Landshut, on
the 10th September, 1809, and acknowledged by his
father. His mother died the same year, and before he
was three years old his father was forced to leave him
in order to join the Russian campaign. The old Baron
von Stromwalter, who enjoyed a retiring pension as
assessor of the council, was an intimate friend of the
Lieut.-Colonel, and with his wife's consent took the
deserted boy under his protection ; and although he
had two children of his own, a married daughter and
a son in the army, he always treated Thalreuter as if
he were his son.

The Baroness von Stromwalter bore absolute sway
over her family and household : her husband, who
was a goodnatured, weak, and foolish man, knew
nothing but what his wife allowed him to know, and
took no part in any affairs except where his signature
was necessary, and this he never ventured to refuse.
In addition to this, the whole of the property was hers
except her husband's pension, which was very small.
She possessed funded property to the amount of

11,000 florins (about 900*l.*), a small estate called Schwaig, and some rents, tithes, &c., from which, however, several debts had to be deducted. The fact that letters addressed to the old Baron were opened and answered by his wife, proves how little he was regarded in his own house. The Baroness was in the habit of treating him with cool contempt, even in the presence of a third person.

The Baroness soon conceived the most extravagant affection for the lively young Thalreuter; she was charmed with the amusing rogueries of the mischievous boy: with her, his rudeness passed for pretty ways, his knavery for innocent childish tricks, · and a lying disposition for the mark of a fertile, precocious, and promising genius.

His foster-parents lived for a long time on their estate of Schwaig, where farmers' sons and ploughboys were the sole companions of the spoiled boy, who thus had ever before his eyes examples of plebeian coarseness, vulgar habits, and still more vulgar ways of thinking.

The foster-mother sent him to the Catholic school, where he is said to have been quiet and diligent. As he was intended for the army, he afterwards received, according to his foster-mother's account, instruction in French, drawing, and mathematics. But it afterwards appeared that Thalreuter had not the slightest tincture of learning or accomplishments; indeed he had made but little progress in the most elementary parts of instruction. He wrote a bad hand, and made the grossest mistakes in spelling. But when only fifteen or sixteen years of age he possessed surprising knowledge of commercial and pecuniary affairs,

added to an inexhaustible talent for the invention
of the most various, specious, and complicated lies,
perfect in their smallest details, and worked up with
masterly skill. This talent was combined with and
assisted by a singularly comprehensive and accurate
memory.

The older the boy grew the more firmly did he
establish his ascendancy over those who lived but
to minister to his pleasures. He was on the most
familiar footing with his foster-mother, towards whom
he felt neither affection, respect, nor gratitude. He
only looked upon her as the person who was able to
afford him the means of gratifying his desires. The
Baroness on her side did everything she could to please
her darling. She gave her money with equal readiness for excursions and pleasure parties, and for the
payment of his debts, or of any damage he might have
wilfully done. Nothing in the house remained closed
or secret from him : he had free access even to the
closet in which the Baroness kept her money. In
short, the blind love of his foster-mother rendered
him absolute master of her person and property.
" He did what he liked with the Baroness," says one
of the witnesses, "sometimes by fair and sometimes
by foul means." His conduct to the poor weak old
Baron, who was now seventy years of age, and who
had treated him like his own child, was the worst of
all. He never mentioned his foster-father but in terms
of contempt; even in the presence of others and in the
public streets he addressed to him the most degrading
insults; nay more, some witnesses had even seen him
strike the old man.

Thalreuter employed the liberty with which his

foster-mother indulged him, not only in making considerable debts on her account, but also in plundering her to a large amount. He carried away a number of things out of the house, and at short intervals of time stole from her bureau, to the keys of which he had free access, as much as 700 florins. When the Baroness at length discovered this deficiency, she determined to let her foster-son feel the whole weight of her displeasure, but she soon relented, forgave him this youthful peccadillo, and merely took the precaution of keeping the keys of her bureau out of his way for the future. This circumstance, added to the reflection that he could only gain possession of trifling sums by mere pilfering, led him to contrive a scheme whereby he hoped to prevail upon his foster-parents to place their whole property at his disposal for the indulgence of his extravagance.

In the beginning of the summer of 1825, Thalreuter let fall first some mysterious hints, and then some more definite expressions, with regard to his own birth, by which he said that he was destined to be something very different from what he now appeared. The inquisitive old Baron was forced to content himself with the information that he, Thalreuter, was the son of a noble Count, but in a confidential moment he disclosed the wonderful secret to his foster-mother. He told her, with tears of joy, that "he was the son of the reigning Duke of B——; that his father had already lost one son by poison, and lest this should happen to him also, the Duke had had him conveyed, as soon as he was born, to Colonel von Rescher, his especial favourite, who had undertaken to bring up his grace's second son. Von Rescher had accordingly passed for his

father, and had observed the most inviolable secrecy."
He related many other circumstances; talked about
a certain Count von Rosenthal, and a General von
D——, and spoke with the greatest affection of a
certain Lieut.-Colonel von Hautbing, also a favourite
of the reigning Duke, who had acquainted Thalreuter
with his real origin.

Notwithstanding the improbability of the whole of
this story, which stood in direct contradiction with
all that the Stromwalters knew of Thalreuter's real
origin—and they even possessed his certificate of
birth—the weak heads of the worthy couple were too
easily turned by the grandeur of the romance, and
the desire of increasing their limited means, not to
give implicit belief to the tale.   From time to time
Thalreuter showed to Baron or Baroness Stromwalter letters, always brought by himself, from his
royal father the Duke, or from the imaginary Von
Hautbing.   In one, the foster-parents were thanked
for their care of the boy; in another, 10,000 ducats and
many other fine things were promised as a reward
for their services : the time of his grace's arrival was
said to draw near, by which the good foster-parents
would be deprived of their darling James.   On one
occasion Von Hautbing announced the arrival of some
money; on another, specious excuses were sent to
account for the non-arrival of this sum, which, however, might very shortly be expected.   All these
letters, of which there were about twenty from his
grace alone, were such illegible scrawls, and so
wretched in composition and style, that the merest
schoolboy could not have failed to detect the impos-
ture.   But the very circumstance of the letters being

so illegible afforded young Thalreuter the excuse for always reading them himself aloud to his foster-mother, and he thus had the opportunity of explaining away any momentary doubts which might arise in her mind. Before long Thalreuter appeared with a costly present of six strings of fine large pearls from his ducal father for his dear foster-mother, which was acceptable not only as an ornament, but also on account of its supposed value, to Baroness von Stromwalter, who was much embarrassed for want of money. Thalreuter prevented his foster-parents and others from having the pearls examined by persons competent to form an opinion of their real value, by representing how offensive such a proceeding would be to his grace. They were accordingly left in pledge with different people for several hundred florins. The fact that Thalreuter had bought mock pearls at a toy-shop for one florin and thirty kreutzers (about 2s.) the string, with money he had stolen—which was discovered when the case came before the court—remained carefully concealed from these simpletons. A small jewel-case, containing a pair of ear-rings, also a present from the imaginary Duke, and bought with Baroness von Stromwalter's own money at the same toy-shop, greatly contributed, if indeed anything had still been wanting, to confirm the belief of the Stromwalter family in the distinguished origin of their foster-son. Thalreuter's inexhaustible fertility in lying kept the credulous old people in a constant state of excitement. He one day showed them a miniature of an officer covered with orders as the portrait of the Duke; on another he brought them landscapes, which he said were views

of the estates purchased by the Duke to reward his foster-parents. One day when the Baroness returned to
the house, Thalreuter met her, exclaiming that " it
really was most unlucky that neither she nor the
assessor had been at home; for that he had at length
seen his royal father, who had driven up with four
horses, and had wished to speak to them, but could
not wait, as he was forced to continue his journey immediately." On another occasion Thalreuter told old
Stromwalter that Hautbing was staying at the Swan
Inn, and wished to speak to him that evening. He
then gave him a note, in which Hautbing cordially
invited Von Stromwalter to crack a bottle of cham-
pagne with him. The old Baron hastened to dress
himself in his best suit, in order to pay his respects to
the envoy of the Duke, but, before the appointed hour
was come, Thalreuter, apparently fresh from the
Swan, brought the message, with many excuses and
compliments, that Hautbing had been compelled to
set out upon urgent business, at a moment's notice.

This extraordinary tissue of lies, transparent as it
was, served nevertheless completely to blind the
Stromwalters; and Thalreuter, not satisfied with being
treated with increased indulgence and more liberally
supplied with money than before, in his character of
a prince in disguise, was encouraged by the complete
success of his first stratagem, to attempt another still
more profitable. He accordingly communicated to the
Baroness as a profound secret, that the Von Wallers,
a distinguished, rich, and noble family in the town
of ——, purposed to arrange a marriage between
their daughter and Lieutenant von Stromwalter, and
that the betrothal had already taken place, and every-

thing would now be speedily concluded. Now Herr
von Waller had never said a word of the matter to
Baron or Baroness von Stromwalter, nor had the
Lieutenant ever mentioned it in his letters to his
parents. Nay, more; the Von Wallers were almost
strangers to the Stromwalters, and did not now make
the slightest overtures towards a nearer acquaintance.
But Thalreuter assured his foster-parents that the
nature of the transaction made it indispensable to its
success that they should behave as if they knew
nothing at all about the marriage—that Herr von
Waller was bent upon taking "papa and mamma"
by surprise. The foolish old people gave ready
belief to this most palpable lie, because the Duke
of B——, Herr von Hautbing, and General D——
wished them joy, in successive letters forged by
Thalreuter, of the highly advantageous match between their son and Fräulein von Waller. Thalreuter
had now brought his foster-parents to the point he
desired.

Ere long he informed the Baroness that her son the
Lieutenant must now pay, previous to his marriage,
into the military fund the sum of 10,000 florins (required in the army as a security for a man's ability to
support a wife); that his father the Duke intended to
pay the greater part of this sum, and that he expected
the parents to contribute only a few thousand florins.
The credulous mother, overjoyed at the prospect of
her son's marriage, without a moment's hesitation
delivered 2700 florins into the hands of this young
rogue, who in a very short time squandered the whole
sum in reckless extravagance. Not long after this
Thalreuter brought the intelligence that Lieutenant

von Stromwalter had had the misfortune to be arrested
for seditious practices, and that his release from prison
could only be effected by depositing securities to the
amount of 1000 florins.   The Baroness, terrified and
distressed, again delivered to the disguised prince
1000 florins for the release of her son.   Soon after,
Thalreuter informed her that young Stromwalter was
involved in most pressing pecuniary difficulties, and
required immediate assistance.   The fond mother immediately sold a quantity of furniture in order to
raise the required sum, which she intrusted to Thalreuter.   A second and still more serious embarrassment of the Lieutenant, which unless instantly relieved
must break off his marriage, filled her with anxiety,
and levied a fresh contribution on her purse;—a girl,
according to Thalreuter's assertion, was with child by
the Lieutenant, and money was immediately required
to satisfy her, and to prevent the affair from reaching
the ears of the Von Waller family.   This invention
put several hundred florins into Thalreuter's pocket.
Another time he extracted money on pretence of buying ornaments for the bride.   The supposed marriage
of the Lieutenant also served as an excuse for taking a
good deal of furniture out of the Stromwalter's house
to set up the young couple, which Thalreuter sold on
his own account.

We may well ask how it was that neither Baron
von Stromwalter nor his wife thought of visiting the
Von Wallers, so as at any rate to sound them about
the marriage.   The old Baron did indeed once express
an intention of so doing; but Thalreuter employed
all his eloquence to prevent him, and drew such a
picture of the danger which his visit would bring

upon the intended marriage, that the weak old man gave up the intention, and abandoned himself with blind confidence to the guidance and direction of a boy of fifteen. Again, we may ask, how it was that the son had so little communication with his parents that the latter did not write to ask him a single question concerning his marriage? How was it that the parents suspected nothing when their own son never let fall a word on such important subjects as his approaching marriage, the money required as a deposit, his imprisonment, his love affair, his embarrassments, and the money which was sent to satisfy all these claims? Thalreuter provided against this also. He intercepted all letters from the parents to the son, and from the son to the parents, or he wrote in the name of the mother letters to suit his purpose, which she, without even reading them, confirmed by the addition of a few lines in her own handwriting. One letter from the Lieutenant, in which he requested his mother to inform him of the truth or falsehood of the reports of Thalreuter's unheard-of extravagance which had reached him at D——, was, in spite of Thalreuter's precautions, given to old Baroness von Stromwalter in his presence. He no sooner saw the handwriting than he snatched the letter out of her hand and wrote in her name an answer to it, in which he disclosed to the Lieutenant the secret of his high birth. Baroness von Stromwalter, who was not allowed to read the letter, added these words: "Thus writes your loving and astonished mother, who rejoices in the prospect of going to D—— with James's father to embrace her beloved son." The son was thus deceived with the aid of his own mother, and Thalreuter did not fail to nourish his hopes and expectations by letters addressed to him from time to time.

Baroness von Stromwalter met the enormous expenditure caused by Thalreuter's knavery and extravagance by selling out of the funds, borrowing money, and selling or pawning her jewels, furniture, &c. Thalreuter employed other means of obtaining money at his foster-parents' expense. He placed before them a paper, the written contents of which he covered with his hand or with a book, and requested them to oblige him with their seal and signatures: this, he added, was merely in jest, and he wanted their signature to this paper in order secretly to prepare for them a very great pleasure. Hereupon the papers were signed and sealed without more ado. It appeared on examination that these papers were bills of exchange for 50, 64, 200, or 275 florins, which Thalreuter instantly contrived to get exchanged. There was nothing in the house which the foster-son did not steal if it suited him to sell or to give it away. Chairs and tables, plate, copper and tin utensils, glass, clothes, bedding, pictures, clocks, watches, telescopes, snuff-boxes, and every sort of article, even to a mousetrap, were mentioned among the list of things he had carried away under various pretences. If he wanted to make a present of the Baron's Cremona fiddle to any one, it was always that convenient nobody Lieut.-Colonel von Hautbing who wished to play upon it: if he cast his eyes upon a hot-water bottle, Fräulein von Waller suffered from violent spasms, and it was immediately sent to her. After having plundered his foster-parents of all their money, he proceeded to squander the little landed property which still remained to them. He persuaded his foster-mother to sell her small estate of Schwaig, asserting that the sale would only be a simulated one; that Von Waller was the real purchaser, and would give it as a marriage portion to his daughter. The sale took place, and the few thousand florins went mostly in the payment of old debts: of the little that remained, Thalreuter took 650 florins for himself, as he pretended to help the son out of fresh difficulties. The old foster-mother still possessed a few tithes and rents; these too were sold soon after, and the few hundred florins which remained to her after the payment of debts were delivered into Thalreuter's hands. The old Baroness now became anxious about the state of her property. Her capital was either gone or intrusted to Thalreuter, and the constantly recurring necessity of borrowing money or pawning her effects, proved to her how desperate her condition really was. But Thalreuter was too good a chancellor of the exchequer not to be able to quiet his faithful parliament by a skilfully contrived budget, and he assured Baroness von Stromwalter that her property had never been in so flourishing a condition as it was then. He made out an accurate statement of her possessions (including the estate of Schwaig which had been sold, and 10,000 ducats promised by the Duke), according to which they amounted to at least 70,000 florins: this statement completely relieved all her anxieties. The last and worst trick he played these unfortunate old people was to make them believe that his royal father had just bought them a splendid house, or rather palace, in the town of A——, in which they were to pass the rest of their lives. Without so much as in-

quiring into the existence of this palace, the childish
old people instantly gave notice that they should quit
the house they then rented, and began to look forward
with joyful impatience to the next Candlemas, 1826,
when they expected the whole mystery to be un-
ravelled, and their fortunes to be established.   Meanwhile Thalreuter, who by his last lie had cheated his
poor foster-parents of the very roof over their heads,
took care that their removal should not be troublesome.   Under pretence of furnishing the new palace
a little beforehand, he carried off most of the few
articles of furniture that were left, a yellow damask
sofa, six chairs, &c., which we need scarcely inform
our readers soon found their way into the pawn-
broker's shop.

The money thus obtained was squandered in
the most reckless and foolish extravagance.   He
entertained his acquaintances, who were men of
the lowest class, in the most sumptuous manner
at different inns and taverns; the most costly wines
were not alone poured out like water at the table,
but thrown into the adjacent ponds and dashed
against the carriage-wheels; the most delicate viands
were thrown out of the window for boys to scramble
for; splendid fireworks were let off to amuse the
guests, among whom he distributed all kinds of expensive presents with the greatest profusion.   One
witness even stated that on one occasion he moistened
the wheels of the carriage he had hired with eau de
Cologne.   The toyman Stang, who was (though not
entirely by his own fault) the constant companion of
Thalreuter and partaker in his extravagant parties of
pleasure, sold him, in one year, goods to the amount

of 6700 florins, among which were fifty florins' worth of eau de Cologne.

This way of life could not fail to lead him into other kinds of mischief, and accordingly, in April, 1825, he was taken up in a drunken brawl and charged with assault and battery, but acquitted owing to want of evidence: two months after, he and several accomplices were tried for poaching.

The company which Thalreuter kept was as low as his own manners, consisting chiefly of coachmen, grooms, &c. ; the only man with any pretension to respectability with whom he associated was Stang, the toyman, who on first witnessing the boy's extravagance thought it his duty to report it to Baroness von Stromwalter, but she replied, "that the expenditure of her James would not appear surprising whenever the secret of his birth and rank should be revealed ; that at present she could only say thus much, that he was the son of very great parents and would have more property than he could possibly spend:" she concluded by saying "that she was very glad that her James, who had hitherto associated only with peasants and coachmen, should have chosen so good a companion and adviser as Stang." The poor toyman was of course overjoyed at the thought of having secured the friendship and custom of a prince in disguise, and no longer felt any hesitation in accepting Thalreuter's presents and joining his parties of pleasure, and from this time forward they became almost daily companions.

Thalreuter's conduct naturally attracted the attention of the authorities of the town, but as the usual explanation was given to them by his foster-parents, of course they could do nothing but look on and await the solution of the mystery.

Nor did they wait long. Thalreuter owed 70 florins for coach-hire to a man of the name of Block, whom he had promised to pay at the end of the year 1825. On the 29th or 30th December Block went in search of his debtor, whom he found in a tavern, and demanded his money. Thalreuter instantly pulled a cheque out of his pocket and showed it to his creditor, saying that it was drawn in his favour for 450 florins by the advocate Dr. Schroll, that he was going to get it cashed and would then pay the debt. The coachman Block conceived some suspicion, and immediately informed Dr. Schroll of the whole affair. The latter declared before the local authorities, on the 5th January, 1826, that he had never held any communication whatever with Thalreuter, much less given him an order for money, and that he demanded an examination into the matter, as a draft in Thalreuter's favour must be forged.

In consequence of this accusation upon oath a search-warrant was issued and Thalreuter arrested on the 11th January. Early next morning Baroness von Stromwalter hastened to the court and begged that her foster-son might speedily be set free. "It was indeed true," said she, "that he had robbed her at various times of sums amounting to not less than 700 florins, but that she had forgiven him this offence long ago, and did not wish him to be called to account for it." She at the same time declared herself ready and willing to be answerable to the whole extent of her property for any injury he might have done to a third party. She said that she had already paid 700 florins for him, and offered, without hesitation, to pay all his fresh debts, which might amount to a few hundred florins more, and then all that had happened might be as though it had never occurred. But the astonishing confessions which Thalreuter made at his first examination soon induced the Baron and Baroness to alter their tone, and to represent themselves as unfortunate victims, who had slept securely on the brink of a precipice and were only awakened by their fall. They now declared that they had always believed their foster-child to be the son and heir of the reigning Duke of B——, but that now he had himself confessed that he, whom they had treated like their own son, had deceived them in the most shameful manner, and had cheated and plundered them of all their possessions, and even of their good name, and reduced them to absolute beggary; that they accordingly renounced all their parental duties towards him, and left him to justice and to his well-merited fate. In spite of this declaration, hopes from time to time revived in them that this manifest reality might after all be only an illusion, and that the Duke might at last appear as a Deus ex machina to release his darling son from durance vile, and them from want and misery.

Thalreuter confessed with the utmost frankness, but without the slightest remorse, or compassion for his poor old foster-parents, not only the forgery of the draft upon Dr. Schroll, but also of an order upon a bank for 445 florins, which, however, he said, was not intended to be presented. He likewise recounted the long series of deceits and thefts which he had practised upon his foster-parents; but it was impossible, accurate as Thalreuter's memory was, to ascertain the precise amount of that which he had robbed from them, as he very naturally had kept no accounts. The old Baron von Stromwalter could give no information whatever with regard to the state of his own affairs, and referred everything to the superior knowledge of his wife, and she, who had blindly committed everything to the hands of her James, had nothing to trust to but the vague and general impressions on her own weak memory. Thus much, however, is certain, that during little more than one year Thalreuter, by various dishonest means, got from them between 6000 and 8000 florins.

Such a varied and ingenious tissue of falsehoods, such a complication of deceits so long and so successfully practised by a boy of fifteen upon two old people of rank and education, seemed impossible without advisers and accomplices; and accordingly Thalreuter, with the same apparent frankness with which he had confessed his own crimes, now met the questions of the judge by the assertion that Stang, the toyman, had persuaded him to the forgery of all the false documents, that he had dictated the false bank order and fabricated the royal seal upon it, and that he had devised the scheme for cheating his foster-parents and had assisted in the execution of it. That among other things Stang had once appeared at Baron von Stromwalter's dressed in a brilliant uniform and covered with orders, and had given himself out as an envoy from Thalreuter's pretended father. He added that a considerable part of the money thus obtained had been employed by Stang in increasing his business and enlarging his shop, and also that many of the things stolen from his foster-parents had fallen to the share of Stang; and, not content with these accusations, he charged Stang with being a cheat and a forger by trade, with carrying on a regular fabrication of forged drafts, lottery tickets, exchequer bills, and tontine scrip, and with selling plated articles stamped with the mark of real silver. All these charges were supported by detailed statements of specific facts. Thus, for instance, he enumerated a long list of bills forged by Stang, specifying the persons by whom they purported to be drawn, the houses on which they were drawn, the persons who accepted them, and the time when the bills were negotiable, accompanying his statements with so many minute circumstances that it would have been easier to doubt the light of the sun at noonday than the truth of his assertions. At every fresh examination these charges were strengthened by new disclosures or new accusations, which, according to Thalreuter, recurred by degrees to his memory. Among other things Thalreuter even asserted that, in order to open a fresh supply to the failing resources of the Von Stromwalters, Stang had proposed to poison Baroness von Stromwalter's rich brother, and that he had prepared the poison, which he kept in a bottle in a place which Thalreuter described.

Stang, a married man, and the father of a family, was not exactly the sort of person whom one would suspect of such actions. He maintained himself, to all appearance honestly, by his business, which he had greatly extended by his activity, cleverness, and economy, and which was quite sufficient to support himself and his family respectably. But previous to the establishment of his toy-shop, which had happened within a few years, his life had not been altogether free from suspicion. He was originally a tailor, and then entered the service of a merchant, who discharged him in a short time, and gave him but a doubtful character. He then wandered about the country as a conjuror. It was notorious that Thalreuter and Stang were continually together, and that the latter took part in all Thalreuter's dissipations, and also that he lorded it in the Stromwalters' house. Moreover it appeared impossible for a lad of fifteen to have conceived or executed all that has been already related, without assistance; and Thalreuter's frank confession afforded sufficient ground for presuming that Stang was his accomplice, and for arresting him accordingly.

Thalreuter's accusations were not, however, confined to Stang; several other persons figured in this story as accomplices in a greater or less degree. Wolositz, a wealthy Jewish merchant, was pointed out by him as the receiver of Stang's bills, knowing them to be forged; and the accusation was supported by a statement of circumstances which gave it every appearance of truth. He likewise named an innkeeper called Brechtal, as one intimately associated in all Stang's criminal secrets, and whose business it was to travel about and pass these forgeries in the disguise of an officer. Thalreuter accused both these men, but more especially Brechtal, of instigating him to rob and cheat his foster-parents, and stated that he had bought for the latter out of the stolen money a horse, a butt of wine, &c.; and that inside of this butt hung a small watertight barrel, in which Brechtal kept Stang's forged bills. Wolositz and Brechtal were accordingly taken into custody, and four other persons were involved in the same suspicion by Thalreuter's charges.

In order to obtain proofs of the truth of the various charges, and to secure the articles designated by Thalreuter as belonging to the Stromwalters, the houses of the suspected parties were searched; Stang's house repeatedly, for no sooner was one search ended than Thalreuter prepared some new charge against Stang which rendered a fresh search necessary. Thalreuter, who was present on these occasions, employed himself in pointing out to the authorities either those things which belonged to his foster-parents, or had been bought with their money, or the materials, proofs, and instruments of the various forgeries. Each search led to fresh discoveries on Thalreuter's part, until at length the rooms appropriated to the purpose were crowded with effects of all sorts. In Stang's private dwelling the authorities seized silver spoons, tin and copper utensils, glasses, bottles and jars, napkins and table-covers, bedding, children's toys, and even articles of clothing, such as Stang's boots and trowsers. Out of his shop they took all sorts of objects of the supposed plated material, and other articles of value, watches, lace, buckles, telescopes, eye-glasses, ladies' reticules, rouge-boxes, cosmetics, scented pomatums and soaps. The innkeeper Brechtal fared no better: they took from him his gun and a pair of waterproof boots (for Brechtal was also a shoemaker); his horse out of the stable, and all the wine out of his cellar.

While these domiciliary visits were going on, the gaoler one day discovered, while changing Thalreuter's prison, seventeen florins concealed in his straw mat-

tress. On examination, Thalreuter confessed that
he had taken the opportunity of one of these visits at
Stang's house, to steal this sum out of his writing-
desk. When asked how this was possible, as one of
the officers of the court constantly had his eye upon
him, he replied that the presence of the officer had
not prevented his gaining possession of the money by
a sleight of hand which he had learnt from Stang
himself.

When the charges against Stang and others came
to be sifted, many of them proved to be utterly false.
A lottery ticket found in Stang's possession, and denounced as a forgery, was pronounced at Frankfort
to be genuine: several bills which he was accused of
having forged and put in circulation, were never presented. It was moreover discovered that no such
firms existed as those on which some of the other
bills were said to have been drawn. When this was
represented to Thalreuter on his twelfth examination,
he not only retracted a great part of his accusation
against Stang, but declared his whole statement about
Wolositz and the four others, who were most respectable persons, to be sheer calumny. His motives for
making all these false charges were various. One
had excited his hatred at a fight, another had abused
him ; a third had found fault with his conduct
behind his back, while a fourth had laughed at his
bad riding. Stang and Brechtal did not get out
of the scrape quite so easily, but every step in the
inquiry was the means of discovering some fresh
falsehoods, more especially with respect to Stang.
For example, all the articles which Thalreuter had
asserted to be plated were found to be real silver :

many of the things said to have belonged to Baroness von Stromwalter were not hers, but were proved to have been long in the possession of Stang and his family. The small secret barrel concealed in Brechtal's butt of wine never could be found, and the bottles said to contain poison for Baroness von Stromwalter's rich brother were filled with most innocent scent and hair-oil. Thalreuter, however, retracted only so much of his accusation against Stang as was proved to be false, and although forced to declare one charge after another to be mere inventions, he still persisted through several examinations in accusing his boon companion of enough to ensure him an imprisonment of several years with hard labour. It was not until his twenty-second examination that he declared all his accusations against Stang to be pure inventions dictated by revenge, adding that he could never forgive Stang for taking advantage of his youthful inexperience, and encouraging him in all his debaucheries and excesses. But these excuses for his false accusations were also false. In his twenty-sixth examination he was compelled to retract even this, and to own that he had no other reason for involving Stang in this criminal prosecution, than that Stang had charged him too much for his wares: neither had he any cause for accusing Brechtal, beyond that he had occasionally scored a double reckoning against him.

Thus it was proved beyond doubt that this young villain not only had no assistance in effecting the ruin of his old foster-parents beyond that of his own wit and the weakness and simplicity of the old people, but that he had also used the criminal court itself as a stage upon which further to display his instinctive talent for stealing and lying.

Those innocent persons who had been taken into custody upon Thalreuter's accusations were immediately released. Thalreuter, in consideration of his youth, was sentenced, on the 25th September, 1826, to eight years' imprisonment with hard labour, for his forgeries, thefts, and other deceits. He was to receive twenty-five lashes on his entrance into prison as a further punishment, and to have warm food only on every third day. Directions were also given that this young criminal should receive all necessary instruction, and that the greatest attention should be paid to his moral and religious training.

Fortunately for the community and for himself, Thalreuter did not outlive the term of his imprisonment. He died in 1828, in the Bridewell at Munich.

THE KLEINSCHROT FAMILY;

OR,

THE PARRICIDES OF THE BLACK MILL.

UPON a streamlet called the Sittenbach, which runs
at the bottom of a narrow glen enclosed within steep
mountains, stands the lonely Schwarz Mühle, or
Black Mill, at about 340 paces from the last house in
the neighbouring village. The miller, Frederick Kleinschrot, a strong, powerful man of about sixty, lived
there until the 9th August, 1817: he and all his
family were Protestants. His business was a thriving
one, and his property, as was subsequently proved,
amounted to a capital of 13,577 florins. He had
been married for thirty years, and had had twelve
children by his wife Barbara, five of whom were
still living. His eldest son, Leonard, was settled as a
master miller at a distance, but the second and third
sons, Conrad and Frederick, the former twenty-
eight and the latter twenty-three years of age, lived
in their father's house, the one managing the farm,
and the other assisting his father in the mill. The
two daughters, Margaret Barbara, aged twenty-three,
and Kunigunda, aged eighteen, supplied the place of
maid-servants.

In the farm-yard belonging to the mill, and not
above twenty paces distant from it, was a separate

cottage, rented at a low rate by a day-labourer of the name of John Adam Wagner. In addition to his rent, he was bound to work for the miller when required to do so, for six kreutzers a-day and his food.

Besides the miller's family and that of the day-labourer, a stable-boy of about thirteen lived at the mill. He slept in a distant stable, so that he could hear nothing that took place there by night.

On the 9th August, 1817, the master miller disappeared. It was not until the 11th October of the same year that his wife informed the provincial magistrate that her husband had left his home nine weeks ago, taking with him all the ready money, and that they were without any tidings of him. She requested that he might be publicly advertized, which was accordingly done, but without success, and that all outstanding claims might be called in. The property of the absent man was accordingly put into the hands of trustees appointed by the court.

About a year after his disappearance, it was rumoured abroad that he had been murdered in the Black Mill. The report no doubt arose out of suspicious expressions uttered by Wagner to one of his fellow-labourers of the name of Wiedman. One day when he was angry with the Kleinschrot family, he said to Wiedman, "If you did but know what I know, you would be surprised : if I were to tell of the miller's family, the mill would be shut up and they would all go to prison. If I want money, they must give it me ; and if I want the cottage, they must give me that too."

On the 1st September, 1818, Metsieder, a gen-

darme, informed the provincial court of this expression
of Wagner's. Suspicion was further increased by the
knowledge of the domestic quarrels which had constantly taken place in the Black Mill, and by the
strangely embarrassed manner of the miller's family
and of Wagner and his wife towards him (the in-
former).

The provincial magistrate had been already made
aware, by former proceedings, of the bitter animosity
subsisting between Kleinschrot and his family. Two
months before his disappearance the old man had laid a
complaint before the magistrate, that his wife and sons
had possessed themselves of his keys and his money,
and assumed the whole management of the house and
mill. That they had ceased to treat him with reverence, or to obey his orders, and had even threatened
him with blows. The wife and children, on the other
hand, replied that the plaintiff was a profligate spend-
thrift who neglected all the duties of a husband and
a father, and wasted his substance on low women.
The magistrate ordered them to submit to him as the
head of the family, and to restore to him the lawful
control over his own household. But on the following
day the miller complained to the magistrate that his
family would not abide by the decision of the court,
and that his children had actually struck him. A commission was accordingly sent to reinstate old Kleinschrot in his rights as head of the house. But even
in the presence of the commissioners, the family
expressed the bitterest hatred towards him, and declared their settled determination to obtain redress
from justice for his extravagance, profligacy, and
cruelty.

These and other circumstances, added to the statement of the gendarme, were sufficient grounds for
a serious inquiry. The provincial judge of the district took steps evincing great zeal in this matter.
On the very night in which this information reached
him, he caused Wagner and Wiedman to be arrested,
and went in person to the Black Mill, to examine the
miller's wife and her sons. Wiedman repeated before
the court the expression used by Wagner, which we
have already mentioned, and the common rumour
that Kleinschrot had been murdered in his mill, and
that Wagner had helped to bury the body in the saw-
mill. On the other hand, Wagner and the miller's
family maintained that old Kleinschrot had privately
absconded. The elder of the parish, who was examined as to the character of the Kleinschrot family,
declared that he knew nothing against either them
or Wagner; and a shepherd of the name of Sperber
stated, that during the hay harvest of 1817 he had
been employed by Kleinschrot to accompany him to
a neighbouring village, and to carry a bag of money,
which from its weight must have contained at least
2000 florins. Hereupon the proceedings were ab-
ruptly stopped. Wiedman was not examined upon
oath, the miller's daughters were not questioned at
all, and no search was made in the saw-mill, which
rumour pointed out as the spot in which the body had
been buried. The provincial judge, contrary to his
bounden duty, sent no report of the case to the central tribunal, and thus the matter rested for three
whole years.

In the autumn of 1821 the provincial judge of the district was suspended from his office on suspicion of mal-

versation. A commission was sent by the central court to direct the inquiry into his conduct, and to instal his successor. The commissioner had scarcely commenced the inquiry, when, on the night of the 11th November, a fire broke out in the record chamber, which was kept constantly locked, and the greater part of the records were destroyed, to the extreme injury of many members of the community. Suspicion immediately fell upon the suspended magistrate, who had an especial interest in the destruction of records which might betray his malpractices, and who moreover was alone able to effect it. The commissioner was directed to inquire into the origin of the fire, and with the view of discovering fresh cause of suspicion, and of confirming those already existing, he set on foot a rigid examination of the records which had escaped the flames, in order to discover those which the suspended magistrate might have had a peculiar interest in destroying. During the course of his research he found a small volume of documents relating to the appointment of trustees for the management of the absent miller's property. The rumour that Kleinschrot had been murdered by his own family, and that the magistrate had received a considerable bribe from them for letting the inquiry drop and hushing up the whole affair, reached the commissioner's ears at the same time. On further search, several other papers connected with the proceedings were discovered.

These were sufficient grounds for fresh investigation, and on the 6th December, 1821, Wiedman's evidence was taken on oath, and Wagner and Anna his wife were summoned as witnesses. Wiedman repeated his former statement: Wagner renewed his

assurances that he did not know what had become
of the miller; but his wife immediately confessed
"that in August or September, 1817, the miller's
sons tried to persuade her husband to assist them
in getting rid of their father: that she would not
suffer it, but that the sons never ceased urging
him, till at last her husband went one night into
the miller's bedroom, and helped the sons to murder
him; whereupon the body was buried in the cleft of a
rock near a field belonging to the miller." John
Wagner, who in the meantime had been given in
charge to a gendarme, in order to prevent any communication between himself and his wife, was examined afresh, and the following confession extracted
from him:—

Old Kleinschrot, who was a cruel husband and
father, and a man of most abandoned habits, lived in
constant enmity with his family. One morning in
September, 1817, his son Conrad informed him
(Wagner) that the Kleinschrot family had determined
to put their father to death, on the following night,
in order to save themselves from utter ruin. Conrad
promised to provide for him if he would assist them
in the deed, and told him how it was to be accomplished. After much hesitation he (Wagner) agreed.
Conrad fetched him at night, and, with the help of
the younger brother Frederick, they murdered the
old man in the kitchen. The body was first buried
in the saw-mill, but was afterwards carried away
from thence, thrown into the cleft of a rock in a field
called the Krumacker, and covered with earth and
stones. The miller's wife and daughters were privy
to the murder.

On the 7th December, the court resolved upon
the provisory arrest of the miller's family, and
proceeded that very evening with a proper guard to
the Black Mill, where the whole family were found
saying grace after supper. When the prayer was
ended, the warrant of arrest was shown to the miller's wife and her two sons : every member of the
family was then arrested, and confined separately.
The mother and her two sons were examined on the
spot, but confessed nothing. They asserted that all
they knew was that Kleinschrot had been gone for
some years, they knew not whither.

On the following day Wagner was fetched from the
prison to show where the body of the murdered man
had been buried. He led the authorities up a steep
ascent to the left of the mill, and across several fields,
till they came to a cleft among some rocks, which
Wagner pointed out as the spot. After removing
several loose stones, they came to some leaves and moss,
whereupon Wagner remarked, "that they must now
be near the body." Under the layer of leaves and
moss were found some tattered scraps of linen, part
of a skull, several ribs, and other bones, which the
physicians pronounced to be those of a man. When
these were taken out of the cleft, Wagner said,
" These must be the bones of the murdered Frederick
Kleinschrot of the Black Mill, for his sons brought
his body here in my presence four years ago, and
threw it into this cleft ; we then covered it with leaves
and moss. Moreover, Kleinschrot had remarkably
fine teeth, just like those in the jaw-bone before us."

The miller's children were then led separately, one
after the other, first to the place where the bones had

been deposited, and then to the cleft in the rock. As soon as Conrad saw the bones, he exclaimed, before a question was asked, "That is my father!" and added, after a pause, "but I am not the murderer." Frederick looked at them without betraying emotion or embarrassment, and on being asked, "What are these?" answered, "Why, what should they be but bones; but whether of a man or a beast I cannot say; I do not know the difference." The youngest daughter, Kunigunda, cried out when led to the cleft, "I know nothing about *this:* I know *that* about my father, but of what happened up here I know nothing; I am innocent, completely innocent." When it came to the turn of the eldest daughter, Margaret, she exclaimed, "I am innocent of the deed, I am innocent. I knew nothing about it till I heard my father's dreadful scream, and then it was too late. I have never had a moment's peace since. Oh, God! what will become of us?"

Thus, then, a mystery was brought to light which had been concealed for so many years—a murder committed by a hired assassin on the person of the miller, in which his wife, sons, and daughters were all more or less concerned as instigators or accomplices.

Barbara, the wife of the murdered man, and the daughter of a miller, was born on the 8th April, 1764. Her parents were, as the clergyman expressed it, "equally wanting in head and heart." Her memory and powers of comprehension were so defective that she could retain nothing at school. The little intellect she had ever possessed was so much impaired by the constant ill usage she had received from her husband during her long and unhappy marriage, that she occasionally sank into a state of stupidity bordering on idiotcy. Her husband's constant complaint was, that he had a wife so stupid that she could not manage her own household. All the witnesses concurred in describing her as a kind-hearted, patient, well-meaning woman, and of spotless life and reputation.

The same was said of her children by the clergyman and many other witnesses, who unanimously praised their piety, integrity, goodness, gentleness, love of order, and industry. But they were all deficient in intelligence, extraordinarily ignorant of everything which did not concern their own immediate occupation, and filled with the grossest superstition. They believed ghosts and witches to belong to the natural order of things. For instance, they were firmly persuaded that Wagner's wife was a witch, and Frederick took some trouble to convince the judge of it. As positive proof of the truth of his assertion, he related how, after refusing her something, she had plagued him unmercifully with the nightmare on the following night, and how she had once in his presence drawn circles round a haycock with her rake, muttering strange words the while, whereupon a whirlwind suddenly seized the haycock, lifted it high into the air, and bore it away as far as his eyes could reach, which plainly must have been witchcraft, as the other haycocks remained quietly standing in their places.

Old Kleinschrot was described as a man of considerable talent and information for his station in life, and as a good manager in a certain sense. He sent his children to school and communicated regularly twice a year; but his character was in every respect the very reverse of that of his kind-hearted wife and well-disposed children. Coarseness, cruelty, brutal violence, quarrelsomeness, and niggardliness, excepting where his own pleasures were concerned, were the principal ingredients of his repulsive and hateful character. He was an unnatural son, and had frequently raised his impious hand against his father, and forced him to take refuge from his violence behind locks and bolts. The son who illtreated his own father was still less likely to spare either wife or children, whom he looked upon as creatures born to serve and suffer under him. All his children on leaving school became his menial servants, and fulfilled their household duties with care and fidelity; in spite of which he refused them decent clothing, and allowed them and their mother to suffer the greatest privations, more especially whenever he left home for several days, on which occasions he left them no money for their daily wants. His ill-humour vented itself not only in abuse, but in actual violence. The peasant Röll, who had lived for twelve months in Kleinschrot's service about twenty years before, stated that the old miller never let a day pass without quarrelling with and beating his wife and sons, who were then boys. In his fury he seized the first weapon that came to hand. He once struck his wife such a blow with an axe that she had her arm in a sling for fourteen days. The daughter Margaret asserted that her mother had lost half her wits from a blow on the head which she received from her husband some fifteen years ago. The old miller's kept mistress, Kunigunda Hopfengärtner, who had formerly served at the Black Mill, had once been present when the miller flung a hatchet at his son Frederick, which must inevitably have killed him had he not started forward, so that it only grazed his heel. The schoolmaster once saw him beat his wife and children with a bar of iron.

The children, who beheld in their father only the tormentor and oppressor of their suffering mother, drew closer around her, and formed a defensive league among themselves, united by affection for the oppressed and bitter hatred towards the oppressor. The children felt bound to protect their mother, and to assist each other against the common enemy, whom they not only hated, but also despised; for they knew that their father, notwithstanding his age, constantly associated with the lowest women, by whom he had several illegitimate children, and upon whom he wasted his money, while his rightful children were suffering want. Kunigunda Hopfengärtner, a worthless creature who was sent to the house of correction soon after Kleinschrot's disappearance, had been kept by him for years, and declared him to be the father of her illegitimate child, born on the 7th April, 1817. When it was known at the mill that she was with child by old Kleinschrot, all the children, with the exception of the youngest daughter, rose up against him, and the quarrel reached such a pitch that the two sons, Conrad and Frederick, came to blows with him; one witness stated that Margaret, on being attacked by her father, snatched up a pitchfork with the words, "You old rascal, if you come near me I will stick it into your ribs." This, however, she strenuously denied.

In order fully to understand the character of the murdered man, and the terms on which he lived

with his family, it is necessary to hear the description which the wife and children gave of him. "You
cannot think," said the wife, "what a bad man my
husband was. He knocked my poor head about till I
quite lost my memory. Once when he had knocked
us down, my son Frederick and I lay all night bleeding
at the head in the hay-loft. He was a mischievous
man, as all who knew him can testify : he illused me
as no one else would use a beast, and for no possible
cause : he was always particularly savage at the holy
times of Christmas and Easter, and his fury against
every one then knew no bounds ; formerly too he
used to go by night to the place where four roads
meet, and where they say three things are to be got—
money, or help in fighting, or something else, and I
therefore believe that my husband stood in communication with the Evil One." The eldest son, Conrad,
drew the following picture of his father. "My
father was a savage man who never treated us as his
children, nor even called us his children, but always
rogues and thieves. When I was twelve years old he
illused me and left me lying in the mill quite senseless, and I bear the mark of one of his blows over my
right ear to this day, where there is a scar and no
hair. Once during harvest he beat me over the loins
so that I was obliged to crawl home and leave the
horses standing in the field. I lay in bed for two
whole days after it, and my father was cruel enough
to forbid my mother to give me any food, as I earned
nothing. No servant could stay with him ; he had
three or four in the course of the year, so that my
brother and I had to do all the work, and we did it
willingly. Every one will allow that we have im-

proved our property by our industry to the amount of 1000 florins and more : and yet he was never satisfied and constantly abused us and said that we cost him more than we earned. He never gave us clothes, and we went about in rags. But ill as he treated us, he treated our poor mother far worse. He was a monster in every respect, he could not endure our mother, called her by the vilest names, and frequently beat her so that she lay in bed for days : she bears the marks of his cruel treatment on her body to this day. Sometimes he kicked and beat her till she was so covered with blood that no one could have recognised her. Thus we lived in constant fear of our lives. Meanwhile he had three illegitimate children by women upon whom he spent the money which my mother had brought him at their marriage, for all the property was hers. We should have sought our living elsewhere long ago, but that we must then have left our mother exposed alone to our father's cruelty. At length we sought for protection from justice, but found none. Had he been like any other father, he might have been happy with his children, for we were honest, industrious, and well-conducted, as everybody knows. But he was a monster whose only pleasure was in tormenting others. He often beat his own father, who endeavoured to secure himself by six-fold bolts and locks, as you may see in the mill to this day, as well as the marks of the hatchet with which he tried to break open the door into the room where my grandfather had taken refuge, although it is now above twenty years ago."

The youngest son, Frederick, expressed himself much in the same manner " He was not a father, but a monster, who hated us from our youth up, and almost killed our mother by ill-usage. His whole way of life was a shame and a disgrace to us : we had plenty of quarrels and blows from morning to night, and but little food or clothing. Six months before he was put out of the way, my father dealt me such a blow on the head with a hoe, that the blood ran down into my shoes, and the wound did not heal for three-quarters of a year : the scar is still there. Once when I was leaving the mill I heard dreadful screams from the kitchen, and on going in I found my father striking my mother with a hatchet and threatening to kill her. He would certainly have murdered her but for me, for she was bleeding violently. I ran forwards, wrenched the hatchet out of his hands, and held him until my mother had escaped. I then let go of him and ran away, but not till I had received one blow on the loins and another on the arm, which prevented my working for several days. My mother and I slept that night in the barn, as we did not dare return to the house. My mother's body is covered with scars. My father's life was scandalous, and had been so from his youth. He had many illegitimate children, although his lawful ones were already grown up ; we even found him in bed with our maid-servant. He stole money from his father to spend in these profligate courses. A short time before his father's death, as I well remember, he seized the old man by the feet and dragged him down the stairs and out at the mill-door, so that his head was bruised and battered and covered with blood. Such was the monster we had as a father. Alas ! ever since we were born we have never known peace ; while our father lived we were tortured by him, and now since his death we are tortured by our consciences."

It is true that these statements were made by the murderers; but the coincidence of their testimony with the character given of the old miller by other impartial witnesses, leaves no doubt of their truth : indeed it is only on the supposition of such a father that we can comprehend how a wife and children, praised by all for their kindness and integrity, could be driven to commit so fearful a crime. He was himself the cause of all that befel him, and must be held morally answerable for a large share of the heavy guilt of the murder. His fate appears but as the act of avenging justice. He who had ill-treated and struck his own father fell by the hands of an assassin hired by his own children.

The following account of the murder and of its immediate cause is compiled from the confessions of the murderers.

The mother and sons had several times, in their impatience to be freed from their intolerable domestic oppression and misery, given utterance, even in the presence of strangers, to ideas of murder. Once, about a year or even longer before the murder, one of the sons said to John Schuster, a forester who accidentally came to the mill, " that he only wished he would shoot his father for a roebuck ;" and the mother added that " he should not then need to buy flour for some time to come." Schuster did not know whether this was meant in jest or earnest, and went away without answering a word. One evening, before Wagner lived in the cottage near the mill, a labourer of the name of Frederick Deininger was at work for the miller's family, and one of the sons said to him, " Whoever would put my father out of the way should be well paid for the job." Deininger is said to have replied that he could not do it, as the old man would be able to master him. The miller's family declared that these expressions fell from them in anger caused by a sense of recent injuries, and not from any pre-concerted scheme. Thus much, however, is certain, that the idea of killing the old miller was not strange to them, and that they would have been well pleased if any one to whom they had said as much in their anger had offered to do it for them. They wished him to be killed, but not by themselves.

An expression which the provincial judge impru-dently repeated several times tended to strengthen their desire for the old miller's death. When the sons endeavoured to obtain protection against the cruelty of their father, or complained of his extrava-gance, the judge dismissed them with the dishearten-ing observation, " I can neither assist nor advise you ; you have a bad and quarrelsome father ; the best thing that could happen would be his death." The mother and children concurred in saying that these words made the deepest impression upon them, and pointed out to them the only way that was open to them. It was evident that nothing was to be hoped from the protection of the law, and that there was no release for them but by their father's death, which now ap-peared to them to be both necessary and justifiable.

Subsequently, when the girl Hopfengärtner accused the old miller of being the father of her child, at which the irritation of the miller's family was so great as to cause the sons for the first time to lay violent hands on their father, these thoughts took a stronger hold of their minds than ever. Just at this time too, unhappily for them, a man was thrown in their way well able to understand thoughts of this kind, and who knew how to work upon men and to place their thoughts in a light which deprived them of nearly all their horror. This was Wagner, the day-labourer, a man exactly fitted to suit those who, without being villains themselves, stood in need of a villain to do that for the which they felt themselves too fainthearted.

John Adam Wagner was the son of a day-labourer, who was still living when the trial took place. He was born on the 9th November, 1769, and was a Lutheran. Common report gave him a very bad character, especially for cruelty. One of his childish amusements consisted in catching birds, putting out their eyes, and then letting them fly. He served first in the contingent of an imperial city, then for twenty years in the Prussian army, and in 1807 in that of Bavaria. He afterwards wandered about Prussia, Hanover, and Bohemia, and returned home in 1808 accompanied by a mistress. He then served for three-quarters of a year in the preventive service, after which he married a widow with two children, and supported himself with difficulty as a labourer. Those whom he served found no particular fault with him, excepting a certain unwillingness to work, owing probably to his long military career. Another consequence of this was an utter want of feeling added to his originally cruel nature, which he exhibited in the most revolting manner upon this trial. A murder, committed with every prospect of concealment, and for which he was well paid, was no more to him than any other task; at least he related all the circumstances of the horrid deed as circumstantially and as coolly as a labourer might do when called upon by his master to render an account of the work done on a particular day. 1817, the year of Kleinschrot's disappearance, was a year of famine, and Wagner had a wife and four children to support, for whom his wages were insufficient to buy bread, and he and his family often went supperless to bed. When, therefore, a prospect was opened to him of present gain and future support, he was ready to do anything.

It was Conrad Kleinschrot's misfortune to be constantly thrown into the company of this man, and while at work with him he often talked freely of the misery of his home and of his bitter hatred towards his father. On the 1st May, 1817, Conrad told Wagner that his father had again left home on the previous night, taking with him all the money, and that his mother and the family knew not what to do. "The best would be," said Wagner, "for some one to follow him, knock him on the head, and take away his money; it would be easy to kill him in the Hinterhof" (a dark ravine about three miles from the mill): "there he might lie, and no one be the wiser." Conrad answered, "Dare you do it?" "To be sure I dare," said Wagner. Conrad then objected that "a murdered man, especially one so wicked, would find no rest in his grave, but would walk the earth as a ghost." But Wagner bade him be at ease, for that "he knew how to lay the old man."

This conversation did not, however, lead to any

immediate result; it was merely an expression of the general feelings and wishes of the family. The same subject was, however, the constant theme of conversation whenever Conrad was alone with Wagner, and the only objections he raised were the possibility of discovery and fear of the old man's ghost. But Wagner was always ready with an answer to every scruple, doubt, or fear.

About six or eight weeks before the miller's death Conrad and Wagner were again thrown together, and Conrad again exclaimed, "How lucky it would be if the old man were never to return." Wagner, who saw that the family were not yet prepared for violence, endeavoured to tempt them to an indirect attempt on their father's life, and proposed to destroy the old man by a sympathetic charm. "He knew," said he, "a piece of magic by which he could make the old man perish like a waxen figure within four weeks." Conrad, who was as superstitious as the rest of his family, replied, "It would indeed be best if we could get rid of my father in this way," and entered heartily into the plan. His mother had already consulted Anna Wagner upon a scheme of this nature, and had given her a pair of old Kleinschrot's stockings, which were to be hung inside the chimney. The mother and sons waited some weeks hoping that the black art would produce its effect, but at length they informed Wagner that his magic had failed. Wagner, who was not easily disconcerted, rejoined, "Well, if magic fails, I must rid you of him by other means."

On the 7th June, 1817, when old Kleinschrot complained to the local authorities of the conduct of his family, he also petitioned that, to maintain his paternal authority and the order of his household, his sons should be sent on the Wanderschaft;* and on seeing that his sons did not obey the verbal order of the court, he renewed the request in writing. The mother and children were in terror lest old Kleinschrot should succeed in this application. She could not endure the thought that her sons, her only protection against her husband's cruelty, should quit her; and the sons, between whom the greatest unanimity prevailed, could not resolve to leave their mother exposed to the inhuman treatment of their father. In addition to this, the family were informed that the girl Hopfengärtner publicly boasted that the old miller was going to turn all his own family out of doors and to take her as his housekeeper: they likewise suspected that he intended to procure a formal divorce from his wife.

During all the early part of August Kleinschrot was busily employed in his own chamber in writing something which the wife and her children imagined to be intended against themselves. The youngest son, Frederick, probably at his mother's instigation, stole into his father's room on the 9th August to discover what he had been writing all. the week, and found a memorial addressed to the provincial authorities demanding the removal of his wife and sons from the mill. Frederick hastened upstairs with the paper and read it to his mother and to Conrad. Their consternation was extreme, especially that of the mother, who lamented at the thought of being divorced in her old days to make room for a harlot.

---

* The custom of travelling for three years, and supporting themselves by occasional work and sometimes by begging.— *Trans.*

Wagner's suggestion was mentioned, and it was resolved that he should murder the old miller on the following night. It is not known who first gave utterance to their common feeling; in all probability it was the mother; at least so Conrad positively asserted. The mother did not deny that she and her sons had consulted together about putting her husband to death; but whether, when the murder was determined upon, she had told Conrad that he might go and settle the matter with Wagner, was more than she could say, as her memory was so defective. She, however, admitted that if her sons said so, they were probably right; she could no longer remember the exact words in which she had consented to her husband's murder; but in all her confessions she repeated that the fear of separation from her children, and of being divorced in favour of a worthless woman, had led her to say to her sons, " that she consented to Wagner's being employed to kill her husband." She even added, " If I had not agreed to it, the murder would never have happened; but I did agree, and I said so to my sons."

The two daughters, Margaret and Kunigunda, had taken no part whatever in the consultation upon the murder. When it was already determined and Frederick was leaving the room, they entered it accidentally and found Conrad with his mother. Their brother then told them what was about to happen, and, according to her own account, Margaret replied, " Do not do this. If our father leads a bad life, he will have to answer for it in the next world: let him live, and leave him to his conscience if he has behaved ill." On hearing that Wagner was to put her father out of the way that very night, she said to her brother, " Do not suffer it; Wagner is a bad man, who will bring you into trouble in order to get money."

Frederick, the younger son, appears to have taken no part in the transaction until the day of the murder. He had no communication with Wagner, and did not remember that his brother had formerly told him that Wagner had offered to rid them of the old man. On the contrary, he repeatedly stated that on the 9th August, after reading the memorial which he had found in his father's chamber, his mother, as he thinks, proposed that the miller should be murdered by Wagner; whereupon he had exclaimed, " Oh, mother, that would be a horrid thing; I would rather go away than that such a thing should happen." But when his brother represented to him that " if they two went away, the miller would marry a worthless woman, and have a number of children and waste their whole patrimony;" and his mother added that " there was no help for it;" he at length gave way, saying, " Well, as you please, if you think it right to do it; I agree to anything."

When the matter was thus settled, Conrad went out, called Wagner, and asked him whether he would still undertake to murder the old man on the following night. On Wagner's replying in the affirmative, Conrad promised to give him 200 florins down, and never to lose sight of him, but to give him something every year.

They passed the afternoon together in the fields, talking the matter over, and devising how the plan was to be carried into execution. Conrad reiterated his former doubts as to whether Wagner really thought it would succeed, and supposing it did, whether his father would rest in his grave, and whether the crime might not be discovered, and their lives endangered. Conrad even desired him to consult his wife on the subject. But Wagner overruled his scruples, and it was definitively settled that the murder should take place on the following night.

On the evening of the 9th August, old Kleinschrot supped in company with his wife, his children, and the Wagners. After supper Wagner and his wife returned to their cottage, and Kleinschrot went into his bedroom, which communicated with the kitchen by a small flight of steps. At about ten o'clock, after his mother and sisters were in bed, Conrad went to Wagner, and told him that everything was quiet. Wagner immediately armed himself with a hatchet, and returned to the mill to earn his two hundred florins. Wagner and Conrad had agreed during their afternoon's walk that old Kleinschrot should be lured into the dark kitchen, and there killed by Wagner. After a long opposition, Frederick consented to ring the mill bell, which would bring his father out of his bedroom. At first he refused, as he knew that his father was in the habit of going into the mill every night, and he thought that Wagner might wait till then. At length, however, he went to the mill, and rang the bell. Meanwhile Wagner stood beside the steps leading from the bedroom, with the axe in his hand, and Conrad went to his own room, and sat on his bed waiting the event.

Wagner stood with his hatchet raised and ready to strike, when the mill bell rang violently. The old

miller came out of the bedroom in his shirt, and when
he had reached the lowest step, Wagner aimed a
blow at his head with the back of the hatchet. He,
however, missed it in the dark, and struck him somewhere else. Either from fright or pain the miller
uttered a loud scream, which was heard by Conrad
and his mother and sisters in their beds, and endeavoured to run back into his room. But Wagner,
having missed his blow, threw away the hatchet and
seized the miller, who defended himself, occasionally
exclaiming, " Oh God ! oh God ! let me go," " Let
me go, my dear fellow, and I will never injure you
again as long as I live." They struggled together
for some time, and such was the old miller's strength,
that Wagner at one time thought he should be overpowered by him. At length Wagner remembered
that he had a clasp knife, and, loosening his hold
of the miller for a moment, he drew it out of his
pocket, opened it against his own body, and thrust
the blade into the old man's side.

On hearing his father scream, Conrad concluded
that Wagner's blow had failed, and rushed out of the
house in terror ; he ran round the saw-mill, but soon
returned, and on hearing repeated cries for help, went
into the kitchen. His father had received the stab,
but still stood upright, moaning. Conrad took a log
of wood from the pile in the corner of the kitchen,
reached it to Wagner, and then ran out into the road
to see if all was safe.

Wagner, who had dropped his knife in the meantime, struck the miller on the head with the billet of
wood. He staggered, and fell back upon the hearth.
But this blow lost part of its force owing to Wag-

ner's proximity to his victim, and the miller still lived, and lay groaning. Wagner therefore snatched up a brick which lay on the hearth, and struck the miller with it on the head, until the brick was broken to pieces. The miller at length ceased from moaning.

Meanwhile Conrad had gone in again, but he had scarcely lain down on his bed when Wagner came and told him that his father was dead, and requested him to bring a light. Conrad went to the mill to fetch Frederick, and the two brothers returned to the kitchen with a candle. They found their father weltering in his blood, but still breathing faintly. Wagner then asked Frederick for a string : he gave him a bit which he happened to have in his pocket, and went away. Wagner placed it round the miller's throat, intending to strangle him, but did not tighten it, as the old man was already dead.

While all this was going on, Margaret went quietly to sleep, and even after her father's fearful scream had awakened her, she did not ask what had become of him. Cunigunda also went to bed at about ten o'clock, at her brother's request, because, as she said, she had done her work, and was afraid to interfere, lest her brother or Wagner should do her a mischief. Wagner and Conrad dragged the dead body into the bedroom, laid it on the floor near the bed, and locked the door. After refreshing himself with a glass of brandy, Wagner returned to his cottage to rest. Conrad went upstairs to his mother, exclaiming, " Oh, mother, if the deed were not done, it never should be done." The mother did not shed a single tear ; for, said she, her husband had used her so ill that she thought that God himself must have inspired her children and herself with the idea of having him murdered. When asked on her final examination, whether she believed that it would go well with her after death, she replied, " Certainly I do believe that I shall be received into God's mercy ; for I have suffered so much in this world, that there would be no such thing as justice if it were not made up to me in the next."

Early on the following morning, which was Sunday, Conrad fetched Anna Wagner. She washed out the blood-stains in the kitchen, and received the bucket she had used as a reward. Conrad and his brother went in the afternoon to the fair at Petersau, not for pleasure, but because they had been invited by their customers, and could not well avoid going. Far from amusing themselves, they stole away to a neighbouring hill, fell on their knees, and prayed to God for forgiveness of their crime.

Early on Monday morning Wagner rolled the corpse in some linen, given him for the purpose by the old miller's wife, and sewed it up in a sack which Anna Wagner had made of some coarse canvas. He then dug a hole at the back of the saw-mill, whither Conrad and Wagner carried the corpse at midday, and Wagner buried it with the assistance of his wife. Frederick stamped down the loose earth over his father's grave, while his mother stood in the doorway praying.

Here the dead body lay for nearly a year ; but about Michaelmas, 1818, when it was rumoured abroad that the old miller had been murdered, and buried in the saw-mill, it was disinterred by Wagner and Conrad. The two brothers carried it on a bier to

some rocks in a field called the Weiheracker, where
they and Wagner covered it with stones aud moss.
Wagner was rewarded for this job with another hundred florins.

_____

This case presented many difficulties; above all,
that of the *That bestand,* or fact of a murder having
been committed.

It was impossible to prove the violent death by
inspection of the remains *(augenschein)*, as the body
was entirely decomposed, and the bones so scattered,
that there were not enough forthcoming to form a
complete skeleton.   The physician supposed that some
of the larger bones lay still deeper and had not been
discovered, but it is more likely that a fox or some
other animal had knawed the body and carried away
the missing parts.

The only fact juridically proved was that old
Frederick Kleinschrot was no longer alive; but according to the Bavarian code the confession of one
criminal is, under certain circumstances, equal to the
testimony of a competent witness;* how much
stronger therefore were the concurrent confessions of
several accomplices, whose statements were evidence
not only against themselves, but against each other?
But this same code further requires† that when a
violent death is not distinctly proved by the remains,
the witness or witnesses shall prove that " the injuries were of such a nature that death must necessarily have ensued from them." This was not the
case with old Kleinschrot: there was nothing to

_____

* Art. 280, No. 3, Part II., of the ' Strafgesetzbuch.'
† Ibid., Art. 269, 271.

show that the stab or the blows on the head were mortal.

Thus, therefore, although no reasonable man could doubt that the miller, Frederick Kleinschrot, died of the injuries which he had received, the legal evidence was incomplete. For although it was certain that he was dead, and moreover that his death had been caused, according to the full confession of the accomplices, by bodily injuries inflicted by themselves, nevertheless it was not proved either from inspection of the remains, or by any witness, or by the opinion of the examining physician, that these injuries were fatal. The Bavarian criminal law requires certainty, and does not admit the ordinary conclusion from *post hoc* to *propter hoc.*

As the murder had not been judicially proved, sentence of death could not be passed upon any one of the criminals; but they were found guilty, according to their several gradations in crime, of attempt to murder.* Wagner had done everything in his power to accomplish the murder; nothing was wanting but the legal proof that his attempt had been successful. Conrad also was evidently a principal : he had hired the assassin and originated the deed, which in his case was more criminal, as the victim was his own father. These two were accordingly sentenced to the severest punishment short of death—solitary imprisonment for life in heavy chains, involving civil death and previous public exposure.

Frederick Kleinschrot was considered as accessory in the first degree, and was sentenced to imprisonment for fifteen years.

* Art. 60, Part I., ' Strafgesetzbuch.'

The mother, Barbara Kleinschrot, as accessory in the second degree and with extenuating circumstances, was sentenced to only eight years' imprisonment in the house of correction.

The elder daughter, Margaret, would have been considered as accessory in the third degree* had the evidence against her been clear; but both she and her younger sister Cunigunda, who appeared to be of very weak intellect, were acquitted for want of evidence.

Anna Wagner pleaded in her justification that she had acted in obedience to her husband. By the Bavarian code,† a person who knows that a crime is about to be committed and does nothing to prevent it, which he may do without thereby exposing himself to danger, becomes accessory in the third degree, and liable to imprisonment in the house of correction of from one to three years' duration.

This was precisely Anna Wagner's predicament; and in consideration of her confession which produced the discovery of this long-concealed murder, the court sentenced her to the smallest amount of punishment, one year's imprisonment in the house of correction.

The sentences against Wagner and Conrad were sent for confirmation to the central court of Bavaria; the others were only to be sent in case of their being appealed against.

When Frederick Kleinschrot heard the sentence pronounced on him, on the 12th August, he was violently agitated. "I cannot bear my sentence, but will appeal against it. I can never endure the punish-

* Art. 78, No. 2, ' Strafgesetzbuch.'　　　　　† Ibid.

ment awarded me, and would much prefer death to fifteen years' imprisonment in the house of correction. Neither am I convinced that it is just to condemn me to so severe a punishment on account of a man who was so wicked as my father. As long as my father lived my home was a cruel prison, and if I am to live fifteen years more in another, I would rather die."

His mother also at first declared that she would appeal, but eventually they both submitted to their sentence.

Frederick afterwards said, "What determines me not to appeal is, that I shall thus be freed from the misery of suspense, and that I have some hope of being released from prison when I shall have proved by my conduct that I am only erring and not corrupt."

On the 16th November the supreme court confirmed the sentence on Wagner and Conrad. They were both exposed in the pillory with placards on their breasts and the irons in which they were to die riveted upon them. They were then led to their solitary cells.

In the pillory Conrad's demeanour was as might have been expected from him : conscious of his guilt, he endured his punishment in silence, with his head sunk on his breast. Wagner, on the contrary, gazed upon the assembled multitude with an air of impudent defiance, and once even held up the placard which proclaimed his infamy, as if to show it to the crowd more plainly.

JOHN GEORGE SÖRGEL,

THE IDIOT MURDERER.

Conrad Eichmüller, of Lenzenberg, a day-labourer seventy-one years old, and feeble with age, had been employed for about a week on a hill in the forest near Hersbruck, in digging and cutting up stumps of trees. He always went to his work early in the morning, and returned home before dark, usually at five o'clock; but on the 7th of September, 1824, night began to close in, and he was not come back. His wife, a woman of sixty-two, became uneasy about him, and sent her son by a former marriage, a young man called Lahner, with some other youths, to look after him. They soon returned with the news that the old man was lying dead in the forest, and took with them some men, and a cart to fetch the body.

Eichmüller was found about three feet from the stump at which he had been working, and in which three wedges were still sticking; he was lying with his face towards the ground; his skull shattered, and both feet chopped off; the left foot still adhered to the body by the boot, but the right lay under a tree at a distance of four or five feet; traces of blood clearly showed that he had been dragged from the spot where he was at work, after he had been killed and his feet had been chopped off: his jacket and his two axes were scattered about, and one of the latter was stained with blood in a manner which left no doubt that it had been used in the murder and mutilation of the unfortunate old man. The wife had charged her son to take possession of the money which her husband had in his pocket, amounting to about two florins, but on searching the body nothing was found upon it save one button in the breeches pocket.

The deed was no sooner made public than the murderer was known and brought before the tribunal at Hersbruck.

On the 7th of September (the day of the murder), Paul Deuerlein, a day-labourer, was driving a cartload of grain from Reichenschwand to Hersbruck, and at about five o'clock in the afternoon he overtook young Sörgel on the road, and called out to him, " Where do you come from ? the Hansgörgle, eh ?" Sörgel replied, pointing to the hill, " A year ago some one buried my blood up there ; I went to look for it last year, but it had not curdled then, and he who had buried it flogged me soundly. To-day I went up there again to look after my blood, and he who buried it was there again, and had horns, but I hit him on the head with the hatchet, chopped off his feet, and drank his blood." Deuerlein, who knew that Sörgel was foolish at times, took no heed of what he said; meanwhile they came to Hersbruck, where Sörgel's father was waiting for him at the door of the poorhouse, into which he and his family had been received.

Sörgel came quietly along with Deuerlein, who told the father, in the presence of a blind man called Albert

Gassner, what his son had been saying. The father scolded his son for talking such nonsense; but he replied, " Yes, father, it is quite true that I knocked a man on the head, and chopped off his feet; I killed him in order to drink a felon's blood; and the man had horns upon his head." Gassner followed Sörgel into his room, where he added, " I also took from him a purse of money, but I threw it away again, for I will never keep what is not mine." Gassner said, jesting, " Oh, you kept the money, to be sure;" whereupon Sörgel was angry, and said, " Hold your tongue, or I will strike you dead."

About an hour later Sörgel went into the barn of the inn next door to the poorhouse, laughing heartily, and said to Katharine Gassner, " Now I am well again; I have given it to some one soundly; I hit him on the head, and chopped off both his feet, and one of them I threw away." Katharine was frightened at this speech, especially as she perceived blood upon his face: when she asked him how it got there, he answered, " I drank a felon's blood;" and he went on to tell her that the man was sitting on the ground filling a pipe, and that he (Sörgel) took up the man's hatchet, which lay beside him, struck him with it on the head, and took two florins which he had upon him.

In the evening he told Katharine Götz, the daughter of the sick-nurse in the poorhouse, that he had come upon a woodcutter who was digging up stumps in the forest, and that at first he had helped him at his work, but that the man then appeared to him to have horns, whereupon he took up the hatchet and hit him on the head, that the man groaned very much, and he then chopped off both his feet, and drank his blood.

Old Sörgel, who looked upon his son's story as a symptom of returning insanity, to attacks of which his son was subject, chained him to his bed by way of precaution. The son bore it quietly, ate his supper, and joined in prayer with the rest of the family as usual, and then lay down; but towards morning he broke out in raving madness, stormed, and tugged at his chain, which he endeavoured to break. In this state he was found by the constables when they went to arrest and take him before the court, and they were accordingly forced to depart without him. Soon after, however, he became perfectly quiet, and his own father and another man took him before the court, unfettered, on the 8th of September.

He was immediately examined in the presence of his father and his father's companion. On being questioned, he stated that his name was John George Sörgel, that he was twenty years of age, a Protestant, the son of a day-labourer, born in the poorhouse at Hersbruck, unmarried, and without property, and that he had learned the trade of a knife-grinder and of a chimney-sweep. On being asked whether he had ever been in custody before, he replied, " Oh, no; who would do any harm to me—I am an angel." He then related the murder as follows :—" I went yesterday with my father to the wood called the Hansgörgle—I left my father, and saw at a distance an old man digging up stumps of trees—I did not know this man; but it seemed to me that my own blood was buried under the stump, and I formerly dreamed that my parents were shut up in that place, and that I must drink the blood of a felon. So I went up to the old man and struck him on the head with his hatchet, and chopped off both his feet. I then drank the blood out of his head, left him lying there, and went home." When asked what could induce him to commit such a deed, he said, " The thing is done and I cannot help it; it was because I thought he was digging up my blood. Sörgel signed the protocol properly, but during the examination he stared about him wildly, showed great restlessness, and fidgeted with his feet and hands; moreover, he continually expressed a desire of becoming a soldier, and could only be kept in the room by the promise that his wishes should be complied with.

On the same afternoon he was taken to Lenzenberg to see the body, which he approached without the slightest air of dismay, embarrassment, or remorse. When asked whether he recognised it, he said, " Yes, it is the same man whom I struck yesterday evening, he is dressed in the same clothes; I chopped off his feet so that he might never be laid in chains again." During this scene he displayed the same bodily restlessness as he had done at his examination. He frequently laughed, and said that he was an angel, and that he had known very well that the old man was good for nothing.

On the following day, 9th of September, the judges went into the prison of the accused to examine him again. When asked how he felt, he said, " My head is very full, and I have bad dreams; among other things I dreamt that I must go up to the Hansgörgle; where there is a clock which strikes very loud." You told us yesterday that you had killed a man : how did you do that? " I saw an old man digging up stumps

in the Hansgörgle, and I went and sat down near
him. I took up his hatchet, which lay beside him,
and struck him with the back of it upon the head, so
that he instantly fell down dead ; then I chopped off
both his feet. He had an old wooden tobacco-pipe in
his hand, which he dropped when I struck him ; I took
the pipe, but threw it away directly. I also took his
flint and steel, and kept them" (these were found upon
him by his father, and delivered to the court). Sörgel
steadfastly denied having taken any money from the
old man, or having confessed to any one that he had
done so, nor was a single coin found upon him. Why
then did you chop off the man's feet? "In order that
he might not be laid in chains." Why did you kill
him? " I struck him because I thought he was going
to dig up my own blood." He then went on to say
that a strange woman had once told him he must drink
felon's blood to be cured of the falling sickness; and
he added that he had felt much better since he had
drunk the old man's blood. I knew, said he, that it
was forbidden to kill people, but I killed the man
in order to be cured by his blood. It happened soon
before five in the afternoon, and I first drank the blood
from the man's head, and then dragged him to a little
distance and cut off both his feet; the left foot remained attached to the boot, and the right foot I threw
away." The blood-stained hatchet was then . laid
before him ; he looked at it attentively, and said at last,
" Yes, that is the hatchet with which I struck the
man and chopped off his feet." He also recognised
the flint and steel which were shown him. The examination concluded with the following questions and
answers :—Do you repent of what you have done?

" Why, he beat me soundly last year, and that is why
he did nothing to me when I hit him on the head."
On what occasion did the man beat you last year?
" I went to the woods once before to catch birds, and
he beat me then."

On the 15th of September the court was informed
that Sörgel had been perfectly quiet for several days,
and that he talked coherently, without any mixture of
foolish fancies. The judges hereupon repaired to his
prison in order to avail themselves of this interval of
reason for an examination. His appearance and manner were totally changed ; when the authorities came
in he took off his cap, and greeted them civilly, which
he had never done before, at the same time addressing
the judge by name. On being asked, he said he had felt
much better ever since he had been bled by order of
the physician. That before that he had not been at all
well, that his head had been dizzy and full of strange
fancies, and that he had dreamt all manner of nonsense.
He was then asked if he knew the cause of his arrest.
" My father," said he, " who generally watches beside
me at night, told me that I ran away from him
in the Hansgörgle and killed a woodcutter, so I suppose that is why I am in prison." Did he remember
going to the Hansgörgle with his father. " No ; I
should know nothing of the matter had not my father
told me about it the other day. I know nothing at all
of having killed a man ; and if I did so, it must have
been the will of God who led me thither." He was
then reminded that he had himself twice told the court
that he had killed a woodcutter with his own hatchet.
" I remember," said he, " that you were here in my
prison, and that somebody wrote at yonder table, but

I know nothing of having confessed that I killed a man." He as positively denied any recollection of having had a dead man with his legs chopped off shown to him, or that a bloody hatchet and a flint and steel had been laid before him, both of which he recognised. Nevertheless, he knew that he had been imprisoned for about ten days, and that it was Saturday. He admitted having heard, as he added, from his mother, who had heard it from some one else, that the blood of a felon was a cure for the falling sickness, but observed that the man he killed was no felon, but rather that he himself must be one. Still he maintained that he never remembered drinking human blood or killing the woodcutter. " Every one tells me that I did so," said he, "and therefore I am bound to believe it, but I must have been out of my mind at the time." During the whole examination his demeanour was quiet and collected, he spoke coherently, and without any confusion of ideas, and his look was open and unembarrassed.

The next examination was deferred until the 28th September, but nothing new was elicited. Sörgel still answered every question by declaring that he knew absolutely nothing of all that he had formerly related to the court and to other persons. The flint and steel were shown to him, but he denied all knowledge of them, or of how they had come into his possession. The axe was likewise laid before him, but he said " I don't know it." The court remarked that during the whole examination the prisoner behaved with composure and propriety, was perfectly easy and unconstrained, and that his countenance was open and cheerful.

It is evident that the utter ignorance of all he had done, which Sörgel professed during the examinations of the 15th and 28th August, was not affected. Falsehood is never so perfectly consistent as were his declarations in the two last examinations, nor can dissimulation ever appear so frank and unconstrained as the demeanour of this young man, who was, moreover, described by all who knew him as a simple, kindhearted, pious lad when in his right senses. At both the two last examinations he showed himself perfectly sane, whereas if he had had any reason for wishing to deceive the judge, nothing would have been easier for him than to continue playing the part of a madman. If his ignorance at the two last examinations was affected, his former madness must necessarily have been equally false, a supposition which is contradicted by all the evidence. None but a Garrick could have acted madness with such fearful truth and nature. Nor was a murderer at all likely first to confess his crime in the assumed character of a madman, and then to affect forgetfulness of the past upon pretending to recover reason. If, again, he were really mad when he committed the crime, when he related it and when he recognised the corpse and the blood-stained axe, he could have no conceivable motive for acting forgetfulness of deeds committed and words uttered during a paroxysm of insanity.

His behaviour in court on the 3rd November, when his advocate's defence was read to him, confirmed the truth of his statement. His advocate pleaded for an acquittal on the ground that he was not accountable for his actions. During the reading of this paper Sörgel's manner was unconstrained and almost indif-

ferent: he listened to it attentively, but without the
slightest emotion. On being asked whether he was
satisfied with the defence, whether he had anything to add, and if so, what ? he answered, " I have
nothing to add, and what yonder gentleman has
written is quite to my mind. As I have often said, I
know nothing about killing any man, and if I did so,
it must have been while I did not know what I was
about. If I had been in my right mind, as I am now,
I certainly should not have harmed any one." To
the inquiry how he felt, he replied, " Very well, but
a few days ago my keeper tells me I was very crazy
again and talked all manner of nonsense, but I do not
know a word of the matter."

As yet we have confined ourselves merely to Sörgel's
murder and trial, but in order to understand his state
of mind and the event to which it gave rise, we must
examine his previous history, as collected from the
evidence of his parents and other persons who observed him shortly before the trial.

John George Sörgel was the son of a very poor
day-labourer who lived in the poorhouse at Hersbruck. He received a proper school education, by
which he profited very well : he was fond of reading
and wrote a fair legible hand.   From his earliest
youth he was always very industrious, helping his
father in his work to the utmost of his power, civil
and gentle towards every one, and very piously inclined. His leisure hours were occupied in reading
religious books, especially the Bible, in which he
was well versed : his mind thus became filled with
vague images of angels, devils, hell, heaven, divine
revelations, and the like, mixed up with a large stock

of vulgar superstition. These images formed the basis of the world of dreams into which he was thrown by madness. In the year 1820 he was apprenticed to a chimney-sweeper. His master gave the highest testimony to his industry, good-will, attention, and morals; but at the end of a year he was compelled to leave his work owing to a violent attack of epilepsy, which forced his master to release him from his apprenticeship and to send him home. From that time he remained subject to that disease in its most virulent form: he not unfrequently had several fits during the day, once even as many as eight. These constant fits weakened his understanding without in the least blunting his imagination, and he fell into a state of morbid melancholy, arising partly from bodily infirmity and partly from the thought that his illness kept him at home a burden to his family, and debarred him from the possibility of occupation or enjoyment.

In the spring of 1823 the disorder of his mind broke out for the first time into positive madness. He lay in bed, ate nothing, stared at one corner of the room, spoke little, except at times when he poured out wild and incoherent speeches almost entirely upon religious subjects, saying that the Saviour had appeared to him and had talked and eaten with him, that his father and mother would go to heaven, where there was no water to drink, but only wine, and sweet things to eat. The constable, Andreas Lauter, who visited him during this attack, said, " Sörgel shouted, preached, and sang hymns without ceasing for twenty-four hours together. He told us that he had been with God and had talked to him. When I entered the room he called to his mother to withdraw, for that I was the devil : he was lying in bed at the time. I reminded him of it since, but he remembered nothing at all of the matter." In this condition he remained, according to his mother's account, for a week ; according to his father's, for a month. He then recovered completely, talked rationally and coherently, and went to work again as before, and for nearly a year he had no relapse ; but in the spring of 1824 he had fresh attacks, which did not at first last long, but gradually increased in frequency and in violence.

"This spring," says Katharine Gassner, an eyewitness, "three young men of the town passed the poorhouse singing and hallooing on their way to foreign parts. This perhaps vexed young Sörgel, who stood at the gate and began as if he were preaching — ' I am the collier lad. . They go forth rejoicing, and I have the falling sickness, and am left behind in grief and sorrow.' He instantly became restless and uneasy, and we saw that some change was taking place in him. The wife of Götz, the attendant on the sick, tried to quiet him and to persuade him to go back to his room, but he struck her twice on the face and went out upon the high road, where he walked up and down with a disturbed and angry air. At this moment a stranger came along the road, and Sörgel went up to him, knocked his hat off his head, struck him with his fist, and trampled the hat under foot. The stranger, surprised at this unexpected attack, was going to beat him, but his mother, Götz's wife, and I, ran up and pacified him by explaining that the young man was out of his senses." Another witness gave the same account of this occurrence, with the addition that he said in a preaching tone, " I am a little hare ; I am the Lord Jesus, and make the grass to grow."

In the course of the following night he secretly got out of the window and ran in his shirt to the church-yard of the neighbouring village.

In the month of May he was working with his father in a hop-ground, when he suddenly began to thrust the iron bar with which holes are bored for the hop-poles violently into the ground, saying, " Now I am thrusting down into hell." He then ran home to his mother and told her that he would tie no more hops, as he was floating between heaven and earth. He then ran away to Scherau, a wilderness surrounded with fish-ponds : on his way he pulled off his boots and left them on a hill. At Scherau he jumped into a pond, pulled off his trowsers and stockings, and threw them into the water. At nine o'clock at night on the 14th May he came in his shirt to a farmer's house and shouted through the window, " Which way must I go to get upon earth again ?" The farmer's son came out and asked him who he was and what he was about, and he replied that he had run away from home because the earth gave way under his feet while he was binding hops. He repeated this answer next day before the magistrate at Altorf, to whom he was taken by the farmer's son, and who sent him home to his parents."

For several months after this he was quite sane, but in the first week of September he exhibited the first symptoms of a fresh and far more terrible attack. " On the Wednesday preceding the murder," said Margaret Götz, to whom Sörgel was secretly attached, " he complained of a great weight upon his heart, but did not seem at all wrong in his mind. On the Thursday, as I was sitting at my work in the court of the poorhouse, he said to me, ' Margaret, this weight is terrible; I never felt anything like it before; I think I must be going to die.' On Friday I observed that he talked wildly. He did not come and sit with me and the other women, but sat apart by himself; he stared wildly, laughed like a madman, and said he was going down into hell. His friend, the blind Albert Gassner, came in; he seized him by the forehead, pulled open his eyelids, and said ' Now you will see;' and when Gassner said that he could not see now nor ever should, Sörgel replied, ' Wait a bit; I will take a knife and cut your eyes open, and then you will see;' which frightened Gassner so that he ran away. On Saturday, 4th September, he stayed nearly all day in my parents' room, where there was a soldier lying sick. He did not seem to like this, and frequently asked the soldier to get up and go away with him. I turned him out at the door several times, but he always returned, and once he gave me such a terrible look that I was quite frightened. On Sunday (5th) he told me that he had a hair in his mouth that reached down into his stomach, and begged me to pull it out. I was going to do so, but his mouth was so full of foam that I was frightened. He then went to the well and rinsed his mouth, saying all the time that he felt so ill he must be going to die. In the evening he lay upon the bench in my room and hung his head down backwards, which I forbid him several times, but he always did it again. On Monday afternoon he kept walking up and down in the passage, and at last threw himself violently upon his face, crying 'Kill me, kill me!' and in the evening he threw himself down in the same manner under a tree, so that his father had to carry him away." Katharine Gassner and Elizabeth Hecklin gave evidence to precisely the same effect.

After his father had taken him home on Monday evening, he again tried to escape through the window, whereupon old Sörgel sent to the constable for a chain and padlock, and chained his son to the wall beside his bed, to which he quietly submitted.

On Tuesday morning young Sörgel appeared perfectly tranquil, and begged his father for God's sake to unfetter him. His request was complied with, and he prayed and breakfasted with his parents. At last he proposed to his father to take a walk with him up the old hill, about three miles from Hersbruck, as it might divert his thoughts and do him good. His father consented and they set out together at about eight o'clock. When they reached the very top of the mountain, young Sörgel jumped down a steep bank, broke through the thicket and disappeared. His father, seeing that it was impossible to follow him, went home, in order to prevent mischief there. What followed our readers already know.

Nothing is more remarkable than that Sörgel's confessions, which were made during his fits of madness, should, with one single exception, tally so accurately in every point with the real facts of the case. His statement was as connected and as intelligible a one in every respect except the fantastic motives which he assigned for the deed, as could have been made by a perfectly sane man. The only one of his assertions which was contradicted by the evidence of others is this, that before the court Sörgel denied having taken, or having ever told any one that he had taken, the murdered man's purse. It was nevertheless certain that the woodcutter had had two florins in his possession, and that this money must have been taken by Sörgel. This was proved by the declaration of the widow and her son, and by the confession made by Sörgel that very evening to the blind Gassner and to Catherine, both parties agreeing exactly as to the sum. It is, however, equally certain that Sörgel did not keep this money; in all probability he took it in a fit of childish avidity, and afterwards threw it away as a useless or forbidden possession.

The perfect unconcern with which Sörgel related the whole transaction, as if it were the most ordinary event, as well as several irrational expressions which he made use of in court, prove him to have been mad, not only when he committed the murder, but also when he underwent the first two examinations. The most remarkable light is thrown upon his condition by the change which took place in him when the fit of madness had passed away. With the madness every trace of the imaginary world which it had called into existence disappeared from his mind. His recovery was like waking from a deep sleep, which left no impression but a vague sense of bad and frightful dreams. So long as his soul was darkened by madness he was as perfectly conscious of his own fancies, motives, resolutions, and actions, as of the real external circumstances of the deed, and was able clearly to describe all that had passed. But these images, motives, and recollections vanished as soon as the spell of madness was broken, and he heard the account with as much surprise as he would have listened to the recital of the strange deeds of some unknown person. He knew only thus much of a period of several days, " that his head was very confused, and that he dreamt all manner of nonsense." He did not even remember the substance of his dreams; only one or two circumstances remained in his memory; for instance, that the judge had visited him in prison, and that some one had written at the table. He was not aware either that he was himself the principal person concerned on that occasion, that the subject of the inquiry was his own deed, or that he had confessed it.

It is well known that in madness or delirium the patient often appears to himself to be a third person, or ascribes his own feelings and actions to some one else. Thus a fever patient begs his nurse to remove that troublesome guest out of his bed, pointing all the while to himself, or says that a friend sitting by his bedside has a violent pain in the side or is thirsty, and requests that something may be given him to drink; while it is he himself who feels the pain and the thirst which he ascribes to another. This singular confusion of persons occurs twice in Sörgel's madness, and proves its reality and the truth of his confession; and also that the confession was made during the paroxysm of insanity, as in it he relates these delusions as positive facts.

The first instance of this delusion was that which prompted him to drink the blood of the murdered man. After he had recovered his senses he was perfectly well able to distinguish a felon from a murdered man. Thus his application of the vulgar superstition that the blood of an executed felon is a cure for the falling sickness, to the man he had himself killed, was no doubt entirely the result of this delusion. His imagination transferred to the person of the murdered man that which he knew himself to have become by the deed he had committed.   .

We find exactly the same confusion in the motive which induced him to chop off the feet of the murdered man. He constantly asserted that he had done this in order to prevent their laying the old man in chains again. Now Sörgel had of late been frequently chained himself, and indeed had but just been released from the chains in which he had lain all night, and possibly still felt the pressure of the rings upon his ankles; and here again his disturbed imagination confounded his own feet with those of the dead man, and in order to secure *himself* from the danger of being laid in chains in future, on the presumption that a man who has no feet cannot be chained by them, he chopped off both the feet of the dead wood-cutter.

The physicians declared their opinion that Sörgel had committed the murder in a paroxysm of madness, when he was not accountable for his actions, and accordingly the court, on the 23rd November, 1824, acquitted him of murder.

For the safety of the community he was confined in the madhouse of Schwabach, where he died in the course of a few months.

GEORGE WACHS;

OR,

THE SUDDEN TEMPTATION.

~~~~~○~~~~~

ABOUT two miles beyond Vilsbiburg, in the district of the Isar, on an eminence at two hundred paces from several mills, stands a solitary cottage called the Raschenhäuschen. This belonged to a poor honest shoemaker of about forty-two years of age, named James Huber, who lived there with his wife Elizabeth and his three children—Catherine, a girl of nine; Michael, a boy of three; and a baby of two months old. One half of the cottage, with a separate entrance, was let to a day-labourer called Maier, and his family.

Maier returned from his day's labour with his wife at about half-past six in the evening of Maunday Thursday, 8th of April, 1819, and was surprised at the unusual quiet of his neighbour's cottage; none of the shoemaker's family were to be seen or heard. Maier's sister-in-law, Maria Wieser, who had stayed at home all day, had seen the shoemaker's wife leave her house at about three and return home at six: she had heard her knock at the door and laugh aloud when it was opened to her, as if she was astonished at finding the door locked so early in the day, or as if some unexpected guest had advanced to meet her as she crossed

the threshold. Since that time Maria Wieser had
seen nothing of the shoemaker's family. On the following morning too the Hubers gave no token of their
existence: no smoke came out of their chimney, the
house-door remained closed ; nothing stirred within,
and continued knocking and calling produced no
effect.

At length, the daughter Catherine, with her face
bloody and disfigured, looked out of the upper window,
but was too much frightened to come down. After
many earnest entreaties she at length opened the house-
door. The first object that met the eyes of those who
entered was the corpse of Elizabeth Huber bathed in
blood. The body of little Michael was next found
rolled up like a hedgehog between the lowest step of
the stairs which led to the upper floor and a chest near
them. The shoemaker's large iron hammer lay on
the floor of the workshop, which was covered with
blood, more especially all round the bench, which was
upset: on the floor of the bed-room, near the bed,
Huber was found lying dead with his face towards the
ground. On the bed, near its father's dead body, the
infant slept unhurt, though half-starved with cold.
All the bodies were in their usual dresses, and the shoemaker had on his leathern apron.

As there were no traces of violence on the outside of
the house which might lead to the supposition of house-
breakers, the first impression was that the family might
have done the deed themselves ; but the overturned
stool, round which was a pool of blood, and the awl
drawn half through some leather which lay upon the
table—these and several other circumstances clearly

proved that the shoemaker must have been struck down suddenly while seated at his work, and afterwards dragged into the bed-room ; besides, the appearance of the upper rooms proved that a robbery had been committed there. Several closets had been broken open with some sharp instrument, their contents tossed about in great disorder, and a hatband and buckle, which was probably of silver, cut off the shoemaker's hat. The first glance, therefore, proved beyond doubt that this triple murder must have been committed by one or more robbers, who had either stolen into. the house during the day, or found some pretext for staying there openly.

The following was the result of the post-mortem examination of the bodies, which took place a few hours after the discovery of the murders.

The corpse of Elizabeth Huber, a healthy woman of about six and thirty, bore no trace of injury except upon the head. Two deep triangular wounds, each three inches in diameter, which penetrated the skull, disfigured her swollen face—one at the corner of the left eye, the other just above the left temple : the forehead and the bridge of the nose were likewise completely crushed—the heavy iron hammer found on the floor of the workshop exactly fitted the wounds.

The corpse of James Huber also showed no traces of injury save about the head, the back of which was completely shattered.

Neither the head nor the face of the boy Michael had any external wound, but were much swollen : the skull was as soft as dough : the frontal bone, the temple, and the occiput were broken into innumerable fragments ; the rest of the body was uninjured.

The daughter Catherine was severely but not dangerously wounded. The left side of her face was swollen and covered with blood, and her eye closed up; an oblique flesh wound, about an inch and a half in length, and a great deal of blood, appeared on the back of her head, and also a contusion on the left shoulder.

There could not be the slightest doubt as to the mortal nature of the injuries inflicted on the three dead bodies. The medical men were unanimous in their opinion that all three had been murdered with the shoemaker's hammer : this was of iron, weighing about two pounds, and the handle was a foot long.

The strongest suspicion against the perpetrator arose simultaneously with its discovery. The daughter who had escaped gave the first link in the chain of evidence. She could not, indeed, as yet be judicially examined, as she was still suffering from fever, and was always either asleep or in a state of stupor; meanwhile, however, the neighbours and others extracted thus much from her, " that she had been struck down in the house by a man with a blue coat and a high hat ; that this man had frequently been at her father's house before; that he had been there on the previous Thursday, and had sat for a long time with her father in his workshop." This information was confirmed by the statement of Maier's sister-in-law. She said that on Maunday Thursday, towards three o'clock in the afternoon, she had seen a young man answering to Catherine's description enter the shoemaker's house. Soon after, the miller's son, James S——, went into the house, as she heard, to cut the shoemaker's hair. She had seen the young man, whose name was unknown to her, but who, as she had heard, lived with Schneeweisser, the carpenter, in the village of Sölling, some fourteen days before in the shoemaker's shop, where his boots were being mended : she had likewise heard from the children of the miller that at five o'clock in the evening of Maunday Thursday he was still at the shoemaker's cottage. The above-named miller's son, James S——, related at his examination of the 10th of April, "that at about three o'clock on the 8th of April he had, at the shoemaker's request, gone to him and had cut his hair ; besides the shoemaker, his wife and children, he had found a young man who he believed lived with Schneeweisser, the carpenter, at Sölling. The shoemaker begged the lad, who had already taken off his boot, to wait until his hair was cut, when he would serve him. The young man said nothing while witness was present, but stared wildly about him, and seemed rather drunk. He had seen the same man at the public-house (the Post) at Vilsbiburg on the day when the murder was discovered : everybody there was talking about it : this lad only said nothing, but kept his eyes fixed upon high, and "I thought," said witness, "that as he took no part in the conversation, it must be disagreeable to him. I don't know what to make of him, but I can't help thinking that he must be the man, otherwise he would surely have lamented over such a misfortune, like every one else : he alone said nothing, although he had been with the shoemaker the day before."

It was immediately discovered, from the accurate descriptions, that the unknown person could be no other than George Wachs, an apprentice of Schneeweisser, the carpenter, at Sölling. He was arrested

during the night of the 10th of April, and several suspicious articles, particularly two silver hat-buckles,
were found concealed in his trowsers. Early next
morning (Easter Sunday), when the gaoler entered his
cell, the accused came forwards of his own accord, and
said, " I must own that I am the murderer of the
shoemaker and his family : it is all over with me : I
should have confessed to-day, and then have given
myself up to justice." He was forced to make his
Easter confession to the judge, instead of to his
confessor.

George Wachs, born of Catholic parents, at Sölling,
in the circuit of Moosburg, on the 17th of April,
1800, and, accordingly, only nineteen years of age
when he committed this crime, was the son of a small
farmer, who also worked as a day-labourer. His
parents, who were both living when their only son was
brought to trial, were generally described as very
worthy people, who had sent him to school from his
earliest youth, and had endeavoured to keep him
straight by their advice and example. His moral
conduct as a boy was not worse than that of others. On
leaving school he was bound apprentice to a miller at
Freising, who was perfectly satisfied with him, and who
gave him his freedom after three years' service, on the
7th of April, 1817. He then served as a miller's boy
at several places in the district of the Isar, everywhere
earning a character for diligence and good conduct.
But his eighteenth year was the turning point in his
moral life. He was out of work from the 16th of
August, 1818, and either stayed at home with his
parents or wandered about the country seeking employment, and working now and then as a day-labourer.

In the following October, while working under a stone-mason at Moosburg, he stole from the wife of his employer fifty florins (according to her account ninety-eight florins), and would have been delivered over to justice, had not his father—perhaps unfortunately for him—been induced for the sake of his own honour, as well as by affection for his son, to make full restitution. At length, on the 25th of December, 1818, he entered the service of the miller Ingerl, at Gerzen, who dismissed him after three months. " I turned the fellow off," says Ingerl, " simply because his labour was not worth a farthing, and he was always running after women ; besides, he was a reckless, dissolute, riotous fellow, who had no regard for Christianity, and was disagreeable to me on account of his impudent and licentious conduct." This young man's immoderate taste for women fully accounts for the suddenness of the change in his moral nature. Wantonness made him riotous, disorderly, and lazy; love of women made him vain and fond of dress, and vanity made him rapacious, until he became first a thief, and then a murderer.

After Ingerl, the miller, had dismissed him from his service, on the 17th of March, 1819, he all at once gave up his business, and bound himself apprentice to a master carpenter at Sölling, of the name of Schnee-weisser, in the hope of succeeding better in that line. But scarce had he been a fortnight in his new trade when he, who had till then been known merely as a wanton, jovial, reckless youth, proved, by a deed of which no one suspected him capable, the truth of the old saying, that there is no propensity, even one apparently harmless, which may not, when fostered by circumstances, grow into an irresistible passion, and hurry a man into the commission of monstrous crimes.

With his master's leave, Wachs left home at eight o'clock in the morning of Maunday Thursday, the 8th of April, with the intention of making his Easter confession at Vilsbiburg. On his way he met Matthias Hingerl, a peasant's son, who was going to the same village to fetch his watch, which he had left to be mended at a watchmaker's, and which he wanted to wear during the approaching Easter festivities.

George Wachs having unexpectedly found an agreeable companion, thought that any other day in the week would do as well for confessing, and spent the greater part of the morning at Vilsbiburg, not in church, but in the public-houses, drinking beer and talking, chiefly about women and his own adventures. Hingerl showed him his watch, which he had fetched from the watchmaker; and although George Wachs said nothing at the time, we may infer from what subsequently happened, that the sight of this enviable possession painfully recalled to his recollection that, although he certainly had good clothes for the next Easter Sunday, he was still without a watch.

At about noon they both went merrily towards home, but stopped by the way at a village, where they drank three quarts more of beer, and then continued their journey. George Wachs, who, as well as his companion, had drunk a good deal, but not enough to affect his senses, was exceedingly merry and noisy, sung and rolled his hat along before him, ran after it, and played all manner of childish tricks. After accompanying Hingerl about two miles farther, he took

leave of him, and said that he was going to turn back,
but did not say whither he was going or what he
wanted. Hingerl had, however, previously remarked
that Wachs walked lame, and on asking the reason,
Wachs told him that he had cut his foot with a hatchet,
and must have his boot mended before Easter
Sunday.

With this object only, so at least the accused declared
on every examination, he turned back and went to the
shoemaker's house, which he reached at about three,
and where he found the shoemaker's wife and children,
and some girls from the neighbouring mill. Before
long, James S—— came in and cut the shoemaker's
hair, after which he went away again. It was not till
then that the shoemaker set to work upon Wachs' boot;
Wachs meanwhile played with the children, and took
particular notice of little Michael, to whom he gave a
carnival-cake. After his boot had been mended, and
he had stayed some time with the shoemaker, he wished,
according to his own account at least, to go away at
about four o'clock, and asked the shoemaker whether
his clock was right? whereupon the latter told him
that it was too slow by a quarter of an hour, and desired his wife to fetch him his silver watch from up-
stairs that he might wind it up. After bringing the
watch to her husband, who wound it up, and hung it
upon a nail in the wall beside him, she left the house
and went to Sölling to buy fish for the next day. The
children also went out to play in the garden with their
companions, and George Wachs was left alone with
the shoemaker in the workshop. Wachs asserted that
he would have gone away with the wife, had not the
shoemaker detained him, saying, " Stop a bit longer ;

you cannot do much more to-day, and I shall be dull all by myself."

The wife was very unwilling to leave the stranger alone with her husband. At Sölling, she told Mary Z——, that " Schneeweisser's apprentice had already been three hours at her house; that the young man was drunk, and that she disliked his way of talking, which was so strange that it made her laugh at one moment, and frightened her the next." A fortnight before this, Wachs had been at the shoemaker's on a Sunday morning to have his boots mended, and she now said to Mary Wiesers, " That fellow is at my house whom I dislike for coming during church time —I cannot bear him." This foreboding was soon terribly fulfilled on her husband, her children, and herself.

" When the woman was gone"—these are the criminal's own words—" we talked over a variety of indifferent matters, and for a long while no evil thought crossed my mind, although the watch was hanging before my eyes the whole time. All at once it struck me how beautiful the watch was. I took it from the wall, examined it closely, opened it, and asked the shoemaker how much it had cost. He told me that, with a silver chain and seal, the watch had cost fourteen florins, but that the chain was up-stairs in the cupboard, as he only wore it on holidays, when I should be able to see it. I remarked that I had a mind to buy them, if I could ever get together enough money, and he appeared quite willing to sell them. I could not get the watch out of my head: I walked up and down the room with my eyes fixed upon it, and the thought struck me that I would run off with it as soon

as the shoemaker had left the room. But he never
stirred from his seat, and continued hard at work upon
the upper-leathers of a pair of shoes. The desire for
the watch grew upon me every moment, and as I
walked up and down the room, I turned over in my
own mind how I could get possession of it ; and as the
shoemaker still sat at his work, it suddenly came across
me—suppose I were to kill him ? There lay the hammer : I took it up before the shoemaker's face and pretended to play with it ; but I did not hit him directly,
because I kept thinking to myself that I ought not to
kill him. I walked up and down behind his back for
some minutes with the hammer in my hand, but still
in doubt. Then my longing after the watch gained
the upper hand, and I said to myself, Now is the time,
otherwise the wife will be here too ! And just as the
shoemaker was most busily at work, I raised the hammer and struck him with it as hard as I could on the
left temple : he fell from his seat covered with blood,
and never moved or uttered a sound. I felt sure
that I could kill him with one blow. I should think
that a quarter of an hour must have elapsed while I
went up and down the room thinking how I could
get the watch : at length I struck the blow, and this
was my last and worst thought."

" It must have been in an unlucky hour that the
desire for the watch took so strong a hold of me. I
had never thought about it before ; nor should I
have entered the shoemaker's house, but for my torn
boot."

" As soon as the shoemaker was down, I put the
watch into my pocket and went up-stairs to look for
the chain. The key was in the door of the closet in

the upper bed-room ; and as I thought that they were
sure to keep their best things there, I looked in it for
the chain, which I did not find; but there were two
sheep-skins, which I took.   Just as I was going down
stairs with the sheep-skins, I saw two other closets on
the landing; I therefore turned back and broke them
open with a hoe: thinking that perhaps I should now
find the chain which belonged to the watch, I turned
everything over, but did not find the chain; however
I did find six florins in half-florin pieces, thirty
kreutzers, and a silver hat-buckle.   In the same place
also was a hat with a silver filigree buckle, which I
cut off, and put in my pocket."   (He then enumerated
all the articles which he had found in the second
closet, and which he had taken ; the value of all he
stole, including the watch, which had cost nine florins,
amounted to about thirty-three florins, or 2l. 15s.)   He
then proceeded :—" My chief object still was to find
the silver chain, and it was only during my search
for it that the other things fell in my way, and that I
took them."

" When I had got all these things, I returned to the
workshop to take a piece of leather, and perceived that
the shoemaker still breathed ; I therefore gave him a
few more blows on the temple with the hammer, and
then I thought that I had better remove him into the
bed-chamber, so that his wife might not see him immediately upon entering the house.   I accordingly
dragged him out of the shop into the chamber near
the bed."

George Wachs had now attained his object, with
the exception of the missing chain.   There was
nothing more to be got; but one crime leads to

another. In this case the words of Macbeth proved but too true—

" Things bad begun, make strong themselves by ill."

After dragging the murdered man into the chamber, and filling his own pockets with leather enough to make a pair of boots, in addition to the other articles, George Wachs was on the point of leaving the house when the two children met him at the door on their return from play. These children had seen him during nearly half the day, and knew him : if they remained alive, he was betrayed. There could be no doubt as to what his safety required: no choice was left him : the thought and the deed were one. He seized the little boy, and dashed him upon the ground at the foot of the stairs with such violence, that the death-rattle was in his throat in a moment. He then flung Catherine with equal violence under the stairs among a mass of wood and iron ; but the girl, after lying stunned for a short time, got up again and endeavoured to reach the inner room to seek protection from her father: the murderer then took up the hammer from the ground, struck the child with it about the face and head, and again threw her under the stairs among a heap of old wood and iron, where she lay motionless, and he concluded her to be dead. Little Michael, however, still breathed. "When I saw," continued the murderer, " that I had thrown him with such violence that he could not survive, I gave him a few blows on the head with the hammer to put him out of his misery. I then threw him between the steps and an old chest, so that they might not find him directly."

This second business was now over ; but, before he

was well aware of it, a bloody harvest had sprung up under his hands from the seeds he had sown.

As soon as the children had shared their father's fate, he again prepared for flight, but first looked out at the window to see whether any one was near who might observe him. Just then a man drove by in a cart, and he was forced to wait until it was out of sight. At last he thought he might escape in safety, but on putting his head out at the door to see if any one was near, he beheld the shoemaker's wife returning from Sölling: she had already turned off the road into her garden, and was only a few steps from the house, which he could not leave without running directly into her hands. It was clear, then, that he must stay and murder her too, as he had already murdered her husband and children. "When I saw the woman coming, I said to myself, Now I cannot escape; I am lost, and must kill her too. So I shut the door, seized the hammer, and held it with one hand hidden under my coat, while I opened the door with the other: the shoemaker's wife entered laughing, and said, Why, you have locked yourselves in! I made no answer. As soon as she entered the room she turned towards the chest which stood near the entrance, and which I had left open after my search for the chain. I stood behind her, nearest the door, and before she was aware of it I struck her such a heavy blow with the hammer on the left temple, that she instantly fell close to the chest, and only cried in a low voice, Jesus Maria! I saw that she could not recover, and gave her several more blows as she lay on the floor, to put her out of her misery. I then dragged her on one side towards the inner room, so that people should not tread upon her as they entered the house."

" I then went into the inner room, threw a napkin full of eggs, which the woman had brought, behind the grate, and the hammer on the ground, hastily took up the little baby which was lying on the bench, and laid it upon the bed in the back room for fear it should fall and be hurt. I then left the house in perfect security, locked the front door, and went straight home to my master's house, where I arrived at about half-past six."*

" The whole affair could not have lasted an hour. It was past five when I struck the shoemaker, and by six the wife was killed."

" If it had not been for the watch-chain, I should not have got into all this trouble, and nobody would have been killed but the shoemaker. I never once thought of killing the wife and the children."

That he was at the time in perfect possession of all his faculties, and not in a state of furious drunkenness, is proved by the nature of the crime itself, as well as by his own confession. " I felt a little the worse for liquor, but I knew all the while what I was about, otherwise I could never have done all I did. I cannot tell what possessed me, but I was very merry and joyous all that day."

An eyewitness was present at the murder of the woman and of the little boy, upon whom the criminal had by no means reckoned—this was the daughter Catherine, who gave her evidence before the court on

---

* It is strange that all these murders left no mark of blood either on the clothes or the body of the murderer: there were only, as he says, a few spots on his boots, which he easily wiped away.

the 30th of April, after she had sufficiently recovered
from her injuries.   It will be interesting to hear the
most important part of the testimony given by this
child, though legally an incompetent witness.   After
giving a detailed account of the arrival of the carpenter's apprentice at her father's house, her mother's departure for Sölling, and the children's going into the
garden to play, she proceeded thus :—" We children
stayed out together a long time, and as we entered
the house the carpenter's man came towards us and
threw us against the stairs : my brother presently began
to move, and the man hit him on the head with my
father's hammer.   I got up again and tried to get to
the inner room to seek help from my father; but the
man caught hold of me, and struck me over my eye
with the broad end of the hammer, and on the back
of my head and shoulders with the sharp end, and
threw me once more under the stairs.   I did not
dare to move again, and pretended to be dead.   The
man then went to the door and looked out, but came
back in a minute and shut the door, and then I heard
my mother call, Open the door !   The man let her in
directly.   I was still in a great fright, and lay as still
as a mouse, and all at once the man struck her such a
blow upon the head with the hammer that she fell,
and I only heard her cry out " Help!"   He then
dragged my mother towards the inner room, and soon
after went out of the door, which he shut after him."

    In all the subsequent examinations the accused ad-
hered to his first confession, and only repeated his first
statements, confirming them by additional details, so
that a perfectly consistent account of the whole transaction could be collected from his various confessions.

On one point only the accused attempted to depart from his first confession, somewhat in his own favour. In the first general examination he confessed in so many words that he had assaulted the two children with intent to murder them. " I should have murdered only the shoemaker," said he, " had not the children come in just as I was about to leave the house; and as they knew me, I was forced to kill them, lest they should betray me : the same thing happened with the shoemaker's wife." It was evidently from shame of his own inhumanity that he afterwards maintained that he wished only to stun the children so that they should not betray him, and that he afterwards killed the little boy out of pity, on seeing that he had hit him too hard. The deed itself, and the motive to it which he had so frequently declared, sufficiently refute this wretched prevarication. In order to prevent the children from betraying him, it would not suffice to stun them : the dead alone tell no tales.

The truth of his assertion that he entered the shoemaker's shop without any criminal intention, and that it was not until the watch was so temptingly exhibited before his eyes that the idea of murder entered his mind, seems somewhat doubtful. It certainly looks suspicious that the same man should have murdered another for the sake of his watch at five in the afternoon, who on the morning of the same day feasted his eyes on a watch in his comrade's possession. And as it appears by the indictment that he had seen the shoemaker's silver watch hanging in his workshop a fortnight before, it seems natural to conclude that the desire of possessing it was then excited, and subsequently much increased by the sight of his comrade's

watch.   By this presumption we may also easily account for his suddenly turning back on the road from
Vilsbiburg, his unusually long stay at the shoemaker's
house, and, lastly, for his wild looks and his strange
way of talking.

These conjectures, however, lose all their weight on
closer examination.   From first to last the criminal
never seems to have acted upon any predetermined
plan, but merely to have obeyed the inspiration
of the moment, and to have yielded to the temptation
of an opportunity created by the coincidence of
several accidental circumstances.   It is impossible
to calculate chances, and least of all a chance made
up of a variety of accidents.   Whoever lays a scheme
for some predetermined object, if he be not less than
half-witted, will found it upon circumstances more or
less within his control, and not upon events entirely
beyond it, and merely dependent upon chance.   The
shoemaker's cottage, though lonely, was no hermit's
cell.   One half of it was inhabited by the day-labourer's
family as well as by his own : the accused must also
have known that the shoemaker was likely to be
visited by a number of customers just before the
Easter holidays.   He could not have entertained the
slightest expectation of finding Huber quite alone, or
of remaining with him for hours undisturbed by the
presence of a third person.   When he entered Huber's
workshop at about three in the afternoon, he could by
no means have guessed that the wife would go to a
distant village, or that both the children would
leave the house and stop out at play above an hour.
A man who goes with the deliberate intention to murder is sure to determine beforehand in what manner

and with what instrument he will commit the crime.
He does not trust to the chance that when he is
on the spot luck will provide him with a knife, a
dagger, a pistol, a hammer, or some other instrument
of death. The prisoner's statement that he went to
the shoemaker's house merely to get his boots mended
was by no means a mere pretence. Matthias Hingerl,
who accompanied him on his way to and from Vilsbiburg, saw a hole in his boot, and heard him say
that he must get it mended before Easter. Thus his
return to the shoemaker's house has in it nothing
suspicious. The long stay of a frivolous, lazy young
man, willing to idle away his time, is nothing unusual, especially when we consider that he had already
passed the greater part of the day in idleness, drinking, gossip, and all sorts of follies, and would not feel
disposed to spend the remainder of so glorious a
holiday under the eye of his master, and perhaps
even at work. The wild look which one witness
(James, the miller's boy) says he observed in him
from the first, is to be attributed rather to drinking and rioting, than to the effect of any wicked
design in his mind; not to mention that a peasant
lad's judgment in physiognomy does not deserve
implicit confidence. The antipathy which the shoemaker's wife felt towards him had been shared by
others long before he could possibly have had any
thoughts of committing murder: indeed, the miller,
Hingerl, dismissed him from his service for no
other reason. George Wachs, by nature coarse, frivolous, and dissolute, and at that moment heated by
drinking, brought the uncouth merriment in which
he had indulged during his walk from Vilsbiburg

with him into the shoemaker's house, where he gave
a loose to his coarse nature in vulgar loquacity, and in
foolish, wanton jokes. This conduct, especially on
a sacred day, and in a person who had already
wearied her by his long stay, must have been disgust-
ing and frightful, rather than laughable, to a quiet,
pious mother of a family.

We may therefore accept his confession exactly as
he gave it: all the circumstances agree so well with
each other, and form so accurate a picture of the workings of his mind, that it would be next to impossible
for a mere peasant to invent a statement so perfectly
true to nature.

The events of the forenoon had already filled his
imagination with the idea of a watch. Hingerl
had gone to Vilsbiburg on purpose to fetch home his
watch from the watchmaker's, and George Wachs had
to wait at the public-house while his companion trans-
acted this business. When Hingerl rejoined Wachs
he naturally talked about the watch, the possession of
which gave him double pleasure now that it had been
mended and was to go particularly well. In order to
make his companion share his pleasure, Hingerl took
the watch out of his pocket and allowed him to
examine it, boasting of its excellence all the while.
George Wachs said nothing, but it was impossible
that so vain a young man should not envy his more
fortunate companion, and long for the possession of a
similar treasure. Thus, without any guilty thoughts
or criminal intentions, George Wachs was prepared,
by what he had seen, heard, and felt that morning,
for the temptation which afterwards met him in the
shoemaker's house. An unhappy chance placed before

the eyes of one whose thoughts and wishes had on that very morning been directed towards a watch, just such another, and the tempter, opportunity, stood by. This second watch was not merely shown to him and then returned to its case, but was hung against the wall, where it continued to excite his desires : he could not avoid seeing it, and the longer he looked the more inviting did it appear. A silver chain and seal like-wise belonged to this watch, which the shoemaker told him were so fine that he only wore them on holidays. This watch, with its fine chain, was far better than that which he had coveted in his companion's posses-sion. To be the owner of such a treasure, to appear before the women thus adorned, to outshine all his companions, was indeed a tempting vision for a vain lad of nineteen ; and in this vision he indulged until liking became longing, and longing ungovernable passion. For a time his yet undefined wishes hovered round their object; he took down the watch from the wall, examined it more closely, and talked of buying it. But when the shoemaker agreed to sell him the watch, thus placing it at his disposal, fresh fuel was added to the flames which burned within him. Nothing now intruded itself between his desires and their object but the want of a small sum of money, which he did not possess and could not hope soon to obtain. But was the most intense passion of his heart, the object on which his mind was fixed, and which he already fancied his own, to be resigned for such a trifle ? The passions always choose the shortest path. There hung the watch before his eyes; he had but to stretch out his arm and it was his : no one was there to prevent him but the shoemaker, who must

quit the room or die. Thus the choice lay between
theft and murder; the former, indeed, rather than the
latter, but he was equally prepared for the one or the
other, according to opportunity and circumstances.

The most striking feature in this case is the
fearful spectacle of a sudden passion, which seized on
his imagination like a whirlwind and hurried him on
to perdition. The blinding, maddening influence of
the passions was exhibited in a remarkable manner in
his conduct. All his thoughts, wishes, and actions,
considered as means for accomplishing his ends, were
so foolish and senseless, that we might call them
childish but for their extreme cruelty. He was so completely wrapped up in the object of his desires as not
to perceive objections which could scarce escape the
observation of an ordinary child. He first waited for
the momentary absence of the shoemaker in order to
seize the watch and run off with it, which would have
been much the same thing as to take it before the
very eyes of its owner: the thief would have been as
certainly known in the first as in the latter case. But
this youth was exactly like the stupid savage, who,
incapable of resisting a sudden impulse, runs away
with a string of beads before the very faces of
the ship's company, and hides behind a tree, where
he thinks himself and his booty safe so long as he
does not see those by whom he is seen. The
murder which George Wachs planned in case the
shoemaker should not leave the room, was quite as ill-
contrived. None but a man blinded by passion could
avoid seeing that detection was as certain as the
murder was easy. He was well known to the family,
and indeed to the whole neighbourhood: the miller's

lad James had met him at the house, and the shoemaker's wife and children had left him alone with his
victim, and must therefore, immediately upon discovering the murder, have fixed upon him as the murderer. Nothing but the most reckless and blind
rapacity, incapable of forethought and reflection,
would have perceived the mere physical possibility
of the deed and overlooked its real impracticability,
and the certainty of immediate detection.

A strange contrast to the heat of his desires is presented by the coolness and presence of mind with
which this youth of nineteen, who probably found
himself for the first time exposed to such temptation,
conceived, determined on, and performed so frightful
a deed. No sooner had it occurred to him to take
advantage of the shoemaker's absence in order to obtain possession of the watch, or should he not leave
the room to murder him, than he was fully prepared
with a plan which cost him not a pang to conceive
and determine. The very hired murderers sent by
Richard to kill Clarence in the Tower shrink back on
beholding their victim, and one of them says, " Faith,
some dregs of conscience are yet within me." They
feel within them " that dangerous thing which makes
a man a coward ; a man cannot steal but it accuseth
him. . . . . 'Tis a blushing shame-faced spirit that mu-
tinies in a man's bosom ; it fills one full of obstacles."*
But George Wachs, though a mere novice in crime,
does not appear from his own account to have felt
any such " dregs of conscience," or any such " mutiny
in his bosom." His continual walking up and down
betrayed, it is true, some inward uneasiness ; but

* King Richard III., Act I. Scene 4.

this seems to have been caused by nothing but the mixture of hope and fear, the impatience of desire, and anxiety as to the success or failure of his plan. He felt no distress, no hesitation at the thought that he could only gain possession of a miserable watch by destroying a poor father of a family, who had never injured him, and with whom he was at that moment engaged in friendly conversation. It is true that he delayed for a while committing the murder, in the expectation that the shoemaker would quit his work for a moment and leave the room, and in this delay a certain amount of humane feeling may have had as large a share as the very natural dislike of adopting the more troublesome and dangerous mode of proceeding, so long as an easier road to his wishes was open to him. The choice between theft and murder by no means depended on his original resolution,—for he was equally prepared for either alternative,—but simply on the accidental turn of circumstances. On being asked at the final examination how he could murder the shoemaker for a watch of trifling value, when he must have known that such a crime would be punished with the utmost rigour, he answered, "I certainly did think of it, but I don't know what came over me. I felt all at once the strongest desire for the watch, and instantly determined to kill the shoemaker. The watch I must have, and the only question was what to do next: upon this I struck him. The longing after the watch was too strong for me; I struggled all along against my desires, for I knew very well that it was wrong to kill any one for such a cause." However ready we may be to believe that he was aware that murder, especially such a murder as this, was a crime deserving heavy punishment, we much doubt whether this knowledge involved him in any contest between his conscience and his desires. .Deep as is the insight given us by the prisoner into the secret origin of crime by repeated and connected statements, we find no circumstance which might induce us to believe that his determination and its execution cost him any particular effort or qualm of conscience. He speaks only of the beginning of his desire, its growth, and final mastery over him. Throughout all these bloody thoughts and deeds, the prisoner retained such perfect coolness and self-possession, that he was able not only to describe the whole tragedy, but even the workings of his own mind, as accurately as could have been done by a dispassionate observer able to look into his soul. Men whose natures have even a moderate share of the milk of human kindness, can seldom bear to look upon a horrid deed so closely : before they can think of it with composure, they must blunt or deceive their natural feelings, unless indeed the struggle between desire and loathing hurries them on to that desperate fury which they are ready to say with Macbeth,

> " Let that be
> Which the eye fears, when it is done, to see."*

But George Wachs was not so chicken-hearted as to flinch before any terrors of the imagination ; he was so strong in purpose, that he needed no assistance save that of his own good clear understanding, which served him admirably, so far as pointing out the shortest means to a given end. With deliberate cunning he took up the heavy iron hammer before

* Macbeth, Act I. Scene 5.

the eyes of the shoemaker, tossed it to and fro in his hands as if in play, stood a step or two behind his victim, and " as he had heard that the most certain way was to hit a man on the temple," he aimed directly at that place, which he struck with such a firm and unerring hand, that the murdered man instantly fell without speech or motion at his feet.

His cool rapacity led him at once to his real object, unmoved by the bloody sight before him : he first seized upon the watch, and then sought for the chain in every part of the house ; he broke open and ransacked every chest and cupboard, took whatever could possibly be of use to him—money, clothes, silver buckles, even a piece of leather for boots,—and concealed them in his pockets. Such was his coolness, that he returned once more to the workshop before quitting the house : such his cruelty, that he completely shattered the head of his victim, who still lay in the death-struggle : such his deliberate, but useless prudence, that he dragged the dead man into the inner room out of sight.

The other three murders (for the attempt upon the girl was a murder in intention) were necessary consequences of the first, and were considered by the criminal—as they really were—merely supplementary, and forced upon him by an unlucky accident. The shoemaker he sacrificed to his rapacity, the wife and children to self-preservation. A man more accessible to human weakness, if he did the deed at all, would have done it with all the signs of one driven by the pressure of cruel necessity to a state bordering on madness. But Wachs, whom nothing could disturb, nothing unman, saw as soon as the children appeared

before him what he must do, and his determination
was as quick as thought itself. He murdered the children without the slightest remorse, and exhibited in
the whole transaction a cruelty and hardness of heart
only equalled by his coolness and deliberation.

The poor mother was the next to fall.

This last action was a mere repetition of the second
and third; only as it was a grown up and vigorous
person with whom he had to deal, the murderer displayed in the execution of his sudden determination as
much cunning as cruelty. No sooner did he see her
approach, than he resolved how to act. He instantly
shut the door, armed himself once more with the
bloody hammer, concealed the handwhich grasped
it, and then opened the door, which he shut upon
her as she entered the house with a jest on her
lips : the moment she turned her eyes from him, he
aimed at the well-known weak place in her head,
and at one blow shattered it with the hammer which
was already stained with the blood of her husband and
her children.

After murdering the father, mother, and children,
Wachs ended this horrid tragedy by carefully carrying
the infant of the murdered woman into the chamber,
and laying it upon the bed. We can scarcely consider this action as the result of any humane impulse,
but rather as a fresh proof of the remarkable coolness
and self-possession manifested throughout by the murderer. No particular sensibility is required to induce
a man to remove an infant from a place where it is in
danger of falling, especially if this can be done with
very little trouble. When Wachs, just before quitting the house, rendered this small service to the

child, whose life could not injure and whose death could not serve him, he merely proved that, in the midst of murder and death, he preserved such perfect composure as to be able to give his attention to a matter of comparatively trifling importance, and to pass at once from the most horrible deeds to a perfectly indifferent and common-place action.

These several murders, which, strangely enough, left no stain on the clothes or person of the murderer, seem to have left as little trace upon his mind, except a perfectly indifferent recollection of the circumstances. After shutting the door of the house of death behind him, he went home with his pockets full of plunder, and at about half-past six presented himself before his master, gave his master's children some apples, and told him with great glee what a happy day he had spent, and how his companion, young Hingerl, had got so drunk that he could neither stand nor walk. He appeared so cheerful and so perfectly at his ease during the whole of that evening, which he passed with his master and mistress until bed-time, that the former expressed in court his wonder how so young a man could do such deeds, or, when he had done them, behave in such a manner. On the following evening, when his master and mistress were talking over the dreadful occurrence at the shoemaker's, Wachs coolly remarked, "that on the day before the murders he had been at the house, and had stayed there some time, while his boots were being mended : he should therefore certainly have to appear before the court, and perhaps people might even think he had done it." He behaved with equal composure on the Saturday, when he met some woman with whom he associated, to whom he gave the watch, in order that she might get a glass fitted to it. He told her that his father had given him the watch, and talked with great animation about several indifferent matters. When she mentioned what had happened at the shoemaker's house, and asked him whether he had heard who was the murderer, he told her, with the most perfect composure, " that both he and the miller's son, James, had been at the house on the very day of the murder, and would therefore probably be summoned before the court." He then proceeded, without any apparent embarrassment, to talk on other subjects. But nothing more strikingly exhibits his want of common sensibility than the circumstance that it cost him nothing to look out of the window while the funeral of the shoemaker, his wife and child, passed by the public-house at Vilsbiberg, where he was. This he himself confessed, and he replied to the judge's question, whether he had, as was commonly reported, followed the funeral procession into the church, to hear the service — " No, for I had on my working jacket; otherwise I should have gone to see the funeral. I wished on all accounts to go into the church. I certainly was sorry for the people, but I could have gone and looked on, for all that." He who could do that could do more than other men, and of such a one, one is tempted to say that he was little less than a devil. During the whole trial he preserved the same indifference about his crime. Although he acknowledged it to be deserving of punishment, he did not once show the slightest remorse or compassion for his victims.

Considered from a merely technical point of view,

the case presented no legal difficulty. The comprehensive and repeated confessions made by the prisoner agreed exactly with the circumstantial evidence, and with the statements of the witnesses.. Most of the articles stolen from the shoemaker's house were found in the criminal's possession ; some were delivered into court by those persons to whom he had given or sold them ; only the silver watch-chain, which had so much contributed to tempt him to crime, was missing, and the accused stedfastly adhered to his assertion that he had not stolen it, for that, in spite of his eager search, he had been unable to find it. There was also a rosary set in silver missing from among the things left in the house ; the prisoner declared that he had not even seen it.

The defence was necessarily confined to a few unimportant formal objections, and to an attempt to prove that the accused was not in the full possession of his faculties, owing to drunkenness. But this plea was contradicted by the direct evidence of several witnesses, as well as by the nature of the crime and by the prisoner's own confession. The advocate would have most effectually served his client, but not the cause of justice, if he had succeeded in convincing the court of the truth of his remark, "that a man who could do such deeds in such a manner from such a motive, could not possibly be in his right senses, and that therefore it was necessary first of all to cause the medical officers of the court to examine into the state of his mind." This plea was, of course, refused, as the court was in full possession of the means of judging whether the criminal were responsible for actions, or not.

The accused was accordingly, by his own confession, pronounced guilty, on the 28th July, 1819,—1st, of a qualified murder (murder accompanied by robbery) on the person of the master shoemaker Huber; 2nd, of simple murder of his son, aged three; 3rd, of a simple murder of the wife; and 4th, of an attempt at the simple murder of the daughter, aged nine,—and was sentenced to death by the sword; which sentence was carried into execution on the 23rd October following.

Notwithstanding the horrid nature of his crimes, Wachs cannot be classed among the criminals of the first rank. Strong and easily excited animal passions, great frivolity, and utter want of cultivation, were the chief elements of his character: in these the horrible deeds of the 8th April had their origin.

GEORGE RAUSCHMAIER;

OR,

THE TELLTALE RING.

In the year 1821 a charwoman of the name of Maria Anna Holzmann, aged fifty-five, lodged in a house belonging to the shoemaker Sticht of Augsburg: she underlet a part of her lodging to George Rauschmaier and Joseph Steiner.

Holzmann disappeared on Good Friday (20th of April). Rauschmaier and Steiner left their lodging some days later, without having given notice to the landlord Sticht, who lived in another street, of Holzmann's disappearance. They afterwards gave out that she had quitted the house early on Friday morning, leaving behind her all her keys, and had never returned.

It was not till the 17th of May that Sticht informed the police of Holzmann's disappearance. Although Holzmann lived chiefly on charity, she possessed a store of good clothes and other property, and was supposed to have saved money. But when the magistrate went with her brother and sister-in-law to take an inventory of the property, and to seal it up, it was discovered that all the best part of her property was missing. The persons present on this occasion were overpowered by an insufferable stench, which they attributed to the accumulation of dirt in the rooms lately occupied by Rauschmaier and Steiner.

The search made by the police, and the inquiries of the city magistrates after the missing woman, were fruitless. Holzmann's brother suggested that she might possibly have gone away and destroyed herself, as it was said that she had lately lost some money which she had lent at high interest. Rauschmaier, who was examined on oath before the magistrate on the 25th of June, stated that Holzmann left her home at eight o'clock on Friday morning in company with another woman; that she had never returned, and that he did not know whither she was gone, or what had become of her. The inquiry was then suffered to rest until some discovery should be made.

The affair remained in this state till the 2nd of January, 1822, when a washerwoman of the name of Therese Beltler, who also inhabited Sticht's house, informed the police that while she and her son were hanging some linen to dry in the loft, they had discovered the thigh and trunk of a human body—probably those of the missing woman. The usual legal commission immediately proceeded to the house, and found, among some rubbish in a corner of the loft, a human leg and thigh; about six yards off, wedged in between the chimney and the roof, they discovered a human trunk without head or limbs. In another corner they found an old gown and petticoat, together with a red neckerchief, all much stained with blood. These were recognised by another washerwoman in the house as part of the dress usually worn by Holzmann. On taking up the floor of Rauschmaier's room they found the other parts of the body. Among these was the left arm bent double, and wrapped in an old shift.

The head alone could nowhere be found : but this was soon accounted for. It appeared that at Whitsuntide, 1821, the inspector of a factory, not far from Sticht's house, had found a human skull in the weir belonging to the factory. After showing it to his brother, he threw it back into the river, the stream of which carried it away. The skull, which was described as small, and as having only two or three teeth in the jaw, was, in all probability, Anna Holzmann's.

The limbs and body appeared as it were smoke-dried, and were much distorted by pressure in a confined space; but after being washed with water and spirits of wine, and thus restored in some measure to their natural form, the remains were put together, as well as possible, for inspection by the proper officers. The arms and thighs had been removed from the sockets with so much care and skill, that it betrayed a practised hand. While the physician employed by the court examined the left arm, and endeavoured to straighten it, a brass ring fell out of the bend of the elbow. It had in all probability slipped from the murderer's finger while he was in the act of cutting up the body, in the keeping of which it remained as a silent witness against him.

Holzmann was described by her friends and relations as a small, well-shaped person, with this distinctive mark, that her right foot was considerably thicker than the left, and that one of the toes had been removed many years before. This description exactly corresponded with the body when put together, and her brother and other relations did not doubt its identity with Holzmann.

The discovery of the corpse in Holzmann's · own house threw a strong suspicion on Rauschmaier and Steiner. It was scarcely possible that any one could have had time or opportunity to commit such a murder, save one or both of Holzmann's fellow-lodgers. Their staying so long in the house in which the scattered remains of the murdered woman were hidden, without communicating what they must at least have known, was an additional proof of the justice of the suspicion against them, especially against Rauschmaier, who had declared on his oath that Anna Holzmann left her home on Good Friday, 1820, leaving the keys with him, whereas it was quite clear that she had been murdered on that very day, in her own house. Before long it was discovered that during Easter week Rauschmaier and his mistress had pawned or sold much of Holzmann's property.

Rauschmaier was arrested on the 2nd of January, as soon as the dissevered body was discovered. Among other things found upon him was a tattered pocket-book, containing a remarkable document printed in the form of a patent at Cologne, and adorned with the effigies of a number of saints: it purported to be a letter written from heaven by Jesus Christ himself, and brought down to earth by the archangel Michael, granting full absolution for all sins and crimes, however horrible,—in short a patent well worthy to be worn by robbers, thieves, and murderers.*

* This impious and superstitious document bears the superscription :—" Copia, or copy from a divine epistle writ in God's own hand, and now hanging before the image of St. Michael, on

On his summary examination Rauschmaier repeated his former assertion that Anna Holzmann had left the house early on Good Friday, and had never returned. His manner during examination, and when the corpse was shown to him in the churchyard, was cool and unembarrassed. He showed no emotion, and professed ignorance of the body exposed to view. On the 22nd of January he requested an audience, in which, however, he said nothing, but that he wished to be soon released. On the following day he demanded another interview, and this time he confessed that soon after Holzmann's departure he had taken several of her things, which he had given to his mistress to carry away. The judge thought it expedient to examine Rauschmaier merely as to the robbery, without the slightest reference to the murder. Several articles

St. Michael's Mount in Brittany, and no one knoweth whereon it hangeth ; the which is writ in letters of gold, and was brought thither by the holy angel Michael. Whosoever willeth to touch this document, from him it turneth—whosoever willeth to copy it, unto him doth it bend down and unfold itself." Christ then writes in his own person, and first of all impresses upon the faithful the absolute necessity of keeping holy the sabbath, hearing the proper number of masses, never working on saint-days, and the like. He then continues, " I say to you, by the mouth of my mother, by the Christian Church, and by the head of John my Baptist, that I, the true Christ, have writ this epistle with mine own divine hand. This epistle shall be copied the one from the other, and should a man have committed as many sins as there be sands on the sea-shore, blades of grass on the earth, or stars in the heavens, if he confesseth and repenteth him of his sins, they shall be forgiven him. Whosoever hath such a letter by him or in his house, his prayers will I hear, and him shall no thunder or lightning harm. Whatsoever woman big with child shall carry this letter upon her, shall be in due time delivered of a fair offspring. Keep my commandments, as I have ordained through my holy angel Michael.—*I, the true Jesus Christ.*"

of dress belonging to Holzmann, which were already in the possession of the court, were shown to the prisoner, and recognised by him as part of what he had stolen. A pair of ear-rings and two gold rings were then placed before him, together with the brass ring which had been found in the elbow of the murdered woman. On seeing these he exclaimed, " The ear-rings and the gold and brass rings are mine! The brass ring I always wore until within four or five weeks after Easter, since when I have worn the gold ones. The brass ring fits the little finger of my left hand."—It slipped on and off with ease; had a doubt remained, the telltale ring must have dispelled it.

On the 11th of March, 1822, Rauschmaier, his mistress Elizabeth Ditscher, and Steiner, were brought before the court for special examination.

At his first examination Rauschmaier repeated his former confession, that he had robbed his landlady. He adhered to the same story at his second examination, but answered the searching questions of the judge in monosyllables, and betrayed embarrassment by his confused and hesitating manner, and his changing colour. On his third examination, which took place two days after, he fell upon his knees, and exclaimed, weeping bitterly, " Mr. Commissioner, I see that you are well disposed towards me. You spoke so kindly the other day, that I will confess my guilt to you sincerely :" and he kept his word.

George Rauschmaier, a turner by trade, was born at Augsburg, of Catholic parents. His father was a baker, and his mother a midwife. At the time of the murder he was about four and thirty. His mother and sister said in evidence against him, that his mind had

been perverted from his youth : he had always been
remarkable for coarse, ill-regulated passions, violence
of temper, love of dissipation, idleness, and expensive
habits.   He could neither read nor write, and was so
ignorant of the first principles of the Christian religion
as to require instruction from a priest before he could
receive the Sacrament, towards the end of his trial.

In his seventh year he was apprenticed to a bricklayer, and during the winter he found employment in a
manufactory.   In his thirteenth year he learnt turnery
at Munich for three years, at the end of which he returned, on his father's death, to Augsburg, and in
1805 he entered the Austrian service.   When the war
was ended his regiment was disbanded, and he returned to Augsburg.   He was occasionally employed,
till 1807, both there and at Munich as a turner ; but
his employers said that he was an idle, insolent, and
dissolute fellow, whom no one could keep long in their
service.   In 1807 he was drawn for the Bavarian army,
but soon deserted to the Austrians ; and in 1809 he
fought against his own countrymen.   In 1809 he again
deserted, and re-entered the Bavarian service.   In
1811 he underwent a military trial and punishment
for theft.   He passed through the horrors of the Russian campaign in 1812 and 1813, which, together
with the observations that he had the opportunity of
making in the military hospitals, completely obliterated
the slight remaining traces of humanity left in his nature.   When his regiment was at Warsaw, on its way
back in 1814, he stole money and property to the
amount of 110 florins from the adjutant, for which he
was sentenced to fifteen months' imprisonment on his
return to his native country   When released from

prison, he returned to Augsburg, where he remained a
year and a half, until his arrest, earning his bread
however he could. He said to the judge, " You see
from this account of my life, how neglected I was, and
how low I have sunk in consequence."

He continued :—" I was always in want of money,
and knew not whence to get it. I wanted to buy clothes,
but would not stint myself of meat and drink. The
thought struck me that I would kill Anna Holzmann,
who, to my knowledge, possessed many good clothes,
and who was supposed to have saved some money.
I determined to strangle her, as that was easiest, left
no trace of blood, and could be done without noise : I
had also heard the army surgeons in Russia say that
the bodies of persons strangled or suffocated bled
but little when dissected. I made up my mind to
the murder some six or eight days before Good
Friday, and since that time I had no peace from
doubting whether I should do it or let it alone. At
length, on the morning of Good Friday, the people of
the house went to church, even Steiner was out, and
by eight o'clock I was left alone in the house with
Anna Holzmann. The opportunity overcame me, and,
without saying a word I walked straight into her
room, rushed upon her as she was going towards the
bed, upon which I threw her and squeezed her throat
with both hands while I lay upon her with the whole
weight of my body. She could make no resistance,
and in five minutes she was dead without having
uttered a sound, nor could she have suffered much as
she was old and weak. When I saw that she was
dead I let her body sink upon the floor.

" I then searched her chest for clothes and money,

but was much disappointed; instead of what I expected, I found only eight kreutzers.

" After the body had lain upon the floor for about an hour and a quarter and was quite cold, I dragged it into the loft which was level with her room.

" To get rid of the corpse I determined to cut it up with a large clasp-knife, which I afterwards threw into the Lech. I had frequently seen bodies dissected in the hospitals in Russia." He then gave a minute description of the whole operation, which he seems to have performed in little more than an hour. He described how he hid the several parts of Holzmann's corpse in the places where they were subsequently found, and threw the head, wrapped in an old apron, into the Lech, after taking off the gold ear-rings. Hereupon he immediately went, at between ten and eleven, to the church of St. Maurice, but could not pray from remorse, fear, and sorrow. In the evening he went to the Calvary. " I knew very well," said he, " that the murder I had committed was a great sin ; but want of money and the desire to possess some blinded me to the heavy consequences of my crime. The murder of Holzmann seemed to me the easiest and most convenient means of obtaining money. I shook from head to foot while I was cutting her up and hiding her remains, and since that time I have had no real happiness, as every one must have seen." When asked about the brass ring, he said he must have lost it while cutting up the body. The judge told him where it had been found, whereupon he exclaimed, " Yes, yes! nothing more likely. It must have slipped off my little finger while I was bending Holzmann's arm, and been left sticking in the bend of her elbow."

After this confession, Rauschmaier seemed much more easy, showed great repentance, and frequently shed tears at his examinations.

While Rauschmaier's example affords a proof that there exist human beings in the heart of Europe as deficient in moral and intellectual culture as the savages of New Zealand, the conduct of the second prisoner, Steiner, shows how little importance can be attached to the statements of a prisoner, more especially when made against another.

Steiner was thirty-four years old and born at Augsburg of Catholic parents. He was a woodcutter by trade: his education had been as much neglected as Rauschmaier's, and in intellect he was even below him. When examined in 1820 as to Holzmann's disappearance, the authorities were forced to dispense with his taking an oath, as he could not be made to comprehend its nature and significance. After his examination the judge remarked, that " the witness appeared utterly deficient in culture, and incapable of forming an idea: he was almost an idiot, and an answer could not be obtained from him without extreme difficulty."

On his first regular examination of the 2nd of January 1821 he asserted not only his innocence, but also his ignorance of the cause of Holzmann's disappearance. The judge again observed, that " his behaviour proved the deficiency of his intellect, and that everything had to be very clearly explained to him before an answer could be obtained from him." He was examined on the 15th of January, merely with regard to his family and to his means of subsistence, when he began suddenly and of his own accord, a long rambling narrative to the following effect :—That he returned home at about ten or eleven at night on Good Friday, and went to wish his landlady good night, as was his usual custom ; but not finding her in bed, he thought that she would not return that night, and thereupon got into her bed himself. During the night he heard a heavy fall over head, and a noise as if something was being dragged backwards and forwards. On the Saturday he came home at about ten at night : his comrade opened the door to him, and would not allow him to enter his landlady's room, but lighted him at once to his own. He had scarcely lain down when something dropped from the ceiling upon his nose, and when he turned in bed, upon his back. In the morning he found that this was blood. He called Rauschmaier's attention to this, who answered that he could not account for it, but that it was of no consequence. At first he thought nothing of it; but, on seeing Holzmann's remains in the churchyard, the thought struck him that she must have been murdered by Rauschmaier. He himself had never harmed her. The judge remarked that Steiner took great pains to make his story intelligible, gave his evidence without embarrassment or hesitation, and showed that he had more sense than had at first appeared. On the 4th of February he requested another audience, and on being asked what he had to say, he replied, " Something has occurred to me : my memory is bad, and I have erred in several matters. Even a horse, which has four legs, sometimes stumbles ; why should not I ? " He now modified his former statement: it was not on Friday, but on Saturday, that he had slept in Holzmann's bed, and the blood had dropped upon his nose on the Thursday night, not on Good Friday.

He had said to Rauschmaier, early on Friday, " Surely, in God's name, you have not murdered our landlady?" whereupon Rauschmaier threatened to kill him if he said a word about the blood or their landlady. He then showed him a thick knotted club, saying, " I will strike you dead with this if you say a word of the matter!" Steiner continued :—" As he thus threatened me, and I was in fear of my life, I never said a word to any one; but, sir, you may be sure that my comrade, who is a bold strong fellow, murdered the woman." He then proceeded, after some interruption, " It now strikes me that the blood must have been wiped up on Easter Sunday with my shirt, which I found in a corner soaked with blood. No doubt my comrade did this on purpose to throw the suspicion on me. It likewise occurs to me that about a week or a fortnight before Good Friday, my comrade wrestled with Holzmann, in joke, of course in order to try her strength. He must therefore even then have made up his mind to murder her. Nobody acts a play until the rehearsal has turned out well." He further added, that a week after Easter he was with Rauschmaier at a tavern, and when they were alone his comrade offered him a silver ring and a pair of ear-rings, to say nothing about the blood or their landlady; but he would take nothing from him.

Steiner's statement had every appearance of truth, and agreed in the main with what was already known : and so long as Rauschmaier withheld his confession it appeared of the utmost importance.

But when the latter was asked, after making a full confession, whether any one was privy to the murder which he had committed, he answered, " No human being; I resolved upon and committed the murder alone, exactly as I have already confessed it, because I trusted no one; if, perchance, Joseph Steiner or Elizabeth Ditscher are suspected, I hereby attest their innocence; nor do I believe that Steiner saw anything, at any rate he never gave me to understand that he suspected me." In the following examination when he was told that Steiner asserted that he had discovered traces of the murder, and that he had taken Rauschmaier to task about it, the latter replied, " It is a thorough lie; he never said a word to me of the matter. The fellow does nothing but tell lies from morning till night. Had he discovered anything, he would have informed against me. Why should not I confess this fact, if it were true?"

At Steiner's third examination the discrepancy between his statement and Rauschmaier's repentant confession was fully explained. The judge called Steiner's attention to some marked contradiction, whereupon he exclaimed, " I am an ass, and have said a great deal that is not true. I must beg pardon for having lied so much. I thought to myself that, perhaps, my comrade murdered the woman, and that I was suspected, although I am innocent; I therefore said whatever came into my head to strengthen the suspicion against Rauschmaier, and to convince you of my own innocence. All that I have said about the blood dropping upon my nose, and my shirt, about the noise of one falling and being dragged over head, and about my observations to Rauschmaier, his threatening words, promises, and so forth, are mere inventions. I neither saw nor heard anything; but I suspected that Holzmann had been murdered by Rauschmaier. I then considered how it must all have been done, and told it accordingly. I wonder how it all came into my head; I should soon have believed the story myself. Forgive my stupidity, I am a mere ass. Only think how stupid!—I now begin to see what trouble I have got myself into by my lies; but I hope I shall not suffer for them, as I did not harm the old woman. I thought I was doing the court a pleasure by saying what I fancied about Rauschmaier, for I still believe him to be guilty."

Rauschmaier's advocate was led by his sense of justice and propriety to confine the defence of his client to an appeal to the mercy of the court. He did not attempt by legal quibbles to gain an acquittal for a man who had already confessed his guilt, but called the attention of the judge to his client's neglected education.

On the 9th of May, 1822, Rauschmaier was found guilty of murder, and condemned to death by the sword, with previous exposure for half an hour in the pillory.

Steiner was acquitted, and Elizabeth Ditscher was condemned to an eight days' imprisonment for receiving stolen goods.

Rauschmaier's sentence received the confirmation of the superior court on the 18th of June; but a royal rescript of the 28th of June directed that the exposure previous to execution should be omitted.

ANDREW BICHEL,

THE WOMAN-MURDERER.

———○———

IN the summer of 1807 Barbara Reisinger, the daughter of Peter Reisinger, a day-labourer at Loisenrieth, left her father's house in quest of service, and disappeared. No tidings of her ever reached her parents.

In the beginning of the year 1808 the same thing happened to another young woman, named Catherine Seidel, of Regendorf. She went out one morning, intending to have her fortune told by a certain Andrew Bichel, and never returned home to her sisters, who inquired after her in vain at Bichel's house.

The disappearance of these two girls remained for a long time unknown to the local authorities. The parents of Barbara Reisinger comforted themselves with vain hopes; the sisters of Catherine Seidel wept her loss in silence. A report reached them that Bichel's wife had sold some clothes belonging to Catherine; but they disregarded these rumours, and contented themselves with inquiring of Bichel himself after their missing sister; with unsuspecting simplicity they gave full belief to his mere denial of any knowledge of her. At length an accident led to the first judicial inquiry. Walburga, the younger sister of Catherine

Seidel, went by chance into a tailor's shop at Regendorf, and found him making a waistcoat for Bichel
of some dimity which she recognised as a part of her
sister's petticoat. This was too suspicious a discovery
to be passed over, and on the 19th of May, 1808,
Walburga Seidel laid information to the following
effect before the provincial magistrate.

She stated that while she herself was from home
about thirteen weeks before, some woman had come
to their house at eight o'clock in the morning with
a message from Andrew Bichel to Catherine, to the
effect that some one at his house wished to speak with
her. Catherine accordingly went to him, but immediately returned, and told her elder sister Theresa, that
Bichel was going to show her her fortune in a glass,
and that she was to take clothes enough to change
three several times; moreover, that the clothes must
be good and fine—the very best she had. Catherine
then packed up her clothes, and went back with them
to Bichel, since when she had never been seen or heard
of. Two or three days after, Theresa, the elder sister,
called at Bichel's house, which she found locked, and,
on asking after her sister, Bichel told her (contrary
to that which he said to others) that he knew nothing
about Catherine save that she had gone away with a
strange man, at whose request he had sent for her.
Bichel repeated the same tale to her sister and herself
about a week since, after they had repeatedly questioned him about their sister. Upon her sister's disappearance, it was rumoured throughout the village,
that a long time ago a cousin of Bichel's had gone to
his house to see her fortune in the glass, that she
had disappeared, and that Bichel had sold her clothes,

saying that she no longer wanted them, as she was now called " my Lady," and wore French clothes.

On the following day, which was the 20th of May, the authorities proceeded to Regendorf in order to institute the necessary search in Bichel's house, to arrest Bichel, and to receive evidence on the spot. When the authorities reached Bichel's house, he was absent, but two police serjeants were sent in pursuit of him into the forest where he was gone. His wife was closely watched in the mean time, while the authorities examined Theresa Seidel at the court-house. She confirmed her sister's statement with great precision and minuteness, and gave an accurate description of all the clothes which Catherine had taken with her to Bichel's house. She likewise named the 15th of February, 1808, as the day on which her sister had disappeared.

Theresa Seidel's examination was not concluded when the police brought into court a cotton handkerchief which they had found on Bichel's person on his arrest. He had anxiously endeavoured first to conceal and then to throw it away. As soon as Theresa Seidel saw this handkerchief, she exclaimed, " Jesus Maria! that belonged to my sister Catherine!" On examining it more closely, she identified it with certainty.

Bichel was immediately examined: he affected to be totally ignorant of the cause of his arrest. He asserted that he had bought the handkerchief in the rag-market at Ratisbon, and the dimity which he had given to the tailor from a strange pedlar. He denied any acquaintance with the sisters of Seidel: and of Catherine he said he knew nothing save that a young man, a stranger to him, had sent for her to his house: that they had probably gone off together, and that he had since heard that she had been seen at Landshut dressed in French clothes. But his whole manner—his evasive, improbable, and often hasty answers—his hesitation and perplexity—his changing complexion, clearly betrayed his guilt. When asked whether he did not possess a magic mirror, he turned scarlet, but denied all knowledge of it, and stated that about a year ago a man with a goître and a swelled chin had come to his house and had shown the girls their future husbands in a peepshow.

The officers of the court then searched Bichel's house, and found in his room a chest filled with women's clothes: many more, which were at once recognised as having belonged to Catherine, were found in the loft. Bichel's wife declared that she knew nothing at all of the latter; those in the chest she said had been given to her by her husband, who had received them from the father of Barbara Reisinger, the other missing girl. Walburga and Theresa Seidel separately recognised a great number of these clothes as their sister's, and many more as Barbara Reisinger's. Several other witnesses proved that Bichel's wife had sold various articles of dress belonging to these two women, and had worn others. It likewise appeared that Bichel, both before and after Catherine Seidel's disappearance, had tried to induce several other girls to go to his house by offering to tell their fortunes; and on the day of Catherine Seidel's disappearance, she had been seen in the neighbourhood of his house with a bundle under her arm at about two P.M.

All this indicated some strange and horrible deed, but proof of a murder having been committed was still

wanting. It was certain that Catherine Seidel had
disappeared : it was equally certain that Barbara
Reisinger had also disappeared ; and no doubt could
exist that some crime had been committed ; but whether
this crime was abduction, manslaughter, or murder, it
was not easy to discover. No dead bodies were to be
found, no stains of blood or other traces of violence
were visible.

The discovery was at length made by means of a dog.
Whenever the police serjeant went to Bichel's house,
his dog ran towards the wood-shed in the yard, and
sniffed at it until repeatedly called off. This excited the attention of his master, who accordingly took
with him some other men, and on the 22nd of May
they commenced digging within and around the shed.
They had scarce turned up the earth in one corner,
where a good deal of straw and litter was closely
heaped together, before they found several bones, and
a foot or so deeper they discovered the lower half of a
human body wrapped in some cotton rags. A large
heap of logs lay just above the shed near a chalk-pit :
when these were removed, and they had dug to a little
depth, they came upon a half-decayed head, and the
upper part of a body, which the police serjeant immediately conjectured to be that of Reisinger. At a short
distance they found, after some digging, a second body,
which likewise appeared to have been cut in half. This
the police and the witnesses present immediately recognised by the features and by the pinchbeck ear-
rings as the corpse of Catherine Seidel. These remains were carefully conveyed into the sitting-room,
where they were guarded by four men.

Andrew Bichel was just about to be examined for

the second time when information of this important discovery reached the court, which immediately proceeded, accompanied by a physician and two surgeons, to Bichel's house at Regensdorf. The spot in which the bodies had been found, and the remains themselves, were carefully examined. From the appearance of both bodies the physicians were of opinion that they must have been cut up the middle with a sharp knife driven in by a hammer : the arms were still attached to the sides; the feet had been cut off just above the ankles. The physician declared in the report which he drew up for the court on the second dead body, "That he found no reason to suppose that the person was dead or· even mortally wounded before she was cut up. She might have been stunned by a blow on the head, but it could not have been mortal, neither was the stab in the neck sufficient to have produced death ; he therefore conceived that her death was occasioned by cutting open and dividing her body."

The second dead body was recognised as that of Catherine Seidel. Her two sisters identified the earrings and some silver buttons which were found in Bichel's house as her's. Humanity induced the judge to spare the sisters the painful task of identifying the body.

Bichel was now examined a second time. He began by declaring that he would now speak the truth, whereupon he told a long story of how Catherine Seidel had been murdered by strangers in his house ; he, however, immediately retracted this, and approached somewhat nearer to the truth. Promising to be no longer obstinate, and to tell all he knew, provided he were not punished, he confessed that in the heat of an angry discussion he had killed Catherine Seidel by striking her with a log of wood. Every succeeding question was answered by a fresh lie, and every lie was followed by a confession of something approaching the truth, which was again disguised by falsehood and prevarication ; until at length, spite of his determination not to confess even the most indifferent circumstances, the court with great difficulty arrived at the conclusion—that he had murdered Seidel for the sake of her clothes, and that he had then cut her up and buried her remains.

When he was questioned concerning the other corpse which had been found in his house, he turned pale, trembled, and again reddened, but stoutly denied all knowledge of the body. On further inquiry, he stated that a distant cousin of his, whose Christian name was Barbara (her surname he professed not to remember), and whose father was a day-labourer at Loisenrieth, had once served as bar-maid at a tavern at Regendorf, that he had lately seen her at Ratisbon, and that she had given him some of her clothes during the past year, partly as a present and partly to sell for her.

During the whole of this examination, in the course of which ninety-one questions were put to him, his eyes were fixed upon the ground, and his manner betrayed the conflict in his mind between wickedness and confusion : at every fresh admission wrung from him by the force of overpowering evidence, he showed great vexation, but not the slightest feeling of sorrow or contrition.

At this juncture the judge reminded the court of a

clause in the royal decree of the 7th of July, 1806, for the abolition of torture, directing the conduct to be observed towards criminals who refused to confess; namely, that the criminal be conveyed to the spot where the murder was committed, and, if possible, examined in the very presence of the corpse.* Bichel was accordingly conveyed to Regendorf. He was first taken to the town-hall, and even there the feeling that he was approaching the scene of his crimes so over-powered him, that he was near fainting, and they were obliged to give him water to drink. The provincial judge then addressed him as follows:—" You are now close to your own home—the scene of your crimes; confess the truth at once, or you will be conducted to your own house, where you will behold the bodies of your victims." But as yet his will was stronger than even the powerful feelings which agitated his mind. He steadfastly asserted that he knew nothing of the first corpse which was said to have been found in his house.

Hereupon he was taken to his own house, where the two dead bodies were laid each upon a board as well as the remains could be put together. On being led up to the first, that of Barbara Reisinger, Bichel trembled in every limb, his face was convulsed, his looks became fearful, and he asked for water. When asked whether he knew the body, he answered with a hollow voice, " No! I never before saw a corpse which

* Feuerbach remarks that this proceeding has generally suc-ceeded in Bavaria. A murderer who had obstinately persevered in denial of his guilt for three years, immediately confessed on being conducted to the spot of the murder. He adds that in cases of child-murder this has never failed.

had lain in the grave." On being taken to the second body, he could no longer stand, but sunk into a chair: all his muscles quivered, and his face was horribly distorted. He then declared that he recognised Catherine Seidel in the corpse before him. " I recognise her," said he, " by the hands, and by the way in which the body is cut open." The judge asked him why he was so much agitated on seeing the first corpse. " I only trembled," said he, " at the sight—who would not tremble on such an occasion?" He persisted in his former assertions of complete ignorance.

Meanwhile, however, the impression left on his mind by this scene did not wear off. In his solitary prison the terrors of his imagination overcame his obstinacy. Two days after, Bichel demanded an audience, and confessed himself guilty of the murder of Barbara Reisinger also. He denied that his wife had any share in or even knowledge of either murder.

After repeated examinations, which in all the circumstances of the murder were completely ascertained by his own confession, as well as by the evidence of witnesses, the report was sent to the court of appeal at Neuburg, by which judgment was pronounced on the 4th of February, 1809, to the following effect:—

" That Andrew Bichel of Regendorf be dragged to the place of execution, there to be broken on the wheel from the feet upwards, without the previous mercy-stroke, and his body to be afterwards exposed on the wheel."

This judgment was confirmed by the central court to which it was sent for revision.

Andrew Bichel was forty-eight years of age, a Catholic, and born of peasants living at Wetterfeld:

both his parents were dead. He married at Regendorf, where he owned a cottage worth about 200 florins. He had no children by his wife, with whom he lived on excellent terms. His reputation was not particularly bad, indeed his faults are best described by negatives. He was not a drunkard, nor a gambler, nor quarrelsome ; nay, more, he was distinguished for piety. On the other hand he was given to pilfering, and was, according to common report, in the habit of robbing his neighbours' gardens. He was employed by the innkeeper at Regendorf for three years; during this time he committed a variety of petty thefts, which his master forgave him, till at length Bichel so far presumed upon his good nature as to steal his hay out of the loft, whereupon mine host discharged him from his service.

These few traits of character are significant of a covetous and abject nature, shrinking from risk and from punishment, though not from crime. Even his easy behaviour towards his wife and his neighbours did not proceed from a kind but from a cowardly disposition : it was the conduct of a man content quietly to suffer wrong, from want of courage to resist it, who dares not injure others for fear of being injured in return, and who patiently endures insults only because he is too timid to revenge them. The outbreak of ferocity in such a nature is all the more terrible when a secret and safe opportunity presents itself. Cowardice is almost always allied with cunning, and usually with cruelty and malice. To men of this character the innocent and the weak seem fitting objects whereon to wreak their vengeance for the injuries which their self-love has received. Nothing is more true than the old saying, that the most abject slave becomes the most cruel tyrant. Another remarkable trait in the character of Bichel was a degree of covetousness which looked upon no booty as too small to be worth obtaining even by the greatest crimes, if they could but be committed without danger. Such a character as Bichel's is made up of cruelty, insensibility, avarice, and cowardice allied to a very limited understanding and to a coarse nature utterly unsoftened by education. A man thus constituted will commit no crimes requiring energy or courage; he will never venture to rob on the highway, or to break into a house; but he would commit arson, administer poison, murder a man in his sleep, or, like Bichel, cunningly induce young girls to go to him, and then murder them in cold blood for the sake of their clothes, or of a few pence.

The first murder of this sort, at least the first which had been detected, was that committed on Barbara Reisinger of Loisenrieth, soon after Michaelmas, 1806. While out of place she lived with her parents, but left them towards Michaelmas in search of service. For this purpose she went to Andrew Bichel, who had promised to get her a place. She found him at home with his wife, and told him the object of her visit. He replied that he just then knew of no suitable place for her; whereupon she said that she would go to Ratisbon and try her luck there. While they were talking, Bichel's wife, according to his own account, went away to her work at another village, whence she was not to return till evening. When he was left alone with Barbara Reisinger, the thought struck him (if, indeed, it had not done so long before) to murder her for her clothes :—it is true that she had nothing with her but the gown on her back ;—but her father had all her clothes in his keeping, and as he knew that his children were acquainted with Bichel, and that Barbara was gone to Bichel's house in the hope of hearing of a place, nothing could be easier than to obtain these clothes under some specious pretext.

Bichel turned the conversation with Barbara Reisinger upon witchcraft, and told her that he possessed a magic mirror, in which every young woman could see her future fate, her lover, her destined husband, and the like; all, in short, that is most interesting to the female heart. The poor girl readily fell into the snare, and was filled with curiosity to look into this magic mirror. Bichel left the room for a few minutes, folded a white cloth round a board, and returned with this pretended mirror, and a small common magnifying glass. He placed them both on the table, desiring her on no account to touch these sacred objects: he then told her that she must allow her eyes to be bandaged, and her hands to be tied behind her back, in order to prevent her from even making the attempt. The deluded girl consented to everything, and Bichel bound a handkerchief over her eyes, tied her hands together, and then stabbed her in the neck with a knife; she fetched one sigh, and instantly fell. He then cut her open, chopped her body to pieces, in order the more easily to conceal it, and buried the remains in and near the shed where the corpses were subsequently found. He then washed the room, which was deluged with blood, and strewed sand and ashes over it to conceal the stains. He told his wife on her return, when she remarked how wet the room was, that he had spilt a bucket of water.

Neither his peace of mind nor his outward demeanour were the least disturbed by this act. He went on with his usual avocations, and in due time contrived in the most cold-blooded manner to reap the reward of his labour. He started during the Christmas holidays for Loisenrieth, in order to fetch the murdered woman's clothes. On his way he was met by Barbara's father going to Regendorf to inquire after his daughter. " Well, how is this? have you not yet sent her clothes?" exclaimed Bichel. " I have already despatched several messages to you desiring you to forward your child's clothes to me. She is in service with an ambassador—she is married, and she and her husband have an estate to manage. She commissioned me to send her clothes after her." The father maintained that he had received no message. " Well, then," continued Bichel, "since I am so far on the way I will return with you and fetch them." He did so. The mother carefully packed up all her daughter's clothes, and gave them to Bichel. The father accompanied him to some distance, carrying the booty for him as far as a certain public-house, where they separated. Old Reisinger afterwards heard that Bichel was selling some of his daughter's clothes. He went three several times to Ratisbon to inquire after his daughter, but of course obtained no information about her. At last he went to Bichel himself at Regendorf, reproached him, and called him a rogue. But Bichel drove him away with threats and told him not to trouble himself any further about his daughter, who was well provided for.

The length of time during which this crime remained undiscovered, can only be accounted for by the ignorance and boundless simplicity of Barbara Reisinger's parents, and of the other persons to whom so many suspicious circumstances were known.

Meanwhile, Bichel sought for fresh victims. The first murder was so easily perpetrated, and so richly rewarded, that he determined to make a trade of it. A man who has once deliberately committed an inhuman action will not, so long as the same motives to crime exist, rest content with his first exploit. Once acquainted with horrors, he will soon become familiarised with them.

Bichel now looked about for other girls whom he might delude by superstition and entice into his power, and within reach of his knife. It is not exactly known upon how many he tried his cunning : the legal authorities, however, heard of several. About Christmas, 1807, he cast his eyes upon a girl of one and twenty, called Graber : he turned the conversation upon her absent lover, and asked if she had lately heard from him. She answered that she had not; and he said, " Well, if you will say nothing about it to any one, you may come to me, and I will then let you look in my magic glass, which will show you whether your lover be alive or dead. But in order to see this you must put on a boddice, which is so holy that it can only be touched with a cloth." He added that she must bring her best clothes, and her finest shift. She promised to go to him, but did not keep her word, and Bichel sent a woman to her a few days before his arrest, to bid her hasten her visit. He also endeavoured by similar representations to induce a certain Juliana Daweck to go to him with her clothes, and repeatedly used the most pressing entreaties to prevail upon her to do so. He laid the same snare for a girl called Margaret Heimberger. These women were saved, some by their want of faith in the wonderful properties of the magic mirror, others by a secret dread of Bichel, and others again by mere accident. Nothing, however, happened to rescue the unfortunate Catherine Seidel, the discovery of whose murder put an end to his wicked deeds.

Some nine months before, Seidel's fine clothes had attracted his attention, while he was coming from Ratisbon with her : he at once resolved to murder her, and immediately began to prepare the means. He entered into conversation with her, boasted of the virtues of his magic mirror, and invited her to come and see it. Why she did not then go,—whether he repeated his invitation several times, and why the plan was not executed until some months afterwards,—is not stated in any of the official documents. We will now proceed in the criminal's own words, which are too remarkable and characteristic to be omitted :—

" On the day of the murder," said he, " I sent for Catherine, and when she arrived I said to her, since we are quite alone I will let you look in my magic mirror. But you must go home and fetch your best clothes, so that you may be able to shift yourself several times. When she had returned in her common working clothes, carrying her other things in her apron, I rolled a white napkin round a board, and brought a spyglass, both of which I laid upon the table, forbidding her to touch either that or the mirror. I then tied her hands behind her with a bit of pack-thread,—the

same which I had before used for Barbara Reisinger,—
and bound a handkerchief over her eyes. I then
stabbed her in the throat with a knife which I had in
readiness. I had a desire to see how she was made
inwardly, and for this purpose I took a wedge, which
I placed upon her breast bone, and struck it with a
cobbler's hammer. I thus opened her breast, and cut
through the fleshy parts of her body with a knife.
I began to cut her open as soon as ever I had stabbed
her ; and no man, however quickly he may pray, could
get through his rosary, or say ten Ave Marias in the
time it took me to cut open her breast and the rest
of her body. I cut up this person as a butcher does
a sheep, chopping the corpse with an axe into portions
which would go into the pit which I had already dug
for it on the hill. The whole time I was so eager
that I trembled, and could have cut out a bit and
eaten it. When Seidel had received the first stab,
she screamed, struggled, and sighed six or seven
times. As I cut her open immediately after stabbing
her, it is very possible that she may still have been
alive when I began cutting. I buried the fragments
of the body, after having carefully locked the doors.
I washed the bloody shift and gown belonging to
Seidel twice, and hid them from my wife, as a cat
tries to hide its young, carrying them about from one
place to another. I put the other bloody things
into the stove, and burnt them.

"My only reason for murdering Reisinger and
Seidel was desire for their clothes. I must confess that
I did not want them ; but it was exactly as if some one
stood at my elbow, saying, ' Do this and buy corn,'

and whispered to me that I should thus get something without risk of discovery."

The sentence of breaking on the wheel from the feet upwards, which had been pronounced in accordance with the laws still in force, was commuted to beheading. This was done, not for the sake of sparing the criminal, whose crimes deserved the extremest punishment, but out of regard to the moral dignity of the state, which ought not, as it were, to vie with a murderer in cruelty.

JOHN HOLZINGER.

JOHN CONRAD HOLZINGER, a Lutheran, was born in 1790, at Ansbach, where he carried on the trade of a vintner. He possessed a couple of houses, mortgaged to half their value, an acre of land, and a wine shop, worth about 1200 florins. By his first wife he had four children.

He was a tall strongly-made man, with a somewhat repulsive countenance. His health was equal to his muscular strength, and he had never suffered from any illness, although he frequently complained of determination of blood to the head, and of nervous agitation. He had received the usual education of his class, and possessed a fair understanding; he was cheerful, obliging, and ready to talk, which made him a generally welcome guest. He was, however, subject to sudden but transient fits of passion, during which he frequently smashed the glasses and crockery, but had never been known to proceed to personal violence.

His friends, relations, and servants were unanimous in their praises of the goodness of his heart. His maid-servants described him as " a kind-hearted man, who would not offend even a child;" and his apprentice said that he was " an excellent fellow, who would do whatever he was asked." The district physician said the same thing, and asserted that Holzinger's wife had more than once described her husband as " a kind good man, from whom everything was to be got with proper management." This sort of praise is doubtful at best, and is generally bestowed upon those who are wanting in real moral worth, and whose easy goodnature is but the sign of a weak and yielding disposition.

In Holzinger this facile temper was rendered still less estimable by being combined with unmanly cowardice, and worse than childish terrors. If any one opposed him with firmness he instantly sank into abject submissiveness, even in the midst of the most violent fits of anger. If roughly addressed, he started in affright. As a child he ran away when his comrades fought, and he did not dare to walk alone after dark in the fields, much less in a wood. A man not half his size once in jest pretended to attack him on meeting him in the dark, whereupon Holzinger ran away in terror.

Lastly, Holzinger was beyond measure licentious and inconstant.

After his wife's death, which took place in June, 1818, her sister Christiana, the divorced* wife of a clergyman, a handsome woman of about thirty, undertook the direction of his household. The most intimate connection was soon formed between them, and Holzinger seriously intended to marry her. He passionately loved her, and became so accustomed to her society as never to be easy without her. He did nothing without first consulting her, and was completely under her dominion.

---

* The reader must keep in mind that divorce à *vinculo matrimonii* is permitted by law in Protestant Germany for causes far lighter than those in which the English legislature interferes. A divorce, therefore, does not necessarily imply adultery.— *Transl.*

According to the testimony of the authorities, her conduct was blameless; but those who knew her intimately spoke of her capricious and quarrelsome disposition. Whenever Holzinger did anything to displease her; if, for instance, he stayed too long at the public-house, or drank too freely, she reproached him in coarse and violent language. These misunderstandings did not, however, at all disturb the connection subsisting between them, and were always quickly over. Holzinger always gave way to her, and endeavoured to appease her anger by fair words and promises of amendment. One of his common phrases was, " Christiana, are you fond of me?" She generally answered him with a kindly " Yes," or with an impatient " What is the matter now? Why should I not be fond of you?" He scarcely ever addressed her without pressing her hand, or putting his arm round her neck in an affectionate manner.

Although Christiana granted every favour to her lover, she steadily refused to give him her hand in marriage, declaring that she had determined once for all not to marry again. This arose perhaps from a desire to indulge her inclinations without restraint, or perhaps her penetration had detected under Holzinger's apparent good nature, qualities which made her shrink from a more permanent union with him.

Thus constantly refused by his mistress, Holzinger was compelled by his position as the father of a family and as a tradesman to look round for another wife, and when his connection with Christiana had lasted about six months, he selected a certain Johanna R—— of Weissenburg, a woman of forty, who had been twice married, and was then divorced from her second husband. This choice did not in the slightest degree interrupt the intimacy subsisting between Holzinger and Christiana. Everything was done by her advice, and it was agreed that the new marriage should not supersede the old love. Christiana was to stay and manage his household until after the wedding, when she was to return to her own home at Wassertrüdingen, where her lover was to visit her regularly once a fortnight.

Holzinger fetched his bride home from Weissenburg a week before the wedding-day, which was fixed for the 3rd of January, 1819. It is more easy to imagine than to describe what he must have felt on seeing this woman of forty or more, contrasted with Christiana who had rejected his suit, and on remembering that the former would remain while the latter would shortly leave him; his passion for Christiana was now mingled with resentment against a woman who could first refuse the hand of her lover, and with perfect indifference see him married to another.

The hope of occasionally visiting Christiana was a poor satisfaction : he placed little confidence in her conduct when absent from him, and foresaw that another lover would soon share his mistress with him, or perhaps entirely supplant him. Indeed, he thought that the favoured lover was already chosen, in the person of Carl Schulz, his future wife's nephew, a youth of twenty, who had accompanied his aunt to Ansbach. Christiana frequently talked with him, seemed greatly pleased with his company, and invited him to visit her at Wassertrüdingen. Schulz became the object of violent jealousy to Holzinger, who determined to get him out of Christiana's way. He accordingly endeavoured by marked incivility to force him to leave his house, even before the marriage. But to Holzinger's great annoyance Schulz stayed, and Christiana's manner towards him remained unaltered.

Christiana rendered the evening before the wedding doubly painful to him by harsh behaviour, which, contrasted with the attentions which she paid to young Schulz, increased his agitation, and entirely got the better of his usual patient good humour. Holzinger had been at the tavern from six to eight, when Christiana wrote him an insulting note, in which she called him " a good for nothing drunken fellow," and desired him to come home immediately. The maid met him on his way thither, and gave him the note in the street. He read and then tore the letter in the presence of Christiana, who scolded and abused him the while. He endeavoured as usual to appease her by soft words and excuses, and was so much hurt as to shed tears; but on her continuing to reproach him, he was seized with sudden fury, dashed a stone jug to pieces on the floor, cursed and swore, and tossed his arms wildly in the air. Christiana was ill-natured enough to represent his conduct in the most hateful colours to the bride elect, whom she dissuaded, even at this stage of the affair, from marrying him. Holzinger saw in this a mark of the contempt and dislike with which he believed that Christiana now looked upon him.

At six o'clock on the following morning the wedding was celebrated in the presence of Christiana and other relations. After the ceremony they went to Holzinger's house, where they sat round a table drinking arrack, and all appeared to be in the best humour. The misunderstanding of the preceding day seemed entirely forgotten, and Christiana's manner to him betokened complete forgiveness and reconciliation.

The forenoon passed without any unusual occurrence. Holzinger appeared cheerful and good-humoured, but was observed to drink more than was his habit. Besides two glasses of arrack on returning from church, he drank beer and wine, and, according to the accounts given by his friends, was intoxicated before midday. Nevertheless, the quantity he had drunk was by no means sufficient to deprive him of reason ; he acted and talked like one excited by drink, but was perfectly aware of what he was about, and in full possession of all his faculties.

At about one they dined : Holzinger ate nothing but some soup. After dinner, Christiana, who was bidden to a christening, sent for the hair-dresser, and when he arrived she took him by the arm, and went into the nursery to have her hair curled.

Holzinger, whose jealous suspicions were roused, soon followed them, and, looking through the glass-door, saw the hair-dresser's arm round Christiana's waist. Holzinger burst into the room, gave the hair-dresser a violent box on the ear, and asked him what he was about. Christiana, enraged at his behaviour, abused him, calling him a coarse drunken fellow. He immediately left the room, and went down to the cellar to fetch some wine for the christening. While there he again drank some wine, and then returned to the dining-room, where he found Schulz, and with him Christiana smartly dressed for the christening. Holzinger went up to her, and putting his arm round her neck, as was his custom, said, " Come here, I have something to tell you." But she, who had not yet forgotten the scene with the hair-dresser, pushed him away, and left the room with the words, " Let me go; you are an ill-conditioned drunkard; I will have nothing more to say to you." Schulz observed no agitation, or anything unusual in Holzinger, who left the room soon after.

"A few minutes after Holzinger had gone out of the room"—these are Schulz's words—"I heard a noise over head. I thought it might be Holzinger and Christiana, who had made up their quarrel and were romping. But before long, in the midst of the noise, I heard groans; I ran upstairs, and on opening the door I saw Christiana lying on the floor. Holzinger was bending over her, in the act of cutting her throat with a knife he had in one hand, while with the other he held her chin, and the blood spouted up from her like a fountain. As I entered, Holzinger started up, and holding the bloody knife high over his head, exclaimed, 'I am the murderer of this harlot!' He then flung the knife upon the ground. I stood a short time aghast at the sight, and then ran down stairs and out of the house followed by Holzinger's wife, sister, and maid-servant, who had come into the room in the meantime. Holzinger followed us, brandishing the knife which he had again seized, and repeatedly exclaiming, 'I am the murderer of this harlot!' Christiana gave no sign of life: she had ceased from groaning, and her arms had sunk upon the floor."

Holzinger, meanwhile, ran about the house and yard like a madman, accusing himself of the murder to every one, and lamenting the fate of his wife and children. When the physician, who had been sent for, arrived, Holzinger fell upon his knees in despair, and repeated his self-accusation, attributing his crime

to sudden anger at Christiana's reproaches. He behaved in the same manner before the police, adding
that he had been driven to murder her by jealousy.

On examination Christiana's throat was found to be
cut almost from ear to ear, and the knife, which was
one commonly used at table, was found concealed in
the bed. It had been carried upstairs to cut the
wedding cake.

At his first examination Holzinger made a full confession in the following words :—" I will confess everything of which I am conscious. I am well aware that
I have committed a dreadful crime, but such a com-
bination of circumstances urged me to it, that in the
opinion of any unprejudiced person I must stand to a
great degree excused. My heart is good, and I never
in my life injured any one in cold blood."

. He then repeated what the reader already knows,
adding that, after the scene with the hair-dresser, he
had gone upstairs intending to reproach Christiana
with her conduct. " She was very angry, and said,
' You wicked man, I will make you burst with jealousy;
I have a good mind to stab you with this knife,' with
these words she pointed to a common carving-knife
which lay on the table beside the cake. At the same
time she spat in my face. I was drunk, and in my rage
lost all control over myself, and could no longer calculate the consequences of my actions. My sister-in-law
struck me on the breast, upon which I snatched up the
knife, and, throwing her on the floor, cut her throat. I
was drunk, and so much enraged by Christiana's behaviour, that I lost all command over myself, and was
in such a state as not to be accountable for my actions.
My sister-in-law was to blame for my drunkenness;

she made me drink half a bottle of arrack besides two bottles of wine and two quarts of beer."

Holzinger, who cried and sobbed during the whole examination, did not seem to be aware that Christiana was dead, and asked with great emotion, whether she could not be saved by medical help. On being told that he was suspected of having drunk the wine and the arrack in order to increase his courage for the crime which he had determined beforehand to commit, he answered, "I had no evil intentions, and I loved my sister-in-law so dearly, that God knows I could never have harmed her on purpose." In the subsequent examination he again referred to the state of his mind when he committed the murder. "I was beside myself; my body acted, but it was without the consent of my will. I behaved like a madman, and knew not what I was doing. I was not even aware that I held the knife in my hand, and it was not till my sister-in-law lay bleeding before me that I came to my senses. Had not the unlucky knife lain on the table I should not have been in this trouble." He did not know that Schulz had seen him in the act, nor did he remember hiding the knife. He denied all recollection of having seen his sister-in-law in the parlour, and of what took place there. He said that owing to the drunken state in which he then was he could remember nothing.

Holzinger had in his confession insinuated so strongly and with so much ingenuity that at the time of the murder he was scarcely accountable for his actions, that the advocate charged with his defence founded his hopes of acquittal on this plea. But in order to ensure success it was necessary that the matter should be taken out of the province of legal jurisdiction, and referred to the medical faculty. Holzinger's advocate accordingly asserted " That his client's brain and nervous system were completely disorganised, and that he was in a state of raving madness when he committed the murder." He therefore demanded a consultation of physicians.

This was not properly a case for reference to a medical board, and the demand ought to have been refused. " In all cases," says Heinroth, " where the motive to the deed is evident, it is more than superfluous to consult the medical faculty. Nor can the assertion of the criminal, or the conjectures of the advocate that the deed was committed from blind impulse, or in the confusion of the moment, be a valid reason for medical examination, when the motives for the action are apparent." * In this case the motive was manifest according to his own confession, and the evidence of other competent witnesses.

It was obvious that Holzinger had killed his sister-in-law in a fit of violent fury, excited by love and jealousy ; and the excuse that the gratification of these passions is a proof of deranged intellect, is inadmissible. Yet in endeavouring to show that he was not accountable for his actions, Holzinger could refer to no derangement of intellect save that arising from those very passions which impelled him to the deed. Among a hundred men who commit murder, manslaughter, &c., there will be found scarce one who will not describe, and describe with perfect truth, his state during the commission of the crime as one of passing

---

* Über das falsche ärtzliche verfahren bei criminal gerichtlichen untersuchungen zweifelhafter Gemüthszustände.—Hitzig Zeitschrift. 1828, 1 vol. f. 125.

madness. But the madness of passion and of crime cannot absolve a criminal of guilt either in law or in conscience, for it is a madness that does not begin until the criminal intention is already formed.

But what proved beyond doubt that Holzinger was accountable for his actions was the fact that he gave the Court a connected and detailed account of the origin and growth of the passions which drove him to commit the crime, and of the state of his mind when he committed it, and entered into a minute analysis of the derangement of his intellect, drawn from his own observation. Holzinger remembered what he had done, and knew that it was a crime. A madman, on the contrary, either rejoices in his deed, or speaks of it as an indifferent event, and, should his insanity leave him, the whole thing appears to him as a dream. That a madman should give an account of his madness from his own sensations is as incredible as that a blind man should relate that which he has seen, or a deaf man that which he has heard.

Nevertheless, the demand made by the advocate was conceded, and both the district physician and Holzinger's usual medical attendant were separately called upon for their opinions as to the state of his mind.

The latter admitted that he had never perceived any symptoms of insanity in the prisoner either before or since the commission of his crime, and that although it was proved that both his mother and grandmother had for many years suffered from hypochondria, it could not thence be inferred that he was actually afflicted with the same disease, but only that, in all probability, he had a tendency towards it. This physician, nevertheless, concluded his opinion by saying that Holzinger was deprived by drunkenness, by the passion of jealousy and by anger, of consciousness and self-controul, and that he was not a free and accountable agent when he committed the murder.   The district physician, on the contrary, gave it as his opinion that there were no certain, or even probable, reasons for supposing that Holzinger's brain and nervous system were disorganised and himself insane at the time of the murder.

In spite of this difference, however, the two opinions tended towards the same legal result; both denied the existence of actual insanity in Holzinger's mind, and according to both he was accountable for the death of his sister-in-law.

Nevertheless, the report of the case was sent for consideration to the College of Medicine, which, on the 20th of April, 1819, sent in a wordy and incoherent opinion, which concluded by saying " that at the time of the murder he was in a state of mental derangement, arising partly from violent passion, and partly from latent hereditary tendencies, which made him irresponsible for his actions."

According to this opinion, then, the innocent and unfortunate prisoner ought to have been fully acquitted—nor was there in it anything which could even justify his confinement in a madhouse for the sake of public security ; for the Medical College itself admitted that he had been in the full possession of his reason during the whole course of his life, with the sole exception of a few moments, during which he went mad in order to murder his sister-in-law, after which he immediately returned to his usual health and sanity.

One of the arguments used by the Medical College

to prove Holzinger's insanity was, that he committed the murder in a place, at a time, and under circumstances which none but a madman would have chosen According to this then, every man who suffers himself to be impelled by passion to commit crimes which he has not carefully planned beforehand, is a madman.

Again, the college strongly insisted on the fact, that after seizing the knife, Holzinger remembered nothing more. Now, even if Holzinger actually made such a statement the truth of it might very fairly be questioned, but his own words were as follows : " I could no longer command myself, and do not know what I did while in that condition; I only remember thus much, that I snatched up a knife which lay upon the table, seized my sister-in-law, threw her upon the floor, and cut her throat."

Among the arguments by which the Medical College sought to establish the fact of the prisoner's insanity, it adduced the prisoner's seeming ignorance of his sister-in-law's death up to the moment when the body was shown to him in Court, contrasted with his frantic behaviour after the deed, and his loud and public self-accusations. Far from being a psychological phenomenon, this was the mere invention of a criminal who from the very beginning artfully endeavoured to represent himself as irresponsible for his actions. After the murder Holzinger twice returned to the room where Christiana lay weltering in her blood ; he told his household that he had killed her, and when the physicians arrived he showed them the corpse himself, but expressed no hope that her life could possibly be saved. Unless, then, his subsequent ignorance of her death was, as we believe, affected, we must suppose that he was sane immediately after committing the murder, and was afterwards seized with a monomania, under the influence of which he believed the murdered woman to be still living, and entertained hopes of her recovery, while on every other subject he was in the full possession of his faculties.

As the foregoing medical opinions failed to establish the fact which they were intended to prove, and were directly at variance with experience and common sense; as, moreover, they contained every defect which deprives a medical opinion of legal authority,[*] and as the deed itself was fully proved, the Court was now called upon to decide whether the prisoner was guilty of murder or only of manslaughter.

The following circumstances appeared to indicate a murderous intention : — In the first place, Holzinger did not kill his sister-in-law by a single blow, stab, or shot, as is usually the case in a completely unpremeditated murder committed in sudden anger. A certain degree of preparation was necessary, and her resistance had to be overcome before her death could be effected ; and though these actions occupied a very short space of time, that was sufficient to throw a suspicion of design upon him. It also looked suspicious that Holzinger excused his unusual drunkenness on the day of the murder by falsely stating that every day since Schulz's arrival he had drunk enough to intoxicate himself, in the hope of dispelling his jealous vexation. No less so is the forgetfulness which he professed of the scene in the parlour, when on endeavouring to conciliate Christiana, he was repulsed by her with hard words, and immediately after which he followed her

* Art. 264, Nos. 3, 4, Part II., of the 'Strafgesetzbuch.'

into the upper room, and there murdered her. One is naturally led to the supposition that this forgetfulness was affected by the prisoner, that this very scene determined him to commit the murder, and that he followed her up-stairs with that intention. His account of her behaviour to him, of her striking him, spitting in his face, and threatening to stab him, seemed, to say the least, exaggerated, and, moreover, he made no mention of any such provocations until some time after the murder—the only motives he at first assigned were jealousy and resentment of her reproaches.

These arguments were counterbalanced by others of equal weight. A premeditated murder is generally committed secretly, so that the very publicity of Holzinger's crime renders it highly probable that the idea first occurred to him when he had reached the upper room, and that it was executed in the heat of the moment: it is also certain that Holzinger followed Christiana unarmed, and used no weapon but the knife which accident threw in his way. His behaviour after committing the deed,—his wild despair and loud lamentations over his dead mistress, were an additional confirmation of the supposition that the murder was unpremeditated.

These last-mentioned arguments outweighed the preceding ones in the judgment of the Court, and Holzinger was accordingly found guilty of manslaughter on the person Christiana R——.

The proper punishment for manslaughter is imprisonment in the house of correction for an unlimited time;* but this may be shortened to twelve or even to eight years, if the deceased had provoked the attack

* Art. 157, Part I., of the ' Strafgesetzbuch.'

by extraordinary insults, or if the deed was committed in a state of drunkenness. In Holzinger's case both these excuses obtained, in consideration of which he was sentenced to eight years' imprisonment in the house of correction.

On the 2nd December 1816, Holzinger was conveyed to the fortress of Lichtenau, where he was treated with unusual indulgence. He had some years before lost the use of one eye from a shot, which procured for him from the surgeon a certificate to the effect that he could not be employed in the work usually imposed upon the prisoners, without endangering his sight. He enjoyed as much liberty as is consistent with confinement within the walls of the fortress, and was employed only in easy tasks. His punishment, in fact, consisted only in the ignominy attached to it, and this he seemed to feel as little as he felt remorse. He accosted his fellow-citizens who came to visit the prison without the slightest shame, either for his crime, or for his prison dress.

Holzinger's conduct while in the house of correction was, however, so good in all other respects, that at the end of six years, when three-fourths of his term of imprisonment had expired, he obtained his discharge, on the favourable report of the governor of the fortress.*

The governor described him as a man of limited intellect and defective education, physically and morally enfeebled by dissolute habits. Six years' residence amongst criminals had done more to harden and degrade, than the punishment had done to amend him.

Holzinger came back amongst his fellow-citizens

* Art. 12, 13, Part I., of the 'Strafgesetzbuch.'

thoroughly indifferent to his crime, which he looked upon as a matter completely settled, and with which his conscience had nothing further to do. He unblushingly forced himself into the society of his fellow-citizens, and even delighted in turning the conversation upon his deed, in order to show how little it weighed upon his mind. He considered that a few years' imprisonment had completely cleansed him from all guilt.

The trial and imprisonment had utterly ruined him, and he was forced to maintain himself by driving a hired carriage (Lohnkutsche). His wife died during his imprisonment, and he was now at liberty to follow his inclinations. He was scarcely out of prison before he formed a violent attachment to a certain Rosina Ott, a well-conducted girl of five-and-twenty. From love towards the daughter he lodged with the mother, who was a washerwoman, and by unceasing attentions and apparent good humour, he succeeded not only in overcoming her repugnance to a one-eyed murderer, but even in gaining her affections. Rosina Ott was endeared to him by the very labour it had cost him to win her, and he soon gave fatal proof how fierce a passion for her had taken possession of him.

Rosina was penniless; a marriage with her was, therefore, out of the question. As Holzinger wanted money, he sought and obtained in marriage a woman of nine-and-thirty, named Margaret Heimstädt, who possessed 600 florins; no inconsiderable sum for a man in his circumstances. He now thought that he had so arranged matters as to gain from a wife what was wanting in the mistress, while the mistress would be to him what the wife could never become. This, however, rested upon the supposition that his wife would allow him to frequent Rosina, and that the mother of the latter would suffer her daughter's connection with the husband of another woman. In both these expectations Holzinger was disappointed. Margaret Heimstädt, who had lived with him as his wife ever since the banns had first been published in church, and had already surrendered the greater part of her property to him, forbade him all further communication with Rosina Ott. On the other hand Rosina's mother interdicted him from any future intercourse with her daughter. As Holzinger paid no attention to the commands of his betrothed wife or of Rosina's mother, they both went before a magistrate at Ansbach, where they met—though without previous concert—the latter to claim protection against Holzinger's importunities to her daughter, the former to break off the marriage, and forbid the third publication of the banns. Matters were, however, privately arranged by the mediation of their mutual friends. Holzinger promised his future wife that he would give up all connection with Rosina, whereupon she consented to retract her declaration with regard to the publication of the banns.

The banns were accordingly published for the third and last time on Sunday, 18th February 1827, and Holzinger now found himself in the same predicament as on the 3rd January 1819. On the one hand a middle-aged woman with whom he must live without affection, on the other a far younger woman, whom he passionately loved, and whom he was forced to resign. His bridal day eight years before had been marked by the death of his beloved Christiana, and now the festive Sunday was destined to be celebrated in a like manner.

On the evening of the 18th February it was rumoured in the town of Ansbach that Holzinger had
killed Rosina Ott by a pistol shot. The aunt of the
unfortunate girl, who was an eye witness of the murder,
hastened to inform the police of it. The corpse was
found lying in the snow close to a shed in a field just
beyond the suburbs; the clothes were still burning in
places, and the fragments of a pistol which had been
discharged and then broken, and the lock of which
was covered with blood and human hair, were found
close by.

Holzinger had been in the habit of visiting Rosina
at her aunt's house after her mother had forbidden him
her own. On the 18th February he went to this aunt
and told her that his wife suspected his meetings with
Rosina, and watched him accordingly, so that he could
no longer meet her at the usual place, but that he
must have a last interview with his mistress, to whom
he wished to present a small farewell gift on taking
leave of her. He, therefore, requested that she would
meet him in the evening at a place outside the town.
Rosina, on being informed by her aunt of his request,
likewise begged to be allowed this last interview,
adding that after this " she would have nothing more
to say to Holzinger." Her aunt went with her at
half-past five to the appointed place, where they found
Holzinger waiting for them. The aunt said that
" their meeting was quite that of two lovers. He
kissed and pressed her in his arms, saying, ' Mine
you are, and mine you must be.' "

On their way home, as they approached the town,
Holzinger desired the aunt to leave them, as he wished
to give the present which he had brought for Rosina

to her alone. At first she refused, and even Rosina did not seem to like the idea of being left alone with Holzinger. At length, however, she gave way, and Holzinger and Rosina walked towards the open fields.

The aunt pretended to remain behind, but from distrust of Holzinger she followed the loving couple, and saw them ascend a hillock. She presently heard loud talking, and Rosina's voice exclaiming in a tone of distress. She hurried up the hill, calling out in alarm, Rosina, Rosina ! " Oh, aunt," answered the girl, " he is going to shoot me ! " At the same moment he fired, and Rosina fell to the ground. The aunt not only saw the flash and heard the report, but distinctly saw Holzinger take aim at Rosina. She screamed aloud at the sight, whereupon Holzinger turned towards her, and called out in a threatening voice, " If you cry out I will serve you the same." This frightened her so much that she ran away.

After, as it would seem, completing his deed by shattering the head and face of his mistress with the butt end of his pistol, Holzinger went to the village of Schalkhausen, about two miles from Ansbach. He got there at about ten o'clock, and went into a tavern where he seated himself at a table in a distant and dark corner, saying that he had come from Langenfeld by a very bad road, asked for a quart of beer, which he drank in two or three draughts, then for a glass of brandy, then another quart of beer, and finally for a bed. The host, to whom such a guest was not very welcome, advised him to go on to the town of Ansbach, but he said that he was very tired, had drunk too much, and that the cold was so intense that he was afraid he might be frozen to death if he went any farther so late at night. The host accordingly gave him a room up-stairs, to which Holzinger retired, carrying with him a third quart of beer. On the following morning, at nine o'clock, Holzinger had not made his appearance, and the host sent his daughter upstairs to look after him. She returned, saying, that she had peeped through the key-hole, and had seen the stranger standing by the window. At eleven o'clock the host went upstairs himself, and on opening the door he saw to his horror that his guest had hung himself on the iron handles of the upper window, and that he was already dead.

The host immediately gave information of the event to the proper authorities, who at once repaired to the spot. On examination it appeared that Holzinger had attempted to cut his throat, and also to stab himself, but it was evident from the appearance of the wounds that the instrument with which he had inflicted them, and which could nowhere be found, was too blunt, and that failing in his endeavours, he had ended by hanging himself with his braces. Holzinger had by his suicide escaped the sword of the executioner, from which, in this instance, not even the physicians could have saved him.

This time there could be no doubt that both the murder and the suicide were premeditated. Holzinger had betrothed himself with a woman who was not only indifferent, but even disagreeable to him, for the sake of her money, of which he had already received and spent the greater part. This woman's jealousy, and the determination of Rosina's mother to suffer no intercourse between her daughter and a married man, at once frustrated the scheme by which Holzinger had hoped to combine the pleasures of love and avarice.

When Holzinger had been summoned before the magistrate at the suit of Rosina's mother, and forbidden all further communication with the daughter, he, nevertheless, went to her house, and when she refused to admit him, he said with a threatening voice and gesture, " You have played me a pretty trick ; but I don't care for the magistrate, and you shall see that Rosina will be mine in spite of you."

Six days later the real meaning of these words was explained. While he was leading Rosina to death he pressed her in his arms, saying, " Mine you are, and mine you must be."

CASPAR FRISCH,

On the 17th of July, 1809, the Jew Parnas Samuel informed the court at Harburg, in the principality of Wallerstein in Bavaria, that Joseph Samuel Landauer had gone the day before to Brünnsee, and that, contrary to his usual custom, he had not returned home. David Levi, his servant, and Andrew Bonländer had gone out to seek him, and had at last found him near the old castle of Wöllwarth quite stiff and cold. The unfortunate man had been conveyed to Harburg, where the physician pronounced him to be dead.

On inspecting the corpse on the following day, great part of the skull and brow were found to be beaten in, and the nose and upper jaw broken; but no injuries were discovered on any other parts of the body, excepting on the third finger of the left hand, the middle joint of which was broken and the skin abrased. The physicians pronounced the injuries quite sufficient to cause death, and conjectured them to have been inflicted with a large stone weighing above six pounds, which was found on the spot covered with hair and blood.

On the very same day distinct traces of the murderer were discovered. It seemed that the murdered man had been seen, on the afternoon on which he was mur-

dered, at the house of a certain Caspar Frisch. One
George Keck had seen a man prowling about the castle
of Wöllwarth soon after, and had recognised him by
his lameness to be Caspar Frisch, who was crooked and
always walked with a stick. This same witness saw
another person, whom he did not know, go to this spot
about the same time, and perceived from a distance
that two persons were beating a third. A young girl
of about thirteen, who also witnessed the struggle from
a distance, spoke of these *two* persons—one wearing a
black smock frock and a peasant's hat, the other a
white frock and a black cap. She also heard the man
whom they had beat groaning for some time after.

They found on the murdered man two acknowledgments of debt, signed by Caspar Frisch, relating chiefly
to some transaction about a watch. His widow made the
following statement concerning Frisch. That "about
ten days previous to the murder, he came to their
house and told her husband that he had buried his
savings some years ago, and for a long time had been
unable to find the spot. But that lately as he was
going to bury something else he had accidentally discovered the first money, consisting of Bavarian kreutzers, which, after paying his debts, he wished to exchange. Frisch then appointed her husband to meet
him on the following Sunday, the 16th July, and to
bring with him some money and two watches which
he wished to buy. He also charged him to say nothing
of all this to his cousins, who would otherwise want the
money to pay their debts with. Her husband at first
thought the whole affair suspicious, but as Frisch protested that he had earned the money by honest labour
he was at last induced to go to meet him on the ap-

pointed day, and to take with him a large sum of money and two silver watches, one of which was a repeater."

The court immediately summoned Frisch and his cousins with whom he lived to appear before it, but only as witnesses. Frisch stated as follows:—"The murdered man came to me at one o'clock, partly in order to bring a couple of watches which he had sold me a week before, and partly to fetch a saucepan lid. About two years before I had bought two silver watches of the Jew for ninety-six florins, which I had agreed to pay in six instalments. I had paid a part of this debt, but not all, as I had never been able to find a sum of two hundred florins which I had buried about five years since during the French invasion. I most unexpectedly found this sum about a fortnight ago while I was new laying the threshold of the old shed, and immediately went to the Jew and offered to pay him the remainder of his debt. On this occasion the Jew proposed to sell me two watches which he then wore, and we agreed that the Jew was to take back the watches which he had formerly sold me, and to let me have the two others in exchange upon payment of an additional sum of thirty-six florins. The Jew came to me yesterday to settle the matter: everything was done as we had agreed, and the Jew then changed what little money was left for twelve-kreutzer pieces. All this was done in about twenty minutes, after which the Jew went away. I stayed at home for a short time, and then went to several places and talked with different persons, from whom I heard that three people had been fighting up at the old castle."

At the conclusion of his examination the judge asked

him how he got the scratches upon his face, which looked as though they had been made by some one's nails. He answered that he had got the scratch over his eye on Saturday, while thatching his cousin's house, and that those about his mouth had been done in shaving.

This evidence was thought sufficient to warrant Frisch's provisional imprisonment.

A number of suspicious circumstances soon appeared against him. Several witnesses were examined as to whether they had seen the scratches on his face on the Saturday or on the Sunday morning : some said they could not remember, but the greater number confidently asserted that at that time there were no such marks upon his face. The wife of a certain Schwerdberger stated that Frisch had come to her while her husband was out, at about six o'clock in the afternoon of Sunday,—the day of the murder,—and, on entering the house, said that his legs trembled so violently and he was so tired, that he must beg her to give him a glass of water. She then observed that there were fresh and bleeding scratches upon his face. On asking him the cause of them, he told her that he had been in the wood to catch squirrels, and had fallen from a tree and scratched his face with the prickly leaves of a fir-tree. Another witness stated that " Frisch had been with him on that very Sunday, at one o'clock, when he observed no marks on his face ; but that at six o'clock, when Frisch again called upon him, he saw the scratches, and said to him, ' You, too, must have been fighting up at the old castle, to get so scratched.' But he denied this, and again attributed the marks to a fall while trying to catch squirrels."

Finally, the physician who examined his face declared that the wounds were evidently produced by a man's nails, and added that on the prisoner's left hand, more especially on the middle finger, there were similar wounds, inflicted beyond doubt with the nails.

Such strong grounds for suspicion induced the court to have Frisch brought before it for special examination on the 19th of July, that is, four days after the murder. It would be useless to recapitulate all the lies and contradictions in which he persisted during the first examination ; but scarce had he returned to his cell when he demanded a fresh audience, and confessed his guilt.

Caspar Frisch, a Protestant, was at this time five and twenty ; his mother had been dead about seven years, but his father was living and had married a second wife. Frisch could not live with his step-mother, who was a well-conducted but severe and violent woman, and who made greater demands on her step-son's industry than he was either able or willing to satisfy. Frisch's right leg was quite stiff, his loins were paralysed, and four of the fingers of his right hand wanted a joint. He could only walk with the assistance of a stick, and was unable to perform common field labour. To make up for this he was very expert in wood-carving and in all kinds of work that did not require much exertion. The incessant contention between his step-mother and himself drove him to seek refuge with his cousins, who willingly received him. He served them as well as his deformity permitted him, as a carter, and in repairing the house and the outhouses, and in his leisure hours earned a little money by his carvings. His cousins were always indulgent towards him; and his neighbours had no serious fault to find with him. The prominent defect of his character was vanity, and a desire to outshine his fellows in dress and trinkets. In these he sought some compensation for the deformity with which nature had afflicted him. As he could not please by his person, he wished to do so by the splendour of his exterior. His crippled body rendered him an object of pity or contempt; but he endeavoured by dress and ornament to turn the scorn of his associates into envy.

More than a year before, he had bought of the Jew, Joseph Samuel Landauer, first one silver watch, then another, a silver hat-buckle and a silver watch-chain, for which he owed him one hundred and thirty-two florins. This sum greatly exceeded his means, but the possession of such ornaments was so tempting, and the term of payment so distant, as to silence all doubts and fears. Frisch could not, however, always pay the instalments when they became due, and the thought would then occur to him that the Jew had cheated him, and had asked more than the things were worth.

About a fortnight before the murder he saw in the Jew's possession a silver repeater, which took his fancy. The Jew offered to exchange it against his old watch and four carolins. Frisch returned home with his head full of this new temptation, and of the old debt. "The repeater is so handsome! I cannot pay for it; and the Jew is a cheat."—Such were the ideas which filled his mind, and which soon suggested to him a contrivance for getting rid of the debt without paying it, and for becoming at the same time the happy possessor of the two new watches: the Jew was to be induced to bring both watches to Frisch's house; and, under pretence of payment, to be persuaded to accompany him to the old castle, where he would pretend to have buried his money—and there the Jew was to be murdered. Frisch declared that his conscience was disturbed, and that he could neither sleep, eat, nor drink during the whole week. This did not, however, alter his determination. He heard an owl hoot one night, and thought that it was intended as a warning to him; but he only said, "Hoot as much as you will, you carrion; I will do it spite of all your hooting." The scheme, engendered by covetousness, fed by pecuniary embarrassment, and strengthened by the idea that Landauer had cheated him, found a powerful apology in his contempt for the Jewish race. —"He is but a Jew! there is no harm done: what business had he to charge so much and to take away all my money?"

About a week before the murder, Frisch went to the Jew's house and told him that he had at length found the money which he had buried in the shed in 1805, when the French entered Germany, and that he would now pay his debt, and give ready money down for the repeater. The Jew then produced not only the repeater, but another small watch besides, which he praised excessively, telling him that it was a most excellent watch, so good a one, that if he bought it, he would thank him for it all his life: that there were not two other such watches in all the country round. He agreed to purchase the repeater, and also a larger and flatter watch, instead of the other, but at the same price. Frisch made an appointment with the Jew for the following Sunday afternoon, when the one was to receive the watches and the other the money.

The Jew came as appointed at about one P.M., when
Frisch's cousins were from home, bringing with him
the two watches. He desired Frisch to give him a
written assurance to the effect that the money was
really his, and the same which he had formerly buried.
The Jew then demanded payment of his debt, but
Frisch told him that the money was concealed up in
the old castle between two rocks, and that he must go
with him to get it. This was in itself suspicious, and
directly at variance with Frisch's former statement,
according to which the money was buried in the shed.
Nevertheless, the simple Jew, infatuated by love of
gain, merely exclaimed, " What! upon the hill ! only
think !" and went on his way thither. He sat down
beside the stream at the foot of the hill to wash his
feet while waiting for Caspar Frisch, who went up
the other side of the castle hill, and beckoned to the
Jew, whom he saw sitting below, to come up. The
Jew, eager to possess the money, ran up, repeatedly exclaiming, " Caspar, where is it ? where is it, Caspar?"
In answer to this question Frisch led him to a spot
where three fragments of rocks formed a sort of cavern,
in which he told him that the money was buried.
Frisch now began to tremble in every limb. He was
himself astonished at the blindness of the Jew in not
taking alarm at his strange demeanour. At length
Frisch stooped to the ground, and began to remove
some stones; but he soon ceased, saying that it hurt
his crippled fingers, and that the Jew must kneel
down and scrape out the earth and stones himself.
The Jew complied, and while he was busily employed
in clearing away the stones, and thinking of nothing
but the treasure which was soon to appear, Frisch

snatched up a stone, weighing, as he said, about three
pounds, and with it struck the Jew on the head as
hard as he could.   His victim fell backwards, but
quickly recovered himself, and attacked his murderer,
striking at his face, and exclaiming in a broken voice
" Caspar, let me go ! "   Frisch now seized him by
the body, or, as he afterwards said, by the leg, threw
him down and fell upon him.   Even then the Jew,
who was undermost, struggled hard for his life, and
would have overpowered Frisch, had not the latter got
one finger of the Jew's left hand between his teeth,
thus depriving him of the use of the hand.   The stones
which lay scattered around afforded ready instruments
of murder.   Frisch struck the wretched man about the
head and brow ; and although at each blow the stone
dropped from his crippled hand, he quickly seized
another, and continued the attack.   He gave the Jew
ten or eleven blows, until his head was crushed, and
Frisch perceived that he was dying : he then robbed
the dying man of his watches and money and left
him.

The accused repeatedly confessed the deed as it has
now been related.   As his confession agreed with the
circumstances stated by the witnesses, and was perfectly
consistent in itself, it needs no further comment.

There was, however, one difficulty which must be
noticed.   The accused asserted that he committed the
murder alone.   It, however, seemed incredible that a
feeble cripple—who could scarce walk without the
help of a stick—should have overpowered a strong
man in the full use of his limbs.   This doubt was
further increased by the statement of two witnesses,
John Keck and Anna Vogt, who affirmed that they

had seen two men attacking a third.   But when we
consider the rapidity of the motions of those engaged
in conflict, one while struggling on the ground, at
another standing; and moreover, that the witnesses saw
the fight from a considerable distance, it appears very
probable that they may have been deceived.   Another
witness, John Löw, who first called Keck's attention to
the contest, stoutly maintained that he had seen only
two persons; moreover, Keck refused to repeat his
statement as to three people, on oath.   The doubt
arising from the disproportion in bodily strength between the murderer and his victim vanishes when we
consider that the first blow fell upon the Jew unawares,
and apparently stunned him : that fear often paralyses
the strong, while passion bestows unwonted strength
and activity upon the weak.   Finally, there was not
the slightest clue that could lead to the discovery of
this third person, and it is not conceivable that Frisch,
who might gain much, and could lose nothing, by
giving him up, should take the whole blame upon
himself, and persist in the assertion, frequently and
solemnly repeated, that he had no accomplice.

The district court, and subsequently the central court
of appeal at Munich, found Frisch guilty of robbery
and murder, and sentenced him to be beheaded.

According to the strict letter of the law, he should
have been broken on the wheel, but the openness of
his confession induced the judges to award the milder
punishment.

There were no reasons for recommending the accused to the royal mercy.   He endeavoured to excuse
himself as follows :—

" I could never get rid of the idea that the Jew had

overreached me: but I always intended to satisfy his demands. It was not until one day when I was at work in the shed that it suddenly occurred to me to murder the Jew, and thus to free myself from my debt. I could never shake off this thought, which constantly troubled and disturbed me. After the first blow I repented, and the Jew might have escaped if he had but gone away, or asked me during our struggle to let him go; besides, I could not have pursued him. But when the Jew attacked me, I thought he would do to me what I had intended to do by him."

This apology affords no excuse or even palliation of his crime. The trouble and confusion which he described must arise in every mind during the contest between desire for any object and the scruples of conscience. The repentance to which he alluded must have been slight indeed, for he confessed that after the first blow the Jew did actually entreat him to spare his life. Nevertheless he again threw him on the ground, and completed the murder. Assuming even that Frisch, according to his own statement, killed the Jew outright only in self-defence, no apology can be made for his crime, as he struck the first blow with a murderous intent.

LUDWIG STEINER,

THE MURDERER FROM REVENGE.

AT about three o'clock in the afternoon, on the 26th of June, 1821, the magistrate Elsperger, of Ratisbon, left his court in the town-hall to take his evening walk. He was crossing the market-place, when he was met by the shoemaker Ludwig Steiner, carrying a piece of leather under his arm. Several bystanders saw that an angry discussion took place between them: Elsperger raised his stick against Steiner; some persons even asserted that he struck him with it; whereupon Steiner drew a pistol from his pocket, and fired at the magistrate, who fell to the earth. The murderer replaced the pistol in his pocket with a contemptuous air, and walked slowly past the astonished spectators until he reached the corner of a street, when, after once looking back at the dead body, he ran towards his own house, which the report of his crime had reached before him. He told his apprentices that he had shot the magistrate Elsperger, laid down the piece of leather in the shop, and hastily left the room, in order, as he said, to give himself up to justice. Before, however, he could leave the house, he was seized by a bricklayer, and after a violent but ineffectual struggle, was delivered by him into the custody of two police serjeants. To these men he said,

" I have accomplished my purpose, and my conscience is now clear : I have long pursued him." He quietly suffered himself to be taken to the police-office, where two pistols were found in his pocket :—the prisoner himself warned the police that one was loaded, " lest any one should be hurt." He said to the police ser- jeant Speiser, who handcuffed and conducted him to prison, " Elsperger utterly ruined me ; he made me miserable ; and at last I have revenged my wrongs on him."

Steiner's demeanour was that of a man who had the most perfect conviction of having performed a glorious deed. On seeing the crowd assembled before the window of his prison, he changed his position, saying, " I must turn about in order that the people may see me ; for although many know me by name, all do not yet know me by sight."

The wounded man, who had instantly fallen speech- less on the pavement, was carried to the nearest police station, where he died within ten minutes after he was shot. The bullet had penetrated the brain, so that there could be no doubt as to the cause of his death. When Steiner was brought into the presence of the corpse, he showed not the slightest emotion, and merely ob- served, " That is the magistrate Elsperger, of this place." He signed the papers which were presented to him with a firm hand, and in his first examination confessed that he had done the deed.

At the time of the murder Ludwig Steiner was fifty- three years of age : he was born of Catholic parents at Alpendorf, in the province of Glatz, in Silesia, and had been settled for many years as a master shoemaker at Ratisbon. He had been twice married, but had no

children.   He was of the middle size, thin, pale, and
of a nervous excitable temperament.   His fellow-
citizens described him as an honourable man, a peaceable good citizen, a skilful workman, and an active
orderly tradesman, who contrived to make a good
living out of a moderate business, and still employed
a few apprentices, notwithstanding his business had
lately declined owing to various causes.   Even as an
apprentice he despised the common Sunday amusements of his companions, and passed his leisure hours
in reading : he set great value on his good name, and
had a very strong sense of honour and justice.

In the year 1817 the shoemakers' guild of Ratisbon
was split into rival factions on occasion of the election
of a master.   Steiner took the part of one whom he
thought unjustly oppressed, and in a quarrel with the
leader of the opposite party so far forgot himself in his
zeal, as to accuse his opponent of a theft in the presence of the whole guild.   An action for defamation
was brought against Steiner, who was condemned on
the 30th of September, 1818, to make an apology to
the man whom he had insulted, to twenty-four hours'
imprisonment, and to costs.   This sentence, against
which he appealed, was confirmed on the 25th of
November of the same year, and Elsperger was the
magistrate who had to pronounce judgment, and to
see it carried into execution.   Meanwhile Steiner was
fully convinced of the righteousness of his own cause.
His self-love explained a sentence so much at variance
with his own convictions and so injurious to his pride
by the supposition that the real papers on which the
judgment should have been founded must have been
suppressed, and false ones substituted for them.   When,

therefore, the judgment confirming the first sentence was made known to him on the 8th of December, he announced his intention of appealing to the central court at Munich. Notwithstanding his eager representations, the magistrate Elsperger would not allow of any delay, but at once proceeded to carry the judgment into execution. Steiner then begged for permission at least to return home before his imprisonment that he might set his house in order, and cut out work for his apprentices; but Elsperger with, perhaps, unnecessary severity, denied this trifling favour, and sent him at once to prison. Steiner came out of prison sick in body, and still more disordered in mind by the injury done to his pride, to his good name, and to what he considered his just rights. He maintained then, and afterwards, that he had undergone excruciating torments from the pestiferous smell of the prison, and the overheating of a stove. This, or more likely his excitable imagination, tended not a little to confirm his belief of the injustice sustained in his person, and to increase his bitter animosity against the magistrate whose duty it had been to pass judgment upon him. But the worst was yet to come : the apology was still due. " The apology which I had to make," said Steiner, " hurt my feelings most of all. I had to apologize against my own perfect conviction, whereas no apology was due; for I had seen with my own eyes the master shoemaker do the very things of which I accused him." Elsperger had also to see this part of the sentence carried into execution ; but summonses, admonitions, and fines were ineffectual for some months. Steiner undertook a journey to Munich in order to obtain a revision of his sentence, at any

rate of that part which related to the apology: he
came back to Ratisbon after a fruitless journey, but
still obstinately refused to obey the orders of the court.
At length, however, when threatened with a fine of six
reichs thalers, he was induced to deliver into Elsperger's hands an apology written by his attorney. From
that time forward Elsperger became the object of his
deadly hate, and he determined either to obtain complete satisfaction for all that he had endured, by an
appeal to the law, or to murder Elsperger in revenge
for the unnecessary harshness and contemptuous
insolence with which, as Steiner imagined, he had
carried an unjust sentence into execution.

Henceforth he thought of nothing but his cause.
His head could only contain the idea of the sentence,
and of the means of obtaining a reversal of it, compensation for his losses, and satisfaction for the injustice he had suffered. These thoughts, on which his
mind was constantly brooding, deprived him of all
peace of mind, and completely altered his nature. He
had no rest at night, and by day he was melancholy
and silent, unless some one touched, however remotely,
upon the subject of his lawsuit, whereupon he immediately broke out into a long-winded statement of the
whole proceeding, pouring out all the vials of his
wrath upon Elsperger and the whole bench of magistrates, calling them rogues, thieves, murderers, &c.,
accompanying these epithets with the most violent
gestures, now looking up to heaven, now crying or
laughing;—in short, behaving like a mad man. His
friend Rubin, who was attached to him by gratitude
for numerous benefits he had received from him, at
length ceased to come near him, as he could no longer

endure to hear the incessant recital of his imaginary
wrongs, and the threats and abuse which he poured
forth upon the magistracy. A master shoemaker of
the name of Magritzer, his benefactor and friend of
many years' standing, incurred his hatred by refusing
to give evidence in his favour in the law-suit. From
this time Steiner, forgetful of the kindness he had
received from him, treated him as his bitterest enemy.
In like manner as he hated the whole magistracy for
Elsperger's sake, he now detested the whole guild
of shoemakers on Magritzer's account. He chose to
imagine that every master shoemaker was his foe,
and accordingly behaved to them with marked cold-
ness or rudeness, and even passed them in the street
without greeting. Every one who attempted to make
him hear reason about his suit received the same
treatment. He was so firmly convinced of the justice
of his cause, which was so closely bound up with his
honour, nay, with his very existence, that in his obstinate conceit he looked upon every attempt to convince his judgment as a personal injury.

The hatred and vengefulness which were working
in his mind, ever since the unfortunate termination of
his law-suit, made him neglect his business: he
sought diversion and repose in reading or in drinking,
dissipated his property, lost many of his customers,
and was compelled to borrow money. Although he
had only himself to blame for these misfortunes, he
looked upon them as entirely the result of the machi-
nations of his enemies, more especially of the accursed
Elsperger. If his apprentices were taken up for any
offence they had committed, he attributed it not to
any fault of theirs, but to the enmity of the magistrate

Elsperger towards himself. If he happened to meet the burghermaster, or any of the magistrates in the street, he imagined that he saw contemptuous sneers or sarcastic laughter in their faces.

In March, 1819, he sent a petition to one of his relations at Munich, requesting him to present it to the supreme court. His relation returned it to him, saying that he could not meddle in any such matters. In May, 1820, he himself undertook the journey to Munich, and laid before the privy council a statement of his grievances. He returned to Ratisbon full of hope and joy, fully persuaded that if there were any justice on earth, the privy council would decide in his favour. He expected nothing less than that the magistrates of Ratisbon would be compelled to give him full compensation for his losses, and to make him an ample and public apology. Soon after his return from Munich, he said to his friend Rubin, whom he met in the street, " My suit must soon take quite a different turn, or else you will hear of my doing something that will make the whole world stare." Rubin could not doubt what he meant by this expression, as Steiner had said to him some months before, while abusing the magistrates, " If the sentence against me be not reversed, my enemy" (meaning Elsperger) " must die; for whoever robs me of my honour, and of my property, shall not live."

As might have been anticipated, Steiner's petition to the privy council was rejected on the 8th of September, 1820. His hatred against the magistracy, and especially Elsperger, was now turned into rage. In the refusal of the privy council he saw a fresh proof of systematic persecution, oppression, and insolence on

the part of the magistracy towards himself. His diseased vanity made him imagine that the whole magistracy were leagued together for his destruction. He
believed, or affected to believe, that they meant to
seize his person, to confine him in a madhouse, and
thus to get rid of his claim upon them for satisfaction
and compensation for his losses. He said to his apprentice Bezold, that he saw by the answer he had
received that all protection was refused him, that he
was as good as outlawed, and that as any one might
shoot or stab him, he must carry some weapon for his
own defence. Thenceforward he always went armed
with a brace of loaded pistols, for the double purpose
of protecting himself from any attack, and of shooting
Elsperger. For months these pistols were his constant
companions, and he made no secret of it. He occasionally fired them off in the presence of his apprentices, for the sake of practice, at some mark in the fields.
It was well known in the taverns which Steiner frequented that he carried loaded pistols, and many persons avoided his company on that account. About
fourteen days before the murder, he related his story
to the master tailor Heimbrand, and, taking a pistol
out of his coat pocket, he said, " If my law-suit does
not turn out to my mind, I will shoot some one." He
had frequently uttered the same threats to his apprentice Keitel, and to a shoemaker of the name of Scheidel,
some seven or eight weeks before the murder. At the
time when Sand was executed for killing Kotzebue, he
said to Dr. H——, who had been his medical attendant for years, " I have lost my honour and part of
my property by this law-suit: I have nothing more
to lose, and will now die like Sand."

The magistrates, more especially Elsperger, were informed of the threats uttered by Steiner; but no notice was taken of him, as they imagined that the very publicity of his menaces afforded security against his carrying them into execution.

A few months before the murder Steiner was summoned to appear before the magistrates for nonpayment of the rent of his shop. The creditor happened also to be a magistrate. Steiner obstinately ·refused to appear, giving as his reason that this was a mere pretext for delivering him into the power of his enemies. The magistrate, his creditor, who learnt from the physician in what an excited state Steiner then was, behaved towards him with the greatest consideration, and requested the physician to persuade him to lend a willing obedience to the commands of the court. This the physician attempted to do with the assistance of Steiner's wife, but with no success. Steiner now imagined that the physician and his own wife had joined in the general conspiracy against him: he therefore turned his wife out of his house as his bitterest enemy. From that time forward she lived separate from him; and Steiner without a wife and without friends, all of whom he had ere now alienated from himself, lived alone in the world, which, in his belief, had not only deprived him of all happiness, but had even conspired to destroy the miserable existence which was all it had left to him.

On the unlucky 26th of June he appeared unusually disturbed and melancholy. Elizabeth Fischer, his maid-servant, saw him sitting at work cutting out a pair of boots, and heard him say to himself with tears in his eyes, " They have made me so poor that I have not enough leather to make a pair of boots, or money to pay for some." This was literally true, and he was forced to procure some leather on credit. At about three P.M. he went to the leather-seller at Stadtamhof, to whom he already owed a good deal, as usual with his pistols in his pocket. Two of his acquaintance met him on the bridge across the Danube: he passed them without greeting, and stared so wildly that one of them said to the other, "Look! there goes that wronghead, that madman, Steiner." He returned home with the borrowed leather under his arm, filled with anger and grief at the thoughts of his reduced fortunes, and furious against the supposed authors of his humiliation, above all, against his arch enemy Elsperger, whom he pictured to himself as rejoicing in his disgrace and misfortunes. The resolution which he had long cherished but had not yet dared to execute, now became stronger than ever. He longed to meet Elsperger : and if he should meet him he determined to speak to him, and, unless he obtained a satisfactory answer, to shoot him. Brooding over these feelings and resolves, Steiner reached the market-place, when his evil destiny threw Elsperger in his way. "Mr. Magistrate," said Steiner, according to his own confession, "Mr. Magistrate, shall I have much longer to wait before I receive compensation for my losses?" Elsperger replied, "What do you want? Go away, you foolish fellow." "What do I want?" answered Steiner; "I am no longer able to support myself." Elsperger then raised his stick and said, "Get along, you fellow!" Steiner now drew out his pistol, pointed it at Elsperger, and attempted, but in vain, to pull the trigger, while Elsperger warded off the pistol with his stick. Meanwhile Steiner returned the useless weapon to his pocket, and quickly drew out the second pistol, which he instantly discharged, exclaiming, according to the testimony of a bystander, "Wait, you villain!"—and the deed was done.

In the fullness of his joy at the death of his mortal foe, and in the first triumph of gratified revenge, Steiner boasted of his long-cherished intentions of murder. But before the court he carefully recalled all expressions of the kind, and endeavoured for some time, with great prudence and skill, so to describe the circumstances attending his crime as to take from it all appearance of premeditation. He did not deny that he bore a deep hatred against Elsperger on account of the unfortunate turn of his law-suit, and the harshness with which he had been treated, more especially with regard to his hasty committal to prison, the heat and stench of which, he said, had nearly killed him. But during several examinations he denied that he carried pistols about him with any particular reference to Elsperger; he wore them, he said, as a protection against any illegal violence which might be offered to his own person ever since there had been a conspiracy among the magistrates against him. At his first examination he described the fatal occurrence which happened in the market-place as the result of sudden and violent anger, and denied that he even at the moment wished to inflict death. Elsperger's insulting language, and the blow which he aimed at him with his stick in the public streets, were so irritating as to cause him to seize first one pistol, and then the other, and to shoot the man who had insulted him. "It was not my intention to kill, but only to wound him," continued Steiner; "I did not expect it to end so fatally." At his second examination he stated that he did not even intend to wound him. "I presented the second pistol to prevent him from attacking me; it suddenly went off, I know not whether I pulled the trigger or not." At his third examination he said, "When Elsperger reviled me, I took the pistol out of my pocket. When he saw it in my hand, he raised his stick and struck at the hand which held the pistol, till his stick split. He then looked at his stick. In the mean time I returned the one pistol to my pocket, pulled out the other, and cocked it, that I might be able to defend myself should Elsperger again attack me. My hand must have trembled as I held the pistol and made it go off— I had no intention of firing." He afterwards returned to his first statement. "I took aim only at Elsperger's leg. I had no intention to kill, but only to wound him, and cannot conceive how I chanced to hit him in the head; I can only account for it by supposing that I must have trembled fearfully." When charged with having uttered threats of murder before several witnesses, he confidently answered that these accusations were impudent lies; that such assertions were really laughable. "It is perfectly true that I have at times been angry with the authors of my misfortunes; —who would not? But I never thought of committing murder. It is a sheer invention that I ever said I would shoot such a one, or do something to make the whole world stare: people often talk among each other, and end by really believing some tale which they have invented themselves. I cannot think what folks would have; the thought of shooting a man dead never entered my head, so help me God." In the fourth examination, he was reminded that he had once said to his friend Rubin, "Some one must die if my law-suit does not take a more favourable turn." He clasped his hands, and looked towards heaven, exclaiming, "Merciful God! I know not whether I said so to Rubin or not. I cannot be certain one way or the other." When reminded that he had once told Rubin that if he lost his cause he would do something to make the world stare, he replied, "Blessed Lord! can folks talk of nothing but making the world stare? It is possible that I may have uttered complaints before Rubin: I may have said that I should be ruined by my suit, and have no compensation awarded me; that it was galling to me to be no longer able to earn my livelihood, and pay ready money for the articles required for my business. When a man is forced to be bankrupt, that is what I call making the world stare. The other shoemakers were envious of me, because formerly I could always pay ready money." He could not help, however, confessing, in answer to repeated questions, that he had frequently expressed himself to several persons to the following effect:—That he carried the pistols about with him in order to shoot some one if he lost his suit; but that he would not shed blood except at the last extremity. The judge exhorted him to say, distinctly, whom he had then alluded to. He answered, "I must confess that it was none other than the magistrate Elsperger, whom I conceived to be the chief cause of my misfortunes." He then recommenced the detail of his griefs: "At length," he continued, "I met Elsperger on the day of the murder. I spoke to him, and he answered me with insults; I lost all power over myself; my blood boiled, and the deed was done." This answer was almost a confession of intentional murder.

At length in his fifth examination he plainly declared that he had long been determined to shoot Elsperger out of revenge. This admission he afterwards qualified by saying that on the 26th of June he had, in a sudden fit of just indignation, shot his bitter foe, not only without any previous plot, but in spite of his determination to the contrary. " It was certainly my intention, if I could not obtain legal redress, to kill him; but I intended first to go once more to Munich. Had not Elsperger insulted and struck me publicly on the 26th of June, I should not have fired at him, because I fully expected to obtain justice at Munich. I will not, however, deny that I had made up my mind to shoot him if I did not obtain justice.

With these ingenious excuses and half confessions he managed to baffle the judge for months, until at length, after a fresh judge had been appointed to investigate the case, he made the following confession in the seventh and two subsequent examinations:—

"The cause of my deed was the sentence which Elsperger pronounced and executed against me. The judgment was unjust, as other papers were fraudulently inserted in lieu of the original documents, in consequence of which the sentence, notwithstanding all my representations, was passed and carried into effect. By this sentence I lost honour and property, whereupon I swore to kill Elsperger unless I could obtain justice. I did not make this determination while I was in

prison, nor indeed until Elsperger summoned me to
make the apology within three days, under pain of
fine and imprisonment. I went to the advocate Eg-
gelkraut, who entreated me to carry my apology to
the magistrate. I did so; and this was the cause of
my hatred towards Elsperger, and of my determination to kill him, so that he might not rejoice and exult
in my misfortunes. I resolved to shoot Elsperger
wherever I might meet him, in the event of my not
obtaining justice from the crown.

" First, however, I endeavoured to get justice done
me by legal means; bloodshed was my last resource.
From my youth up I could never find it in me to
injure any one. When a boy, I was grieved when a
bird which I had hit lay dead before me. As soon as
my arrest was at an end, I went to Munich, but returned without success. In 1820 I again went to
Munich, fully resolved to kill Elsperger if I again
failed in my object, as I could no longer bear his
tyranny. On the 4th of June, 1820, when I returned
from Munich, I heard that my suit was prospering,
but could learn nothing certain. I then went to the
burghermaster." He repeated a long conversation
with him, which we need not insert. " I afterwards
went to the police-office, where the registrar told me
that no answer had come, and that I must write again
about it: a week later came the refusal.

" I related all this and my opinion on the matter to
various people whom I thought my friends, in order
to excite their sympathy: and then began the conspiracy against me. They wanted to drive me mad,
and then to shut me up in a madhouse. It is easy
enough, if many conspire together, to declare a man to

be mad. They say to each other, 'See! see! how he mixes up one thing with another, and what nonsense he talks!' Every one asked me about my law-suit, and I told it to them all, in detail; and then they gossiped about me, and called me a madman, and yet I was no more mad than I am now. Even Dr. H—— helped them to drive me mad, and threatened, if I would not give way, to say that I was a madman, if his opinion were asked. The magistrate H——, too, said publicly that my excellent wife ought to be protected.

"Ever since the conspiracy against me began I have carried pistols, not quite every day, but usually, so as to have some means of defence in case of my being attacked, and also in order to use them against Elsperger.

"The rent which I owed to F—— was made a new subject of persecution to bring me before the police. Had I gone to the office, some harsh expressions on my part would have afforded a sufficient pretext to the police to lay hold of me and shut me up as a madman. For this reason I did not go, but lived in constant dread of arrest, and of being dragged out of my own house and thrown into prison.

"I still hoped to obtain justice against Elsperger from higher quarters. But when all means had failed, and my money was exhausted, so that I could neither write another petition nor go to Munich—when even my wife turned against me, and I was compelled to put her away, and was left alone in the world,—then it was that, should I meet Elsperger, who had used me so ill, and spoken to me so harshly, I determined to shoot him—and succeeded.

"During the whole day I had been sorrowful, be-

cause I was forced to provide myself with leather, and
had no money wherewithal to buy it.   In the afternoon
I went to Stadtamhof to fetch some leather, and put
the loaded pistols in my pocket, in case of being attacked or of meeting Elsperger.   I was much excited,
as I knew not what would become of me: I could not
beg, and was unable to earn my bread as a day-
labourer.   I thought within myself, ' If I see him I will
speak to him, and shoot him dead if he refuses to help
me.'   I was desperate.   I had taken a piece of leather
on credit from the leather-merchant.   It grieved me
to remain in his debt for the leather, but I could not pay
him, for I wanted even a little money for the maid who
cooked my daily food.   That I, who had been a man
of property, should be so reduced as to owe more than
I could pay, enraged me.   In this frame of mind I
returned to Ratisbon, on my way to my own house."

He then related how he unexpectedly met his
enemy in the market-place, and on addressing him
received a harsh reply, whereupon he shot him.
When asked why he had addressed Elsperger in the
public street, he replied, " I would have spoken to him
about my business wherever I might have happened
to meet him, have told him my condition, and have shot
him on his refusing to satisfy me.   I had nothing left
to live on, and was determined that he should not live
to exult over my misfortunes.   I thought to myself I
will shoot him, as he will neither give me compensation nor restore my lost honour ; at any rate he shall
not rejoice at my misfortunes.

" I well know that it is unlawful to kill a man : I am
as fond of life as other men ; but I would rather die
than submit to such oppression as I have endured from

the magistrate Elsperger. Had any one four years ago foretold to me that I should have done such a deed, I should have laughed in his face, for murder is hateful to me, and I well know that it is the worst thing that a man can do."

This short account of one of his examinations sufficiently shows the coolness, dexterity, and cunning with which Steiner evaded making a full and true confession. He distinctly saw what was dangerous, and either denied all suspicious circumstances, or adroitly gave them such a turn as would make his crime appear to be no more than manslaughter. He well knew that he had committed murder, and what would be the consequence if his crime were proved. We see in his confession a disturbed and excited imagination, but we also perceive the existence of a clear sound understanding, perfectly conscious of what he had done, and of his motives for doing it: he analysed the thoughts, feelings, and passions which had first excited his desire for vengeance ; and he so accurately described their origin and progress until the fatal murder, that if Steiner was mad, it is impossible to say who is sane. If a madman can act with so much discretion, who is to point out the difference between a man of sound and one of unsound mind ? There can be no doubt that Steiner had for several years brooded over his imaginary wrongs, that he had long made up his mind to murder his oppressor, and that he went armed with loaded pistols for the purpose.

There can be no legal doubt that Steiner was guilty, and that he fully deserved death. But since physicians have exercised their ingenuity in endeavouring to prove criminals insane, there is scarce any one—be

his guilt as clear as the noon-day—to whose assistance
the physicians do not bring a store of mental ailments,
and such assistance was not wanting to the litigious
and revengeful, though honest Steiner.

Steiner's family physician, Dr. H——, who was examined as a witness, could not assign to his patient
any particular infirmity of mind : he confined himself
within the proper limits. " Steiner," he said, " was
of an excitable, nervous temperament : of late I seldom
visited him ; but when I did see him, I remarked that
his mind was occupied with but one idea—his unfortunate law-suit. He narrated the whole case to me,
and I endeavoured to bring him to a better frame
of mind, but entirely lost his confidence. I always
believed him to be a man of plain good sense ; but
after his law-suit, malice and revenge took such complete possession of his mind that he lost all control
over himself. I will also add that his is a case in
which violent excitement might possibly end in momentary madness."

What Steiner's medical attendant suggested as a
possible explanation, the physician employed by the
legal authorities asserted as a positive fact. In a long
written statement which he presented to the court on
the 25th of October, 1821, he stated that Steiner had
been suffering from partial madness and melancholy
ever since his imprisonment. He concluded that on
every point, save his unfortunate law-suit, Steiner's
intellect was sound ; but on this subject his ideas
were so distorted, his language so exaggerated, and his
actions so eccentric, that Steiner was, in his opinion,
a madman, who could not properly be held responsible
for the crime of murder.

According to this theory, the number of those who are irresponsible for their actions is enormous : there are few men who have not some particular crotchet, some ruling idea, ludicrous or melancholy, which they carry with them to the grave. Fortunately, however, for society, neither law nor public opinion affords indulgence and impunity to all who are led by their erroneous impressions to overstep the limits at which self-control ends and madness begins.

All that the physician adduced as evidence of Steiner's madness merely proved that he had for years suffered his mind to be completely swayed by impulse and passion. Inasmuch as violent emotions tend to disturb the balance of the mind, and to endanger the authority which should be exercised by the reason over the passions, they may indeed be looked upon as diseases, but these moral diseases are beyond the power of medicine. For them,—when the restraints of reason, religion, and morality, and even the fear of transgressing the laws, have been ineffectual,—the proper cures are the prison, and finally the scaffold.

Steiner's ruling passion was a stubborn adherence to his own opinion—a passion which had its origin in his overweening self-esteem—and which caused him to persevere to the utmost in his endeavours to obtain his imaginary rights. There is a large class of men who, like Steiner, are so fully convinced of the justice of their cause, and so determined to have what they call their rights, that they cannot rest until these fancied rights are obtained. They cannot conceive that anything can be otherwise than as they believe it to be, and as they imagine the justice of their claims to be as evident to others as it is to themselves, they look upon all that is said or done contrary to their own conviction as an intentional and manifest injustice. If their sentence be adverse, they attribute it to the hatred or partiality of the judge, or to the bribery the opposite party: they are persuaded that the witnesses have been tampered with, and that their case has been most unfairly tried, as they must otherwise infallibly have gained their suit. They consider every one concerned, from the judge to the crier of the court, as their personal foes, and their anger vents itself, according to their several dispositions, in scornful and intemperate language, or sometimes, as in the present instance, in desperate deeds.

It was perfectly natural that Steiner should visit upon Elsperger the whole weight of his anger : Elsperger had refused to wait while Steiner could appeal to a superior court, from which he confidently expected a revision of the sentence against him, and he therefore considered this magistrate as the real cause of his imprisonment, which he looked upon as unjust. The loss of his law-suit, and the stain which he imagined to rest upon his character—all the misfortunes which subsequently befell him—were laid to Elsperger's charge. The more he thought over the loss of his suit, the more convinced was he of Elsperger's injustice and oppression, and the more intense grew his hatred and his desire for revenge.

Steiner had always expected ultimately to obtain a favourable decision, and to receive some reparation from the whole magistracy : nothing short of this could satisfy his obstinate self-will, his wounded pride, and the hatred he felt towards the whole body of magistrates.

The court of appeal to which Steiner's case was sent, again referred it to several medical colleges, according to the opinion of which learned bodies, given on the

22nd of January, 1822, Steiner " was in a state of melancholy madness, and therefore not responsible for his actions, when he planned and committed the murder."

According to this opinion, all crimes arising out of passion, that is to say, about seven-eighths of those that are committed, must be altogether withdrawn from legal jurisdiction, and referred to the medical faculty, unless, indeed, the passions can be schooled into a behaviour as cool, measured, and rational as if they were no passions at all.

The central college of medicine contradicted the opinions of the physician attached to the court, and of the district college of medicine, and gave the following opinion :—

" That at the time of the murder committed on Elsperger, Steiner was not affected either by monomania or by melancholy madness, to such a degree as to render him unaccountable for his actions, as stated by Dr. N——, and confirmed by the college of medicine."

By this opinion it was determined that Steiner was free from mental disease; the medical college properly had nothing further to say in the matter, and Steiner's conduct had now to be judged by the legal authorities; nevertheless, the medical board continued as follows :—" That although Steiner was by no means insane when he committed the murder, or utterly unaccountable for his actions, his mind was so much troubled and affected, that his freedom of action was impaired or limited, in consideration of which his sentence ought unquestionably to be mitigated."

A medical opinion exceeds its proper functions by making use of the expression that a criminal is responsible or not responsible for his actions, as that is a question for legal decision, and does not come within the competence of a physician; still less can it fall within the province of medicine to prescribe to the judge where he is to seek for extenuating circumstances. Furthermore, if once this doctrine of a limited freedom of action be admitted, there is no saying where it is to stop, and under what circumstances a man is to be considered wholly accountable for his actions, and under what others he has only a half, a third, or a fourth share of responsibility. As far as human experience reaches, every crime that has been committed was not only an immoral and illegal, but also an unwise action. And in by far the greater number, the very passions by which the freedom of action has been limited and impaired, can be distinctly traced in their origin, growth, and final effects; notwithstanding which, most great offenders have very properly been executed.

The three medical opinions failed to convince the court of appeal, which, on the 9th of July, 1822, pronounced Steiner guilty of the murder of the magistrate Elsperger of Ratisbon, and sentenced him to death by the sword.

The advocate charged with Steiner's defence determined to carry his case before a second court of appeal, and after a second reference to physicians, and a more detailed defence, the papers were sent to the second court of appeal, which, on the 31st of August, 1824, pronounced Ludwig Steiner guilty of murder, and sentenced him to imprisonment for life.